That's Alright, Elvis

Scotty and Elvis onstage (Photo © 1996 EPE, Inc.)

That's Alright, Elvis

THE UNTOLD STORY OF ELVIS'S FIRST GUITARIST AND MANAGER, SCOTTY MOORE

AS TOLD TO JAMES DICKERSON

SCHIRMER
TRADE
BOOKS

A PART OF THE MUSIC SALES GROUP

EW YORK/LONDON/PARIS/SYDNEY/TOKYO/BERLIN/COPENHAGEN/MADRID

Schirmer Trade Books
A Division of Music Sales Corporation, New York

Exclusive Distributors:
Music Sales Corporation
257 Park Avenue South, New York, NY 10010 USA

Music Sales Limited
8/9 Frith Street, London W1D 3JB England

Music Sales Pty. Limited
120 Rothschild Street, Rosebery, Sydney, NSW 2018, Australia

Order No. SCH 10158
International Standard Book Number: 0-8256-7319-4

Book design: Rob Carangelo and Len Vogler

Printed in the United States of America

To Bill Black
(1926-1965)

CONTENTS

AUTHOR'S NOTE

When Scotty Moore and James Dickerson began this project, Scotty was asked if he wanted to do the book in the "usual" manner biographies are done, which is to say written in the first person. "So it would be 'I did this' and 'I did that,'" he said. "And people would sort of think I wrote it?"

Scotty thought about it a few days, then asked if the book could be written in the third person, so that people would not think he was trying to be something he was not. His life story was interesting enough, he thought, without being pretentious about the authorship of the book.

James Dickerson spent countless hours with Scotty, discussing his life with him, going over documents and photographs, talking to his friends and associates, and planning the structure of the book. Often Scotty came up with names of people who could be interviewed; never once did he veto the name of someone Dickerson thought could make a contribution to the book. As Dickerson finished work on a chapter, Scotty read it for mistakes and looked for places in which additional information could be added. Never once did Scotty suggest that a passage could be deleted because it depicted him in a less than favorable light. Never once did he ask that his role in an event be expanded or glorified.

The result is a painstakingly researched, intimate look at a life that changed the course of American music history. Scotty asked that his story be told in an honest, straightforward manner—and it was.

ACKNOWLEDGMENTS

The author would like to thank the following for their help in putting this project together:

Ed Frank and Cathy Evans of the Mississippi Valley Collection at the University of Memphis, John Bakke for authorizing use of the Jerry Hopkins Collection at the University of Memphis, James Lewis, Bobbie Moore, Andrea Weil, Lee Rocker, David Briggs, Mary Frawley, Emily Sanders, Evelyn Black Tuverville, Gail Pollock, Tracy Nelson, Hugh Hickerson, Reggie Young, Ronnie McDowell, Rose Drake, Robbie Dawson, Gary Tallent, Ralph Moore, Jerry Schilling, John Carroll, Fred Burch, Marshall Grant, Keith Richards, Conrad Jones, Chips Moman, Tammy Wynette, D. J. Fontana, Billy Sherrill, Mary Ann Coscarelli, Sherri Paullus, Jack Soden, and Todd Morgan at Graceland for their most helpful cooperation, the Naval Historical Center, Analee Bankson, the Jordanaires (Gordon Stoker, Ray Walter, Neal Matthews, and Duane West), Frank Parise, Merle Parise, Debra Rodman, the Memphis/Shelby County Public Library and Information Center, the Jean and Alexander Heard Library at Vanderbilt University Library, the Public Library of Nashville and Davidson County, Edwin Moore, Evelyn Lewis, Louise Moore, and Gerald Nelson.

For giving the reason to undertake the project in the first place, James Dickerson would like to give special thanks to Vicki and Emmo Hein.

PROLOGUE

Rolling Stones guitarist Keith Richards was thirteen the first time he heard Scotty Moore play guitar. It was late at night and—against his parents' orders—he was in his bedroom behind closed doors listening to Radio Luxembourg on a transistor radio. One minute the reception was fine, the next it was riddled with nerve-shattering static. Suddenly, from the bottomless depths of a wave of white noise emerged the music of Elvis Presley: the song was "Heartbreak Hotel."

Keith literally chased the song about his room as he ran from one corner to the other, holding the radio up over his head to snare a few additional uninterrupted moments of music. In an instant, "Heartbreak Hotel" had energized him and forever changed his life.

"I had been playing guitar, but not knowing what to play . . . without any direction," Keith says. "When I heard ["Heartbreak Hotel"], I knew that was what I wanted to do in life. It was as plain as day. I no longer wanted to be a train driver or a Van Gogh or a rocket scientist. All I wanted to do in the world was to be able to play and sound like that. Those early records were incredible. Everyone else wanted to be Elvis. I wanted to be Scotty."

For forty years, Keith dreamed of playing on a record with his hero. On July 9, 1996—forty years, two months, and eighteen days after "Heartbreak Hotel" first topped the charts—that dream came true when Keith went to Woodstock, New York, to meet Scotty and drummer D. J. Fontana for a recording session at a studio owned by Levon Helm, who had made his own mark on music history as a member of The Band.

Of the original Elvis Presley trio, known at the time as the Blue Moon Boys, only Scotty is still alive. Bill Black, the bass player, died in 1965; Elvis died in 1977. D. J. joined the group a little over a year after Elvis, Scotty, and Bill first recorded at Sun Recording Studio in Memphis, and for years it was the three of them—Scotty, D. J., and Bill—who provided the music that catapulted Elvis to fame.

Scotty and D. J. were at the Woodstock studio to record a new song, "Deuce and a Quarter," with the three surviving members of The Band: Levon on drums, Garth Hudson on keyboards, and Rick Danko on bass. Also joining in the session, which was booked by Nashville promoter Dan Griffin, were more recent Band members Richard Bell on piano, Randy Cairlante on drums, and Jim Weider on guitar. Producer Stan Lynch, for more than two decades the drummer with Tom Petty's Heartbreakers, was there to supervise the session. The song, which was

Scotty Moore and Keith Richards, 1996 (Courtesy of Jim Herrington)

written by two Nashville songwriters, Gwil Owen and Kevin Gordon, was for a compilation album that also featured the BoDeans, Cheap Trick, Steve Earl, Tracy Nelson, Jeff Beck, and Ron Wood.

D. J. was ailing somewhat when they arrived at Woodstock, but after a visit to the hospital emergency room he was ready to get down to work. "We did the track the first night," says Griffin. "Then the second night Levon came in and sang and we did overdubs."

"The Band was great to work with," says Scotty. "They reminded me of the early days when we started bringing extra musicians into the band. Nobody was there to try to be a star or show someone else up. Everyone wanted to do it right and make it work."

At around 6:30 the third day, Keith Richards arrived at the studio accompanied by a rather large bottle of vodka, a generous supply of orange soda, and his eighty-two-year-old father, Bert. Scotty and Keith greeted each other in the center of the crowded studio, and Keith introduced Scotty to his father, a diminutive man with bushy white hair set off by a jaunty red cap.

Scotty took to Bert right away. "I don't know if he is Scottish or not, but he looks like he is," says Scotty. "He looks like you expected a bunch of sheep to come in right in front of him." Scotty noticed that Bert was very interested in the session, watching every detail from a choice spot in the balcony of the studio, but he didn't find out why he was so interested until later. Keith said that when he first told his father about the session, he insisted on attending, explaining that he just had to meet the man who had kept his son glued to the radio forty years ago.

During rehearsal, Scotty and Keith sat in chairs facing each other: Keith with his vodka and Orange Crush, and Scotty with his Johnnie Walker (Red). "Deuce and a Quarter" is one of those bluesy, old-time rock 'n' roll songs that marches to a rockabilly cadence. Keith and Scotty resembled consummate craftsmen as they faced off on the floor of the studio, rocking to the groove of the music, their graying hair adding an unexpected dignity to the song.

When time came to do the vocals, Keith asked Scotty to stand next to him and give him direction. Levon sang the first verse, Keith did the second, and they shared the third. Also there were Marshall Crenshaw and Memphis rockabilly pioneer Paul Burlison, both of whom had been invited to the session. Says Griffin: "With Scotty and D. J., you had the best band of the '50s. The best of the '60s, the Stones, the best of the '70s, The Band, and from the '80s, the drummer for Tom Petty and the Heartbreakers. You had the elements of the best bands from four decades—all playing together. It was the crowning achievement of my life. If I had died right after that, I would have accomplished everything I wanted to do."

At around 3 A.M., after the session was done, Scotty, Keith, and D. J. sat around and talked a while longer. For Keith, it was "the final cycle" of a lifelong ambition. He explained that the two people he wanted to work with most were Chuck Berry and Scotty Moore. Having said that, he paused, looking at Scotty with admiration. He said he didn't know why Scotty had started playing guitar, but he knew why he had started— and it was because of Scotty. Then, becoming the interviewer, he asked Scotty who had influenced him.

"Everyone who played," said Scotty, "especially jazz guitarists."

Surprised, Keith looked at him, yet another newfound bond uniting them. He, too, had been influenced by jazz, he said, although he confessed, somewhat apologetically, he had become a "hillbilly cat." Keith said that while Elvis Presley had knocked him out as a performer, it was Elvis's band that had attracted him to the music.

"Everything that goes around comes around," said Scotty. "Like you and Charlie and Ron and that singer in front."

Keith pointed out that while they both had worked with front men their entire careers, his front man was still alive.

"What's his name?" asked Scotty, a glint in his eye.

"I don't remember," deadpanned Keith. Then, after a pause, he added with a hint of resignation in his voice: "We all need one, man."

By the end of the session some eight hours later, Scotty had finished off his jug of scotch and Keith had dipped well into his second. "Keith came to have a good time," says Scotty. "He and Levon hung out until daylight. He was still there when I left. I had met my match—and I can hang in there with the best of them."

Later in the year Scotty and D. J. went to Ireland to add another musical notch to their CD: this time a song with guitarists Jeff Beck and Ron Wood. They recorded the song "Unsung Heroes" at Wood's home at Bigbee Bridge in Sallins County. The Beck-Woods-penned song is a medium-tempo narrative tribute to Scotty, D. J., and Bill Black.

"I had met Ron before, but I'd never met Jeff," said Scotty. "But it was like old home week for both of them. We stayed up until daylight for three days in a row. It was a party. D. J. played his fanny off. He had a ball. The boy was up for it; let's put it that way."

When it comes to Scotty's place in rock 'n' roll history, Keith Richards is emphatic: Scotty is Number One. "First of all, he was laying the licks down for my generation," he says. "He gave us the grounding. If you are my age, he was the beacon. You heard a lot of other cats later, but Scotty is the one who turned you on."

Before doing the interview with me for this book, some six months before the Woodstock session, Keith spent an entire day revisiting Scotty's early work with Elvis. "It was the same feeling I got the first time," he said during the interview. "I've been listening all day. Such tasteful licks and so ominous . . . such delicate finger picking. It was just a guitar and an upright bass and an acoustic. The use of space . . . silence is our canvas, which a lot of cats don't realize, but Scotty certainly does."

For his part, Scotty takes praise today much as he took it in the beginning: with a grain of salt. To his way of thinking, some forty years after he helped lay the foundation for a multimillion-dollar music industry, it still has a surreal quality to it: not the music, but the history of it, the way it happened as he lived it day to day. When he says "walk a mile in my shoes" if you want to understand the music, he does so with both conviction and humility.

CHAPTER 1

ONION SEED
AND THE
CHICKEN AGAINST
THE WORLD

The penny postcard was done in pastels. "Go Woman!" read the caption, then beneath it, a quote from the poet Milton: "Fairest of creation, last and best!" There was a drawing of a beautiful woman, reclining as if in sleep. Whispering into her ear was a blond cherub. On the reverse side, written in bold script, was the address—Miss Mattie Hefley, Route 10, Humboldt, Tenn.—and a message. "Hello, Mattie: How are you this cold morning? This little token sent by me to bring best wishes dear to thee."

The postcard, which was postmarked January 10, 1908, was unsigned, but sixteen-year-old Mattie knew who the card was from. It was from Winfield Scott Moore, Jr., an eighteen-year-old farmer's son who lived up the road, also on Route 10.

At the turn of the century, agriculture was the economic mainstay of rural West Tennessee. Everything revolved around farming. Courtship and family were not undertaken for entertainment or for fulfillment of some vague inner quest for self-identity; economic survival required a successful courtship, followed by successful child rearing. A man who aspired to success as a farmer also aspired to success as a family man: the two went hand in hand.

Winfield Scott Moore, a strapping six-footer, had met Mattie Priscilla Hefley the year before, probably at a school or church picnic. By January 1908 he was wooing her with a passion and devotion to duty that was typical of the times. Couples didn't court by telephone or automobile in those days (there were none); they sent postcards. Depending on where you lived on the postman's route, your musing would be delivered the next day, or possibly the same day if you were one of the postman's first stops. In the beginning Mattie was reserved in her responses to Scott. She followed up his "Go Woman!" card with a stand-offish view of Confederate Park in Memphis:

Undated postcard sent to Scott Moore from Mattie Hefley
(Courtesy of Scotty Moore)

Hello Scott,
Will you allow me to drop you a postal? I received your card OK
after so long a time. It was cute. How are you by now? OK, I
hope. I don't never see you. Do you stay at home all the time?
Your friend,
Mattie

Scott stepped up his postcard attack. As the weeks passed, the cards became more intimate. Once he sent a card that bore a photographic image of a woman with her arms lovingly placed around a man's neck. The caption read: "Your kiss is love supreme."

Mattie sent a card with a romantic image of a well-dressed couple and a cryptic message that read: "Listen, Scott, I will be at Kate's Saturday night, if I am still alive . . . you ought to see me now." Then on February 25 Scott sent the following card:

Hello Mattie,
How are you by this time? OK, I hope. Would like to see you.
When you are sad and lonely and think of the past, just know
that I am your friend as long as life shall last.
Your friend,
Scott

By then Mattie was head over heels in love. She sent Scott a card with roses on it. In her message, she fondly recalled the days that they had spent together, and she looked to a future life together. She ended by saying, "I hope to spend them all with you."

Postcard sent to Scott Moore from Mattie Hefley on April 22, 1910 (Courtesy of Scotty Moore)

Scott and Mattie were married on August 7, 1910. They settled on a 150-acre farm located in a sparsely populated section of Crockett County about five miles from Gadsden and five miles from Humboldt; Memphis was about 70 miles to the southwest, and Nashville was about 120 miles to the northeast. On the gently sloping farmland they planted cotton and corn, and raised cows for milk and hogs for slaughter. And, of course, they started a family. Their first child, born August 31, 1911, was a son; they named him Carney. Then came a daughter, Mildred Lee, born August 14, 1913. Two additional sons followed: Edwin, born January 24, 1915, and Ralph, born May 2, 1917.

As Scott and Mattie worked to establish their farm during the '20s, the ground rules followed by their parents and their parents before them seemed to have less and less meaning. For generations cotton had been the main cash crop in West Tennessee. But by the '20s the crop had come under relentless attack from a new enemy: the boll weevil. By the end of the '20s farm life had become progressively more difficult because of the devastation caused by the insect. To make matters worse, the Great Depression loomed ahead, a dark shadow that danced menacingly across the graves of their ancestors and threatened to destroy their best laid plans.

ONION SEED AND THE CHICKEN
AGAINST THE WORLD

In the midst of the doom and gloom, tragedy struck the Moore household. Mildred Lee, Scott and Mattie's only daughter, became ill with pneumonia. She died on May 16, 1928, at the age of fourteen, sending Mattie into a deep depression. The family carried on the best it could. Life on a farm has a natural rhythm that is unsympathetic to tragedy.

Scott's release was music. A natural born musician, he had taught himself to play the fiddle and banjo; in turn, he had taught his sons to play the guitar. In the evenings after work and on Sunday afternoons, they sat on the porch and performed for each other.

Unfortunately, Mattie didn't have a release for her grief. What she needed was another daughter to fill the void left by Mildred's death. By 1930 Scott and Mattie had decided to have another child. She was thirty-eight and he was forty. They knew the neighbors would talk, but by God they wanted a daughter—and a daughter they would have. Sure enough, Mattie got pregnant. No doubt her pregnancy was an embarrassment to her sons, by then fourteen, seventeen, and twenty years of age, but Mattie was headstrong and knew what she wanted out of life.

Two days after Christmas, on December 27, 1931, Mattie gave birth at her home, as was the custom in those days. To her surprise—and disappointment—she had another son, whom she named Winfield Scott Moore III. "I was a mistake," says Scotty today with characteristic good humor. "Boy did I fool them."

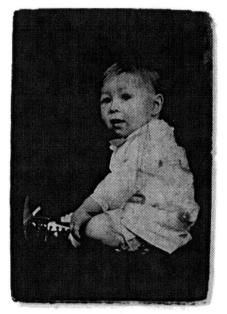

Scotty Moore at about three months
(Courtesy of Scotty Moore)

Scott and Mattie never let on that they felt his birth was a mistake. They raised him with the same love and affection they gave their other children. Even so, Scotty (they called him Winfield; he didn't become "Scotty" until after he left home) grew up in relative isolation from his siblings. Carney had left home two years before Scotty was born to work for the Piggly Wiggly grocery chain in Memphis. Edwin joined the Navy when Scotty was two. Ralph joined the Navy when Scotty was five, just before Scotty started school, and, as a farewell gift, gave him his guitar. Later, he sent him a miniature sailor's suit, which Scotty wore with great pride. "I showed him the chords on that guitar before I left, that was the main thing," recalls Ralph, who is now retired and lives in Paducah, Kentucky.

Scott and Mattie were hit hard by the Depression. There were a couple of years when they couldn't afford to make the payments on the land they rented for farming. When the bottom fell out of the cotton market, Scott looked for other ways to supplement his income. One way was to use his horse-and-mule teams to haul logs out of the lowlands. For that he was paid twenty dollars a day, very good pay for the times. Another way was to perform at square dances and parties when his sons could get home.

5

**Scotty Moore in the sailor suit sent to him by his brother Ralph
(Courtesy of Scotty Moore)**

ONION SEED AND THE CHICKEN
AGAINST THE WORLD

"I wasn't old enough to play, but I can barely remember going to a function or two when they were all playing," says Scotty. "My daddy was old enough to where he wasn't interested anymore. I'm sure his hands were starting to get stiff on him. I remember he showed me one chord on my guitar, and I thought that was the most beautiful chord I ever heard. I used to just sit there and play that thing over and over again."

At about that time, Scotty was befriended by his next door neighbor, James Lewis, who was four years his senior. Their relationship was cemented in later years when James's half sister, Louise, married Ralph Moore. Her most vivid memory of Scotty is of their ride to school in her father's wagon. "I was older and I drove the old horse," she recalls. "My brother and [Scotty] would make a racket and that poor old horse would just run and run."

James's first recollection of Scotty was when the Moore family came over on Saturdays to perform. Scotty was just a toddler. "Back in those days they had ice-cream suppers, and the only entertainment was family bands," says James. "[The Moores] would come over to our house. That was what inspired me to play guitar. His whole family was musically inclined and they had a family band. His dad played the banjo and one of his brothers played the fiddle and the others played guitars."

Everyone in the community, it seemed, played a musical instrument. The same year Scotty got his first guitar, a neighbor, an old man named Rip Brown, taught James to play his first tune, "Little Brown Jug." James's parents bought him a Sears, Roebuck guitar. "I learned to play well enough, they [later] bought me a Gibson," he recalls. "I remember they paid $80 for it and that was a pile of money back then."

James and Scotty used to meet at Rip Brown's house (he lived on the farm between them) and pick up pointers from him. But the neighbor who probably taught them the most, according to James, was Oscar Tinsley, who lived in a log house about a mile up the road. Oscar was the most serious guitarist in that part of the country. He dreamed of playing on the Grand Ole Opry, and he sometimes bought time on the nearest radio station during which he would perform in hopes of being discovered by a scout from the Opry.

"He was a pretty good country guitarist," says James. "He showed us some chords, and finally we got to playing together." In later years, being called an "Oscar Tinsley" in that area was the equivalent of being branded a hopeless dreamer. All the kids wanted to play like Oscar, but no one wanted to be like him.

What Scotty wanted most was to play with his family band, but he was too young and inexperienced. Still, the rejection stung. He couldn't understand why, if he was a member of the family, he wasn't allowed to perform with them. That exclusion was made even worse by the fact that the neighborhood boys all looked up to his father. "Mr. Scott was one of the best bass singers I have ever heard," says James. "Us boys would all line up behind him at church and imitate him singing bass. He was good, and he wasn't bashful at all. Of course, at the Church of Christ, they sang a cappella."

Because of their devotion to music, the Moore family gained a reputation for eccentricity. Sometimes, instead of working in the fields with their neighbors, they sat out on the porch and played music. "We'd go by on our way to the fields and Mr. Scott and the boys would all be sitting out on the porch playing guitars," says James. "We made fun of them because they did that. It wasn't meant as criticism. People just talked about them because they sat out on the porch and played."

When Scotty and James weren't learning new songs on their guitars, they were getting into trouble. "There were a bunch of families around that had kids our age," recalls James. "What we did for entertainment was wander the fields and hunt possums. This one particular day, we found a half-pint bottle full of whiskey. There were three or four of us boys, Scotty included. We all took us a drink. Scotty was afraid to go home. He was afraid his mother, Miss Mattie, would smell it on his breath, so he ate him a bunch of wild onions to cover the odor on his breath. Of course, when he got home smelling like an onion patch, his mother knew something was wrong. From that, we named him Onion Seed, which was one of his nicknames. I had an uncle who called him Wimpy, after J. Wellington Wimpy from Popeye." James had his own nickname, the "Chicken."

Scotty escaped detection that day, but he was not so lucky the next time. He was nabbed stealing communion wine in church. This time he got his "butt whipped," he recalls, just as soon as his family got him outside the church. The Moore household always observed Sunday as a special day, but rarely celebrated holidays such as Christmas. "My whole family more or less saw it as just another day," says Scotty. "You had to feed the hogs and do all that good stuff. I guess I've always been that way."

Scotty remembers his mother as being more serious than his father. "Since my brothers were so much older, they would never tell me any dirt on him, but there were indications he was pretty tough in his earlier days," says Scotty. "But when Miss Mattie got ahold of him, she straightened him out pretty good. He was very jovial. I can't remember ever seeing him completely lose his temper. He would make up his mind about something, and that was it. He would go ahead on. My mother spent most of her time chasing me, usually with a stick of stovewood in her hand."

One of the things he did that irritated her was to play with the black children who lived on the farm as sharecroppers. "We played baseball in the pasture, using the typical bases—piles of cow manure," recalls James. Because there weren't always enough white kids to make up a team, they invited the black kids to join in. "His mother didn't approve of him playing with them. She objected to him playing with 'niggers,' though it wasn't a derogatory name at that time, it was just another word."

Scotty started school at the age of five at a one-room schoolhouse in Coxville. Before the year was out, however, he was transferred to a larger school in Humboldt. "Some things I liked, some I didn't," he says. "I guess I was average. Some things I didn't get as good a grade as others, like math, but I loved geography, prose, and poetry. English and math were probably my worst subjects."

One hot summer afternoon, Scotty and James decided to walk home from school instead of riding the bus. As they meandered along the road from town, they were passed by a slow-moving pickup truck towing a trailer. The temptation was too much to ignore. On impulse, they swung up onto the trailer to hitch a ride. Scotty, who was eight, remembers it as if it were yesterday. "James said, 'When it slows down for the bridge, just hang off the end and drop off.'" Scotty did as he was told, but the truck didn't slow down when it crossed the bridge. Scotty fell to the ground, bumping his head against the concrete pavement. The accident left him with a knot on his head and a swollen right eye. Mattie gave him hell for being careless, and he stayed home from school the next day to nurse his wounds.

He had received a BB gun the previous Christmas, and he went out back to play with it. Nestled among the farmyard debris he found a rusted barrel that was pocked with holes. In an attempt to fire BBs into the rusted barrel, he aligned his gun with the holes. As he was shooting the gun, one of the BBs ricocheted back into his face, striking him in his left eye. "They say you can't remember pain," says Scotty. "Bull. I still remember that." Scott and Mattie took him to a specialist in Jackson, but there was nothing the doctor could do to save his sight. Ever since the accident, Scotty has been legally blind in one eye. "Needless to say, the BB gun got chucked. My daddy took care of that."

The Depression gnawed away at the West Tennessee economy, but life went on. The Moores, like most families in the region, were able to survive because they grew their own vegetables and raised hogs, the mainstay of protein in the South. Some researchers estimate that the average Southerner in those days consumed two entire hogs a year. Traditionally, the hogs were slaughtered during the first cold snap, and the hams, shoulders, and sides of bacon were cured in smokehouses. Properly salted and cured, the meat lasted indefinitely. Usually, it was fried or boiled with vegetables such as green beans, sweet potatoes, butter beans, or turnip greens and served with well-buttered cornbread and fresh strawberries for dessert when they were in season. The exception to that routine usually occurred on Saturday when Scott and Mattie went to town to do shopping for the entire week. Mattie did not cook lunch on those days. Instead, she served store-bought baloney on white bread. "That was absolutely a treat," recalls Scotty.

Most of the plowing was done with mules, an animal as unpredictable in its behavior as it was dependable in its labor. Sometimes the mules on the Lewis place would break free and make a dash to Miss Mattie's flower bed. No matter what the hour—traditionally, 3 A.M. was the time favored by the mules—Miss Mattie would call the Lewises and demand that they remove their mules from her prized flower bed. The Lewises retaliated in later years by selling their mules to the Moores.

Scotty's brothers and parents. L to r: Edwin, Scott, Carney, Ralph, Mattie, and Scotty (Courtesy of Scotty Moore)

"They'd get out and then they'd come back home and we'd get the pleasure of calling Miss Mattie and telling her to come get her mules," laughs James Lewis.

Seventy miles away in Memphis, Carney Moore was carving a niche for himself in the business world. The unemployment rate seemed to double each year. When Carney arrived in Memphis in 1930, there were fewer than 4,000 unemployed, but within two years it had climbed to 17,000. Carney had the good luck, or the good sense, to find work with the most progressive and visionary food market chain in America, Piggly Wiggly.

Clarence Saunders opened his first Piggly Wiggly store in Memphis in 1916. By 1923 there were 2,600 stores nationwide, bringing in more than $180 million a year. Saunders invented the concept of the supermarket, and his marketing techniques revolutionized the American grocery business. Stable work conditions at Piggly Wiggly enabled Carney to support himself and his wife, Auzella, until he could find employment more to his liking. Eventually he took a job with Model Laundry and Cleaners, working as a route man until he could afford to open his own laundry and cleaners, University Park Cleaners. It was located in midtown on North McClean Street near the zoo.

When Ralph Moore was discharged from the Navy, he went to Memphis and worked for Carney at the cleaning plant as a spotter. However, America was soon embroiled in World War II, and experienced Navy men were in great demand. Although he already had served a stint in the Navy, Ralph was drafted to serve another tour of duty. He took the news with characteristic aplomb: "They were short of men, and I guess they needed me." The Navy trained brother Edwin to be a machinist. One day he fell from one deck to another and busted his ankle, earning a medical discharge. He used his newly acquired skills to get work as a machinist at a shipyard in Mobile. From there he was transferred to Huntsville, Alabama, where he earned a reputation as a top-of-the-line tool and die maker for America's space program.

On November 27, 1944, when Scotty was twelve, the Chicago Bridge and Iron Company shipyard at Seneca, Illinois, launched a 329-foot cargo ship that was christened the USS *LST-855*. With appropriate ceremony, the ship, with its crew of nine officers and 104 enlisted men, was turned over to a ferry crew, whose job it was to get the ship to New Orleans by way of the Mississippi River. On December 10, the *LST-855* left Seneca on the Illinois River and made its way to the Mississippi River, passing through West Tennessee and then Memphis about mid-December before arriving in New Orleans on December 20. The *LST-855*, which stood for

Landing Ship Tank, was placed in full commission and turned over to its military crew, who prepared it for its voyage to San Diego by way of the Panama Canal. This ship would play a pivotal role in Scotty's life not too long afterward.

At the time the *LST-855* passed Memphis, Scotty was in the eighth grade and still riding to school in a horse-drawn wagon. Tramping around the countryside were bluesmen Sleepy John Estes and Hammie Nixon, who were born in nearby Brownsville. Twenty miles to the south, rockabilly legend Carl Perkins, who was four months Scotty's junior, traveled the same countryside, taking in the same experiences. About twenty-five miles to the west at Nutbush, Annie Mae Bullock, who later would change her name to Tina Turner, was coming of age. For a time, Scotty, Tina, Carl, Sleepy John, and Hammie traveled the same roads, popped in and out of the same country stores, and sweated under the same sun—all without ever meeting.

As Scotty and James advanced through the school system, they continued to get in trouble on a regular basis. A slender youth—James describes him as a typical "towheaded country boy"—Scotty was quiet and introspective, happiest when he could avoid being the center of attention.

"Being older and meaner than a snake, I was a bad influence on him," says James laughingly. "But he was respectful of his parents. Actually, he was a little afraid of his mother. Back then, corporal punishment was in style. If you didn't do right, you'd get your butt paddled."

One day Scotty and James decided to become chemists. "We got a hold of some sulfur and we managed to start a fire in their old house," says James. "We ran out, with the fumes chasing after us. I guess we were going to invent something." Whether it was the acrid smell of burning sulfur, or the stinging they felt in the seat of their pants, neither Scotty nor James ever again aspired to be chemists.

From that point on, Scotty confined his experiments to music. What James Lewis remembers most about Scotty's guitar playing was this inner drive he had to do something else with a song. James liked to play the music slow, the way it was written; Scotty wanted to go fast. He wanted to play music you could dance to. It was as if there was some, yet undefined, inner rhythm simmering inside him, something wild and raw trying to break out into the light of day.

Sometimes James and Scotty argued over the right way to play the music. In the end, Scotty would offer his own version of compromise: "You do it the way you hear it, and I'll do it the way I hear it."

Scotty and James were inseparable. They worked together, went to church together, and played music together. Usually they went to school together. "There was a man who hauled us to school in the back of a pickup truck," recalls James. "It had this tarpaulin over the sideboards. He was a cow buyer and he didn't always manage to wash out the truck before he took us to school. Sometimes we rode to school in a truck that smelled like cow shit."

That got old with Scotty. By 1945 he had his own horse to ride to school. His maternal aunt lived directly across from the school, so his father built a stable on her property and bought Scotty a horse that Scotty named Roy. The horse soon became a source of lively debate in the Moore household when Mattie decided to display her equestrian talents. It made Scott furious. "Mattie, you're going to hurt yourself on that horse," he said. "You're too old to be doing that." But Mattie, who was fifty-three, didn't think she was too old. She threw a saddle on Roy and rode off, Western style, leaving Scott behind to fret over her headstrong ways.

One day after school, Scotty saddled up Roy and headed back to the farm. Earlier that afternoon a thunderstorm had dumped enough rain to soak the fields. When he reached a thirty-foot-wide drainage ditch that he had often forded on the horse, he saw that the water level had risen considerably, but he decided to cross anyway. The current was stronger than he realized, and he was pulled from the saddle. Somehow he managed to hang onto the horse, and they both made it to the other side. "That little horse took me on across," says Scotty. "I told him when we got up on the bank, we won't do this any more."

Scotty was an average student, but by the time he finished the ninth grade he was thoroughly bored. He had no close friends at school, and he hadn't started dating yet. "If you saw a girl, it would be at a school function or something," he recalls. "I can't remember ever taking anyone to a movie on Saturday. Distance was the big deal, living out in the country and not having a car."

Scotty asked his father if he could quit school and work on the farm. His father agreed to let him do that and paid him an acre of cotton for his labor. That year's work netted him a bale of cotton, which he sold. He used the money to buy his first professional guitar, a big, black, jumbo Gibson. James Lewis remembers the guitar. "It was black and had sort of a sunburst on the front of it. It had a crack down the front. I don't remember how he got ahold of it, but I remember sitting in his bedroom with him playing it."

The Moore house was build on a slight incline just off the main thoroughfare, a dirt road that connected all the farms in the area. Later, the road would be graveled and then eventually paved. Today, one stretch is called Tinsley Road, a tribute to Oscar the dreamer, who never made it on the Opry but at least got his name on a road sign.

Scotty's bedroom was in the back of the house, just off the living room and the kitchen. Scott and Mattie's bedroom was in the front of the house. To the side of the house was a large oak, with a second oak providing shade not far from Scotty's bedroom. Even at midday the room was shadowy and dimly lit, a natural-built haven for young dreams and secret fantasies. From his vantage point in his bedroom, Scotty could pick on his guitar and see everything that was happening in the house, with the exception of Scott and Mattie's bedroom. If Scotty's guitar picking interfered with Mattie's work in the kitchen, he was asked to go outside to the barn or beneath the oak trees. Also out back were the toilet, called an outhouse, and a large, No. 2 galvanized washtub that was allowed to fill with rainwater. The best time to bathe, recalls Scotty, was at the end of the day, after the sun had heated the water.

Tired of his life as a farmer, Scotty returned to school the next year and entered the tenth grade. But school still wasn't for him. He had had a taste of independence, and he felt restricted by all the rules he had to follow there. The defining moment of his young adulthood probably occurred when James married his sweetheart, Evelyn. On their wedding day, Scotty went to visit James with guitar in hand, but not until he arrived did he realize something important had changed. "All of a sudden, it seemed, he turned up married," says Scotty. "I was over there trying to get him to play on the night of his honeymoon."

James laughs when he remembers that night. "He really didn't know what girls were all about." James and Evelyn consummated their marriage, but no thanks to Scotty's interruptions. Two or three nights a week Scotty went over to James's house and played guitar with him, usually until midnight. Later, when Evelyn was pregnant, Scotty's father tactfully warned him that he was going to "run into a party over there" if he didn't stay away. The fact that his best friend had a sex life never occurred to Scotty. Luckily, Evelyn was forgiving of his ill-timed intrusions.

"She tolerated our music making, you know what I'm saying?" says James. "She still tolerates my picking. It's embarrassing to her, I reckon. She calls me 'Oscar Tinsley.' We had this one tune we were pretty good on—at least we thought we were—the 'Hillbilly Boogie.' Evelyn would say, 'Ya'll just play it one more time before you quit.'" James laughs. "She didn't mean it. She was being sarcastic." Fifty years later, Evelyn still has an opinion of their guitar picking. "It was tough on me," she says. "I had to do all the cooking and tend the children when he was picking and grinning with [Scotty]. Scotty's mother used to call him home and he would usually stay another hour after that."

"Guitar playing was an obsession with us," explains James.

Evelyn smiles when she talks about Scotty. "He was a pretty good boy," she says. "He was at home when he came to our house. He used to say, 'I'm going to quit and go home after I play this one.' Then he'd finish and start all over again."

Midway through the tenth grade, Scotty awoke one morning feeling he was at a dead end. School wasn't for him. James and Evelyn were forging a new life. Despite their hospitality, Scotty knew that their plans did not include him. It only deepened his sense of isolation. Everyone seemed to have a purpose but him. Music was the dominant force in his life, but no one, not even Scotty, considered it a potential avocation. "It was something we did for entertainment," says James. "I don't think [Scotty] had any inkling of ever becoming a professional musician."

By January 1948 Scotty had made a decision. He would do as Ralph and Edwin had done before him: he would join the Navy and see the world. "I just had ants in my pants," Scotty says. "I had tried farming, and I thought, 'I'm not digging this.' I didn't dig school. I think my brothers had something to do with it. I wanted to do everything they did." Before he could enlist in the Navy, there was an obstacle to overcome. The minimum age was eighteen—or seventeen, with a parent's permission—and Scotty was only sixteen. For him to enlist, there would have to be a major conspiracy between himself and his parents.

"I went to Jackson [Tennessee] and enlisted," he recalls. "A buddy of mine, a great big ole boy, a six-footer named Sonny Evans went with me. He was older than I was by a couple of years." Scotty figured that his friend, by comparison, would make him appear older. Scotty signed on the dotted line, swearing up and down to the recruiting officer that he was seventeen and had his father's permission, but the Navy recruiter, suspicious of his slender build and youthful face, told him he would need proof of his age.

"The only lie I know my daddy ever told was he wrote a false birthday in the family Bible," says Scotty. "They came out to the house to check with him." There it was, right there in the family Bible, proof that Winfield Scott Moore III was seventeen years of age. Who was going to question the veracity of a family Bible? Certainly not the U.S. Navy.

Satisfied that Scotty was of age, the Navy recruiter sent him to Nashville for his preliminary physical. Despite being legally blind in one eye (although he didn't know it at the time), Scotty was sent to Chicago for additional processing. "From there, we took a train across the Rockies to San Francisco, then went south to San Diego." Almost overnight, Scotty was as deep into the Navy as a man could go, and a long, long way from his West Tennessee roots.

CHAPTER

2

CHINA AND KOREA:
SOWING THE SEEDS
OF REVOLUTION

By the time Scotty entered the Navy in 1948, the number of enlisted personnel had dropped from 2.9 million in 1945 to a little more than 300,000. He could have been sent to boot camp at one of three training centers: Baltimore, Maryland; Waukegan, Illinois; or San Diego, California. By the luck of the draw, he got San Diego, also the training site for the U.S. Marines.

San Diego was more than half a continent away from West Tennessee, but for all its cultural and geographical differences, it might as well have been on the other side of the world. Standing five-feet nine-inches—and weighing 136 pounds—Scotty presented himself for eight weeks of rigorous boot-camp training, a slender, hawk-faced, square-shouldered youth away from home for the first time. No sooner did he arrive than they slapped him into a barber's chair and shaved his head. Then the medical technicians prodded and poked his body, asking the most personal questions imaginable.

After his second physical, he was called into the doctor's office. Scotty was afraid his fraud had been discovered. He was sixteen, and he looked his age. Maybe that trick with the family Bible hadn't fooled the Navy after all. Maybe they were smarter than he thought. Maybe he was in big trouble. The doctor told him to have a seat.

"Do you think you'll like the Navy?" he asked.

Scotty squirmed. "Yes sir."

"Legally I can't pass you," said the doctor. "Because of your eye."

"Yes sir."

Scotty Moore in the Navy (Courtesy of Scotty Moore)

The doctor gave him a penetrating gaze, as if he were searching for some semblance of truth, honor, or courage. He must have liked what he saw. "I tell you what—I'm going to leave it up to you," the doctor said.

"Yes sir."

"If you want to go home, we'll let you go," he said. "Or, if you want to stay, you can stay."

"I'll stay."

At the time Scotty went into the Navy, blacks had not yet been fully integrated into the armed forces. They had been allowed into previously all-white programs on an experimental basis since the end of World War II, but for the most part they were still assigned to duties as cooks.

While Scotty was in boot camp, he got into a fistfight with another recruit, a white sailor from a different company. "It was like one of those things where the whole damned rest of the company is following you and egging you on," says Scotty. "I mean, we were going over bunks, throwing each other down the stairs. We fought all up and down the barracks. We were about the same size, but I ended up getting the best of the guy. It was like one of those movie fights."

After the fight, Scotty took a shower to clean up. Standing under the water, he sensed that someone was watching him. He turned and saw he had a visitor. "This big ole black guy from [the other boy's] company comes in and just slaps the dog shit out of me," says Scotty. "Apparently, he didn't like the way the fight turned out. He was taking up for the other white guy."

Scotty suddenly found himself in a new world that only days before would have been beyond the comprehension of any sixteen-year-old from West Tennessee. Not only was he away from home for the first time, he was standing buck naked in a shower with a black man who was his equal, a man who could freely attack him without fear of reprisals from the Navy. Scotty took the bruises and chalked it up to experience.

Somehow he survived boot camp. Before being assigned to a ship he was given leave to go home. On the way back to Tennessee, he was involved in a bus accident in Texas. "There was a hill and a curve, and this big truck came down the hill and went over the line," says Scotty. "The bus driver pulled to the right, trying to get on the shoulder, and the truck hit the back of the bus and cut it clean off at the wheels. It killed a couple of people. Just ten minutes before that I had been sitting on the back seat. For some reason I got up and walked up to the front."

Although he had only been gone three months, his family and friends saw a pronounced change in him. To the surprise of James Lewis, Scotty tried to renew an affair with a married woman while he was home on leave. It was a woman he had a crush on before he went into the Navy. She was only a couple of years older than Scotty.

"Do you know she's married?" James asked.

"Yes," said Scotty. "But I don't care."

Looking back on it, James still marvels at his friend's boldness. "You just didn't do things like that back then," James says. "He had it pretty bad for her." But if Scotty shocked his friend by chasing after a married woman, talking about racial integration, and showing off scars of fistfights, it would not be the last time. There were more surprises to come.

19

On the day Scotty enlisted, the lead story in *The Commercial Appeal* bore the headline "Britain Denounces Reds/Moves To Create Bloc/Halt 'Ruthless' March." The story quoted the British Foreign Secretary as accusing the Russian Kremlin of propelling the world toward global war through its efforts to "dominate" Europe.

The Cold War had begun in Europe. Halfway across the world, nasty words had become nasty deeds. The Nationalist government of China, under the leadership of Generalissimo Chiang Kai-shek, had come under increased attack from revolutionaries allied with the Chinese Communist Party. The struggle had been going on for years, long before the Japanese attacked Pearl Harbor. President Roosevelt had tried to align China with the Allies during World War II, but Chiang Kai-shek, who had two potent enemies at that time—the Japanese and the Communists—limited his support of the United States to logistical contributions. The Americans could use China to establish bases from which to fight its war with Japan. That's as far as the Generalissimo would go.

By January 1948 it was clear the Communists were gaining the upper hand. Fearful for the safety of Americans in China, Secretary of State George Marshall sent a telegram to the American embassy in Nanking ordering officials there to prepare for possible evacuation. American naval officers stationed in China were not happy with that decision. After the end of the war in 1945, more than 130 American naval vessels had been transferred to China, along with 50,000 Marines who were put ashore at Tientsin and Tsingtao. The Navy ferried Chiang's troops north to fight the Communists, clearly a violation of the United States' public policy of neutrality in the Chinese war.

As the Nationalist cause looked more and more hopeless, American naval officers grew frustrated with their own government. For years the President had held them back, preventing them from becoming more involved in the war; now the State Department was putting out word that the Navy would no longer be able to protect American citizens. Never before had war policy been such an emotional issue for American servicemen. Not until Vietnam, twenty years later, would it reemerge as an issue.

As Scotty was leaving boot camp on leave for his visit to Tennessee, Chinese Communists captured four American Marine fliers after their plane made a forced landing in Tsingtao. It was the third time the Communists had captured American soldiers. Eight days earlier, the Communists had released four Marines they had held for three months.

The *LST-855*, on which Scotty served in China, and its officers
(Courtesy of Scotty Moore)

When Scotty returned to San Diego, he was pumped up over his visit to Tennessee. He had had about as much fun as a sixteen-year-old could have. Within two months of his sixteenth birthday, he had thrown his first drunk, had his first fight, and scammed, by virtue of his forged birth date, the most powerful government in the world—in short, he had become a man. Now he was ready to flex a little muscle. On his return to the naval base, he was assigned to the USS *LST-855*. He was flown in a seaplane to San Francisco, where he caught a transport to Hawaii, then on to Guam, and finally to Tsingtao, where the *LST-855* was based.

Since it had passed through Memphis in 1944, the USS *LST-855* had an interesting, if undistinguished, war record. Scheduled to be part of the Okinawa invasion, it developed problems and was dry-docked for repairs. In July 1945 it was sent to Pearl Harbor, from which it ferried troops and supplies to Guam. In 1946 the *LST-855* was assigned to duty in Tsingtao, China, where one of its first actions was to evacuate Marines from the city of 2.7 million. The *LST-855* made frequent trips from China to the Philippines during 1947, and made a regular run between Tientsin and the coastal cities of Tsingtao and Shanghai.

Crew of the _LST-855_. Scotty is in the bottom row, second from the left, next to John Bankson (Courtesy of Scotty Moore)

Scotty reported for duty on the ship in June or July 1948. If he thought the shocks he had undergone at boot camp were over, he was mistaken. No sooner had he put away his gear than he was told by the other men that the ship had just experienced a court martial. Two men aboard the ship, he was told in hushed tones, had been convicted of sodomy. He was warned to be on the lookout in the shower. As if to further emphasize the changing times, President Truman signed executive order number 9981 in July, ordering an end to racial segregation in the armed forces. Thus Scotty became a member of the nation's first fully integrated armed forces.

Scotty's rank was fireman III, one grade below third-class petty officer. He was assigned below deck to monitor the ballast tanks, the electric pumps, and the generators, which were powered by diesel engines. The petty officer who had held the job previously had just retired. "When his hitch was up, they said to me, 'We're going to put you there,'" Scotty recalls. "I was a one-person division on that ship. They never got another chief or petty officer."

Once he learned the ropes, Scotty made friends with a twenty-year-old electrician, Merle Parise. "He was still wet behind the ears, just a kid," recalls Merle. "We all knew he had fudged on his age to get into the Navy." Apart from his age, Scotty stood out from the others because he played guitar. Usually, he played his guitar below deck, but sometimes he found a private spot on the stern. During those moments of solitude, Scotty allowed his guitar to express the turmoil he felt inside.

When he played songs the way they were written, they somehow came out different— faster, more energetic. On the outside, Scotty was cool and collected, a shy country boy. On the inside, he was bubbling with emotion. Music was his release. No one had ever heard music the way Scotty heard it; no one had ever felt it the same way.

"I was never an instrumentalist," he says. "There's not a song that I could sit down and play you the melody all the way through. Most of the stuff I heard I would try to do my own way and capture the feel of it. I never tried to copy a song note for note. People ask me, 'How did you come up with that lick?' I tell them I was stretching, out on a limb, and that's what came out."

Throughout the summer of 1948 the *LST-855* carried cargo up and down the Yellow River, the Wang Po, and the Hai Ho. Usually, the ship would load at Shanghai. "Our job was to supply the missionaries," says Merle. "We'd deliver rice, mail, food, anything that would help sustain their livelihood in the back country. As the war got worse for the Chinese Republic, our trips became more frequent. It got to where we were hauling tons and tons of rice from Shanghai into Tsingtao. They would off-load the rice, then send it to the front lines for the troops of the Nationalist government. We even hauled coal to supply the steam trains on the coast."

By the end of the summer Scotty and Merle were best friends. They did everything together. They especially liked to get drunk together when they got shore leave. "Scotty had him a White Russian girlfriend in Shanghai," says Merle. "Once we went to the French Quarter of Shanghai to visit her in a Catholic hospital. She had appendicitis. They were pretty close. If the law had allowed, I think they would have gotten married."

As the Nationalist army disintegrated in the face of Communist opposition, the seaport towns resembled wild west frontiers more than they did the ancient cities of Chinese lore. Nationalist soldiers jammed into the cities, along with refugees from the countryside, shedding their uniforms as they deserted, breaking into stores, when necessary, to get civilian clothing. Amid the chaos, Scotty roamed the streets with Merle, and a new friend, John Bankson.

"There were certain sections you had to stay in," Scotty says, recalling the danger. But there was also an upside. "If you had a carton of cigarettes, you could sell it for $25," says Scotty, laughing. "You'd see the captain get off the ship with his pockets bulging with cigarettes."

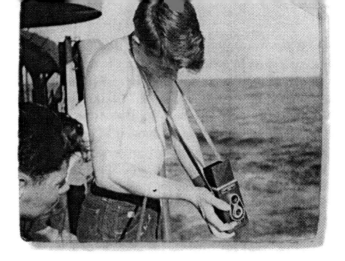

Scotty with camera aboard the *LST-855* in the China seas
(Courtesy of Scotty Moore)

That fall it became clear that the Communists would be victorious. The Truman administration had two options: it could send in American combat troops on a large scale and try to prop up the Nationalist government, or it could give the order to pull out. Truman decided to cut his losses. To the dismay of the Navy, he gave the order to evacuate American embassy personnel and dependents. The long-standing conflict between the Navy and the State Department over China policy snowballed into unseemly confusion as senior officials argued over who was in charge of the evacuation.

On October 23, 1948, the ambassador told the consulates in Peking and Tientsin to issue a formal evacuation warning to all American citizens in the cities. On that same day, the consul general at Tientsin requested help in evacuating the American citizens who remained. He specifically requested Navy LSTs for the operation. He estimated that there were 177 Americans left in Tientsin.

Three days later, Edmund Clubb, the consul general at Peking, cabled the secretary of state advising that December 15 would be the last date possible to take personnel out of Peking by river. Noting that LSTs draw thirteen feet of water, he said that the river now stood at fifteen feet. Tientsin harbor normally froze solid by mid-December. Time was running out.

By the time the *LST-855* arrived in Tientsin, the Communists and the Nationalists had squared off against each other along the river. As the ship made its way up the narrow Hai Ho channel, Scotty recalls shells flying overhead. "They weren't firing at us, but you could hear the shells and see them exploding," he says. "They did most of their firing at night, it seemed like. We were watching a movie one night and had to quit because it got so noisy with all that shelling going on. It was an antsy time. You could see the bodies washed up on the bank of the river. You'd see bodies everywhere you went."

The only ships that got fired on, says Merle, were British. "They put a good sized hole in the side of the *London*," he recalls. "When she came up the river, she came right by us."

Scotty's *LST-855* made several trips upriver to Tientsin to pick up evacuees, but on December 15 it picked up its last load, meeting Clubb's deadline to the day. "There were hundreds of people on the main deck," recalls Scotty. "It was loaded to the gills."

It was during the last trip that Scotty, working below deck, made a miscalculation on one of the valves. He inadvertently overfilled the ballast tanks, dumping water onto the deck and down into the passageways. Scotty doesn't remember exactly what he was doing at the time, but you've got to wonder if he was thinking about that guitar as the icy water from the Hai Ho poured into the ballast tanks. When Scotty heard the screams, he ran into the engine room to see what had happened. "The exec came running down and said everyone was screaming," says Scotty. "They thought the ship was sinking."

"It scared the passengers to death," says Merle. "We all thought we were sinking. I was standing watch over the generators at the time. When I heard the commotion, I went up the hallway and there was water all over the place. I wasn't too scared. If we were sinking, we were sinking. When I found out who was involved, I started laughing like hell."

That December, as the fighting centered around Tientsin, Scotty turned seventeen. With the remaining Americans and their dependents gathered at Shanghai, Scotty's LST, along with the remaining ships in the fleet, continued to carry out missions in the Yellow Sea and the East China Sea, taking supplies in and out of Shanghai. By January 8, 1949 (the day on which Elvis Presley celebrated his fourteenth birthday) fighting was fierce in the streets of Tientsin. On January 15 Tientsin fell to the Communists.

Throughout the summer and into the fall, as Mao focused his efforts in southern and southwestern China, Scotty's LST meandered about in the Yellow and East China seas, keeping a sharp eye out for Nationalist "mistakes." They were safe from the Communist navy—because the Communists had none—but the Nationalists still controlled a fleet of about one hundred ships.

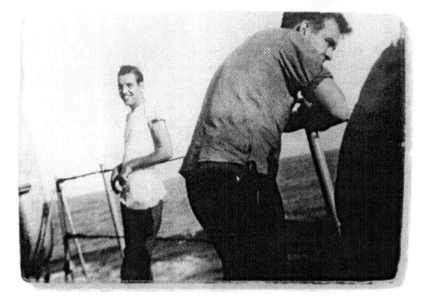

Frank Parise, left, and John Bankson aboard the *LST-855* on the way to Shanghai, c. 1948 (Courtesy of Frank Parise)

Scotty continued to play his guitar. There was a growing urgency to his music. The guitar style of the day offered two possibilities: rhythmical strumming or cleanly fingered "picking" that stressed the resonance of individual notes. Something inside Scotty was making him "pick" with rhythms instead of individual notes. If Scotty had been thinking it, he would have realized it was a radical concept, but since he was feeling it and not thinking it, he simply went with the flow.

With the Chinese ports now off-limits to American servicemen, shore leave was confined to Formosa and Hong Kong. When the LST was at sea, the only recreation Scotty and his friends Merle and John could find was on the ship itself. "The bow doors on the ship were closed at sea, but it was a free flooding area," recalls Merle. "There were a lot of ladders. As the ship pitched up into the air, we would go down and hang onto the ladders and let the water come rushing up in there. It was a good way to go swimming without going overboard."

By December it was obvious that China was a lost cause. The Communists were firmly in control. The Navy was ordered to take out one last load of refugees, then to head home. Scotty's LST was dispatched to Tientsin, where American officials estimated there was only one month's supply of food left. Defeated Nationalist troops from Manchuria had holed up in the city and were making a last stand. When Scotty's LST arrived, fighting in the streets was still vicious. Two supply ships, the *Butterfield* and the *Swire*, had been machine-gunned as they entered the harbor. A number of bullets hit the bridge of the ships, but no one was injured in the attack.

On December 15 the *LST-855* had loaded 90 percent of the remaining 400 people waiting for evacuation. Most of them had come down the river to Tientsin from Peking. As it pulled out of the harbor, the Communists cut the Peking-Tientsin railroad behind them. The ship went to Shanghai, picking up one final load of evacuees before heading for the open seas. Merle, who stayed in the Navy, eventually retiring a lieutenant commander in 1970, said the *LST-855* was the last Navy ship to leave China. It is tempting to think of Scotty with his guitar on the stern of the ship as it left Chinese waters, strumming furiously, the first, infantile guitar licks of rock 'n' roll wafting overhead as the sun set on an old way of life.

❊ ❊ ❊

After stops in Formosa and Japan, the *LST-855* was sent to the Aleutian Islands to rid Attu and some of the other small islands of large deposits of live ammunition and bombs left over from World War II. The ammunition was taken out to sea and dumped in deep water. From there the ship went to Bremington, Washington, for decommission.

Scotty with early band in Bremington. L to r: Johnny, Sparky, Scotty (Courtesy of Scotty Moore)

Located across Puget Sound from Seattle, Bremington offered yet another cultural shock to Scotty. As Scotty waited for the boat to be decommissioned—a process that took about six weeks—he and Bankson formed a band they named the Happy Valley Boys. Bankson died twenty-nine years later of cancer contracted after he boarded a ship that had been used in the testing of hydrogen bombs in the Pacific in the 1950s. His widow, Analee Bankson, recalls the days of the Happy Valley Boys with fond, if not embarrassed, memories.

"I told them they didn't have any talent," she says with a laugh. "I'll never live that down. But they would never play anything all the way through, and that irritated me to no end. They would start something, then go into something else."

While Scotty awaited his next assignment, he formed a new band. For this one, he recruited a steel guitar player named Johnny and a vocalist/guitarist named Sparky. They were good enough to get their own weekly fifteen-minute show on radio station KPRO in Bremington.

"We did a live show, two or three songs and that was it," says Scotty. "We probably didn't play them very well, but we were about as good as anyone else around, so it didn't matter."

The band also played at clubs and private parties off the base. It was at one of those parties that Scotty met a five-foot-four brunette named Mary Durkee. That January they started dating. She was eighteen and still living at home with her parents. "I liked him," she says. "He was good-looking, and he was nice to be around."

Mary, who was out of school and without a job, quickly fell in love with Scotty. To her disappointment, Scotty did not want to rush the relationship. "He said he didn't want to get serious with anybody," she recalls. "I started flirting with his buddy Johnny, and he got jealous and said he didn't want me to go with anyone else. Music was his life. He loved music. That's why he didn't think going with me would be good because music was his first love."

Mary remembers Scotty at that age being very concerned about his appearance. "He had this wave in his hair in the front," she says. One day she talked him into getting a home permanent in the belief that it would make the wave go away. Scotty didn't care for the experience, complaining that the chemicals smelled like "rotten eggs."

Scotty got his next assignment during the first month of his relationship with Mary. He was attached to the USS *Valley Forge*, an aircraft carrier that, because of its huge size, was one of the most impressive vessels in the Navy's fleet. Knowing he was going to be shipped out soon, Scotty proposed to Mary. They were married on March 12, 1950.

USS *Valley Forge* (Courtesy of Scotty Moore)

"My stepdad wasn't too keen on the idea," recalls Mary. "My mother wouldn't buy my outfit until the night of the wedding. She didn't think I was really going to get married."

Scotty and Mary spent their wedding night at her mother's house. On the second night, she calculates, she got pregnant. After a few days at her parents, they went to live with Johnny. Mary laughs when she thinks about it today. "We slept in the same bed with Johnny," she says. "There wasn't much hanky panky going on then."

Shortly after Scotty and Mary got their own apartment, he received his orders. On May 1 the *Valley Forge* shipped out for deployment in the Far East. Bankson also was assigned to the carrier. However, Merle was transferred to a submarine and Johnny was sent to San Diego. Incredibly, Merle's nineteen-year-old brother, Frank, whom Scotty had never met, was assigned to the *Valley Forge*.

"Scotty was standing in the chow line—and they had 2,000 or 3,000 men on that ship—and he had on one of my old dungaree shirts with my name on the back," says Merle with a laugh. "This guy tapped him on the shoulder and said, 'What do you mean wearing my brother's shirt?' It was my brother Frank."

Scotty and Frank became inseparable friends. Scotty was assigned below deck, where he helped take care of the auxillary motors and engines. He had numerous opportunities to obtain a higher rank but turned them down because he expected to be discharged in a few

Scotty, second from left, with Frank Parise at an NCO club in Japan, c. 1950 (Courtesy of Scotty Moore)

months. Frank was a yeoman in the engineering office. Frank looked up to Scotty, who, though still in his teens, had picked up a China Service Medal, put together his own radio show, found a wife and gotten her pregnant, and—perhaps most important of all—played guitar like a bat out of hell. In the space of a year Scotty had gone from a wet-behind-the-ears kid to a man's man.

"We went ashore together a lot in Japan," says Frank. "And San Diego. Once we decided to get a hotel room because we didn't want to sleep on the ship. We bought some scotch. I had never tasted scotch before. We had some water glasses and we drank the scotch out of the water glasses."

On June 25, 1950, the *Valley Forge* was anchored in Hong Kong harbor when it received the electrifying news that North Korea had sent troops across the 38th parallel into South Korea. The next day the carrier steamed north to Subic Bay, where it took on provisions and headed straight for Korea. Late in the day on June 30, President Truman authorized the commitment of American troops to defend South Korea. For the second time in his brief naval career, Scotty was headed for a war zone—and his length of service was extended another full year.

Eight days after being notified of the North Korean attack, the *Valley*

Forge launched the first carrier air strike of the Korean conflict. As outnumbered South Korean troops fought to repel the invaders, wave after wave of Skyraiders, Panthers, and Corsairs from the *Valley Forge* slammed the North Korean rail yards, airfields, and fuel storage depots. Between July 3 and November 19, when the *Valley Forge* headed back to San Diego, the carrier sent over 5,000 combat sorties into Korea.

It was during this time that a training exercise got out of hand. Scotty and Frank listened with amusement to the ship's public address announcement that the *Valley Forge* had been sunk by an enemy torpedo. The "sinking" was part of the training exercise. Back in Bremington, however, the sinking was reported as fact. "I was working for this woman, cleaning up her house, when I heard about it on the news," says Mary. "It knocked me over. I thought I had lost him. I thought I was a widow—a pregnant widow."

Below deck, life went on as usual for Scotty. He played his guitar, channeling his emotions into his music. Frank played harmonica and for a time he and Scotty, and a black serviceman who had a talent for singing, formed a band to amuse themselves. "One evening we got together in the radio shack, and the three of us recorded a song," says Frank. "It was probably the first recording Scotty ever made. I can remember Scotty played 'Double Eagle' on the guitar. He was fantastic." Today Frank laughs when he thinks about the recording: "I wish I had kept it."

The *Valley Forge* arrived in San Diego on December 1, 1950, only to be ordered back to Korea. The Chinese Communists had entered the war with a wave of troops that sent United Nations forces reeling to the south. "Oh, no," Scotty thought. "Not those guys again." On December 16, shortly after he returned to the war zone, a little more than a week before his nineteenth birthday, Mary gave birth to their first child, a seven-pound girl they named Linda. Mary gave up their apartment in Bremington and moved to San Diego to live with Johnny and his wife. When that didn't work out—they got into an argument, the substance of which she no longer remembers—she and the baby went to live with a couple who employed her as a babysitter.

The Chinese sent a blitzkrieg into South Korea that leveled everything in its path. Over the next three months, the *Valley Forge* fought back with some 2,580 air sorties against North Korean targets. By the end of January, the Communists were pushed back north of the 38th parallel. On March 29 the *Valley Forge* headed back to San Diego for repairs. When they arrived in San Diego, Scotty was transferred to the second carrier in the Seventh Fleet, the *Boxer*, but after thirty days aboard that ship, he was assigned to the San Diego naval base when the carrier received orders to go to sea. Considered a short-timer at that point—his enlistment was up in January—the Navy didn't want to ship him out on another long engagement.

Scotty recalls neither his time on the *Boxer* nor his time on the base at San Diego with fondness. "When you're a short-timer you're the dregs of the crew," he says. "A guy told me, with that short time left, go find yourself a file folder and fill it up and just keep walking." Scotty laughs when he thinks about it today. "I did and it worked. Just look busy. That's the secret."

Since Scotty couldn't live with Mary and the baby at the babysitter's, and his discharge was only months away, they decided it would be best if Mary and the baby went to Tennessee to live with his family until he was discharged. Scotty took her to Los Angeles to catch a plane to Memphis. When they arrived at the airport, they were given the unsettling news that the plane Mary was to board had crashed on its way to Los Angeles. They spent the night in Los Angeles, and the next day Scotty put Mary and the baby on a plane for Memphis. Mary still remembers the flight with a certain amount of horror.

"The plane had no heater, and it was cold, and we stopped at every airport along the way," she says. She had a really bad feeling about the plane. She was afraid something bad was going to happen. She couldn't get the plane crash out of her mind. When the plane stopped in Kansas City to take on passengers, Mary and the baby got off and bought a train ticket to West Memphis, Arkansas. There, she was met at the train station by Scotty's brother Carney, who lived in Memphis, and his father, who had driven down from Gadsden to pick up his new daughter-in-law and granddaughter.

"He was chewing tobacco," Mary remembers about her first meeting with Scotty's father. "He kissed me with tobacco on his mouth. Ugh, that didn't make a very good impression." Back at the farm, Mary underwent culture shock. As Christmas approached, she learned not everyone felt the same way she did about the holiday. "His family was a lot different from my family," she says. "They didn't believe in a lot of things my family believed in—like Christmas."

On January 4, 1952, Scotty was discharged from the Navy. He boarded a bus in San Diego and headed east to Memphis with his duffel bag and two medals—he had since added a Korean Service Medal to his collection. He was free at last to follow his dream: to become a performing musician. All he needed was a singer, someone who could do with his voice what he could do with a guitar.

Scotty with unidentified musician friends on board the *Valley Forge*
(Courtesy of Scotty Moore)

CHINA AND KOREA: SOWING THE
SEEDS OF REVOLUTION

3

MEMPHIS BAPTISM: LOST SOULS ON THE ROAD TO NIRVANA

During the four years Scotty had sailed the Pacific, experiencing the horrors of war, the sensual and sometimes bizarre pleasures of foreign cultures, and the boredom of life as a below-the-deck seaman, the America he left behind had undergone radical changes. There were no parades to greet him when he returned to Crockett County. For the first time, he was faced with the day-to-day tedium of life as a married man. He had a wife and a daughter to support. He had served with honor in the China and Korea campaigns; now it was time to find a job and get on with the rest of his life.

Scotty renewed his friendship with James Lewis, but they had both changed in four years. James had become a serious farmer and husband, and Scotty . . . well, he hadn't. "He wasn't the [Scotty] I knew," says James. "I had never seen him like that. He had discovered women. He and [Mary] couldn't keep their hands off each other. I remember my wife and I talked about how lovey-dovey they were together."

Scotty and James jammed on their guitars, but it just wasn't the same. "His guitar playing had improved," says James. "He had left me behind. I had gotten busy trying to make a living."

With no opportunities for employment in Crockett County, Scotty took his job search to Memphis. He went by the Greyhound Bus terminal, hawking his naval experience with diesel engines. "The guy said, 'Yeah, we'll hire you.' He said they used the same kind of engines I worked on in the Navy. The only difference, he said, was that theirs were air cooled and the ones I worked on were water cooled."

'Come over here,' he said. 'Let me show you something.'

"We walked out into the garage. There was this guy taking a big ole tire off a bus."

"'I'm not gonna kid you, that's what you'll be doing for six months before we can get you on the engines.'

"Those big ole tires were bigger than I was. I said, 'Thank you very much—but no thanks.'"

Once, Scotty and Mary went to Memphis together to look for work. James and Evelyn offered to babysit Linda. "We kept her one night," says James. "I remember trying to rock the child to sleep and she was screaming bloody murder. She was just learning to talk. She kept saying, 'bed, bed,' and I put her in bed and she went right to sleep."

Mary had a hard time adjusting to life on the farm. Southerners had their own way of doing things, she discovered; things that were obvious to them were incomprehensible to her. "She was strictly not country like we were," says James. "She was a different type of person. She was nice, but she was not our kind of people, if you know what I'm saying." Forty years later, James pondered that remembrance a moment, then laughed in a self-effacing way that made it apparent why he and Scotty were such close friends. "We were all rednecks," he said with a grin.

James Lewis and Scotty at Scotty's home, c. 1953
(Courtesy of Scotty Moore)

Scotty's parents had a similar reaction. Although they made it clear they would love Mary like a daughter, they did question his judgment. "What'd you marry a Yankee for?" they asked him. At times, Scotty felt like a referee. "She was used to going out dancing on Saturday nights and so forth," says Scotty. "As far as my mother and daddy were concerned, that was a sin. The Church of Christ had no music."

Eventually, Scotty found work in Memphis at an engine repair shop, overhauling and rebuilding small engines. To Mary's relief, they left the farm and found an apartment in the city. For the first time, after two years of marriage, they were living together—alone—as husband and wife. It wasn't an easy adjustment for either of them.

Four years in the Navy had convinced Scotty that a certain degree of regimentation was the best way to deal with life on a day-to-day basis. He folded his shirts a certain way. He rolled his socks a certain way. He placed his clothes a certain way in the dresser drawers so their usage could be rotated. Mary was just the opposite. For two years, she had the freedom, as a married woman, to do as she pleased. When Scotty was at sea she conferred with him by letter on the small matters of married life, but when he was in port, they didn't waste time talking about mundane matters: they made love. Now, almost overnight, everything changed. She was no longer free to go as she pleased. To her dismay, she discovered Scotty wanted her to do things his way.

"He didn't like me wearing pants or shorts," says Mary. "He liked me dressed up in heels and I didn't like that. Scotty wanted everything perfect. Everything had to be clean and spotless. He used to put my clothes out, what I had to wear. He was very finicky and fussy. He was different from anyone I knew."

Scotty's job at the engine shop ended after a short while. He was offered a job on a tugboat on the Mississippi River, but it would have required him to be gone for six weeks at a time, so he turned it down to look for something closer to home. Finally, he decided to take a job with his brother Carney at the dry cleaners until something better came along. He was made the official hatter. His job was to dissemble the hats for cleaning—that is, remove the band and the lining—then put the pieces back together after cleaning and block them into their original shape.

Scotty also made hats from scratch. "They came in big cones that looked like dunce caps," he says. "You would take the fabric you wanted in whatever size you wanted, then you would steam it and block it. Some places made them with machinery, but we did it by hand. You would work the fabric, making it pliable, then you would add the flange, which was the brim—and we had all different types of brims—then you would

**Mary with Donald, one month old, and Linda, twenty-five months old
(Courtesy of Scotty Moore)**

put the brim over the top and work it out on the flange. When you got
to the point where you had it stretched out pretty good, you would cut
off the excess. If they wanted a binding on it, you would do that with a
sewing machine. Then you would put the lining inside and attach a sweat
band—and you were finished. I made all kinds of hats. I even made
women's hats out of the scraps from the men's hats."

Once Scotty had settled into a routine at the dry-cleaning shop, he
turned his attention back to his music. He doesn't remember what happened to the guitar he had in the Navy—actually he bought several
inexpensive Japanese models over the years—but by the time he set up
housekeeping in Memphis he no longer had a guitar. As soon as he could
afford to, he purchased a Fender Esquire guitar and a Fender Deluxe
amplifier. Knowing how he felt about music, Carney told him he could
practice during his lunch break at the shop. Soon Scotty got into a
routine of doing his work with the hats, then taking a break to play his
guitar, then finishing up his day's work and going home to pick up where
he had left off on his guitar.

University Park Cleaners was in a prime midtown neighborhood.
Located at 613 North McClean Street, north of Poplar Avenue, it was
near the city zoo and Snowden Elementary School. The neighborhood
contained a mixture of small businesses and residential buildings, both
single family dwellings and apartments.

Every day after school, nine-year-old Emily Evans stopped by the market next door to the University Park Cleaners and bought a dill pickle to eat on the way home. Scotty sometimes stood in the doorway to the cleaners, watching the traffic go by. Emily smiled at the handsome young man as she passed, entertaining a third grader's romantic fantasy or two, and they exchanged greetings. Fifteen years later, when she had matured into a striking redhead, she would marry the man in the doorway, but for now, he was a regular part of her after-school routine.

Poplar Avenue was one of three east-west thoroughfares that connected downtown Memphis with more densely populated East Memphis; Union Avenue was south of Poplar and Summer Avenue was to the north. Most of the black population was centered in an area south of Union, with some pockets of black residences north of Poplar and Summer. About a mile southwest of University Park Cleaners, in a neighborhood beyond the white mainstream, Elvis Presley and his parents lived in a federally funded housing project called Lauderdale Courts.

That summer, as Scotty adjusted to his new life as a hatter, Elvis tried to adjust to being a teenager. He had another year to go at Humes High before graduation. He had no idea what he wanted to do with his life. For a while, he talked about being a famous singer and driving Cadillacs, but his friends laughed at him, so he stopped being so free with his talk. That summer he entered his "zoot suit" phase.

Jimmy Denson, whose family lived at the Courts, recalled that almost overnight Elvis underwent a transformation from a skinny kid to a decked-out fashion hound. "This was his version of what the 1942 zoot-suiters had been, only he was ten years behind the zoot-suiters," said Denson. "His hair was very short until the zoot suit. Then he started putting that greasy Brilliantine on it. It was greasy and dirty looking and long with long ducktails in the back . . . Apparently, he read an old magazine and would see old people of the zoot suit era. He liked that." Johnny Black, brother of Bill, knew Elvis at that time and sometimes went to house parties with him. The women were impressed by Elvis's zoot suit phase, recalls Black, but the men were not. Says Black: "All these guys with crew cuts and muscles resented a pretty boy."

Elvis began showing up at Ellis Auditorium, located downtown at the west end of Poplar, to attend gospel concerts by the Blackwood Brothers Quartet, a local group with a national following. The Blackwoods attended the same church as the Presley family and Elvis had gotten to know several of them quite well. He also began attending the East Trigg Baptist Church, a black congregation led by Reverend W. Herbert Brewster, who also directed a radio show, the *Gospel Treasure Hour.* B. B. King attended services during this time, so it is likely they were sometimes in church at the same time (although there is no record of their meeting). Elvis was testing the waters: of what, exactly, he wasn't sure.

If Mary thought she finally had her husband settled into a job and a family way of life, she was sadly mistaken. Scotty formed another band that summer. Actually, it was sort of a movable band, with a membership that changed as the demands of the job changed. Today, he doesn't remember if the band even had a name. Says Scotty: "How I met the people I started playing with, I don't know. I'd do a Saturday night here and there. Back then I can only remember one or two groups in town in which the players were always the same. The rest of the bands were all little, makeup groups. You'd have all kinds of combinations of instruments. We had to play country, R&B, pop, whatever was popular. You had to play stuff people could dance to. It was a mixture. People just called it honky tonk. Some days we might have an accordion and a trumpet and a guitar, most any kind of combination you could think of."

Soon Scotty realized that being a floating musician "wasn't gonna get it." He had played a few gigs with Bill Black and they had become close friends, so he talked him into joining a more stable group he was putting together. Acting as their manager, Scotty began booking the band. "We played a few club dates," he says. "Sometimes we played out of town. I remember one fall we almost froze to death playing on the rooftop of a drive-in theater. There was frost on the ground."

If Scotty and Elvis had crossed paths in 1952, Scotty, with his straight-arrow dress code, probably would have been appalled by Elvis's outlandish appearance. It is not surprising they never met until a fateful day in July. As a family man with a day job in a nice part of town, Scotty traveled in circles not open to Elvis. As a musician, he performed in honky tonks that would not have admitted Elvis because of his age. He occasionally went to church, but he didn't share Elvis's bent for gospel concerts. He shared Elvis's appreciation of the blues, but there were no blues clubs in Memphis at that time open to whites. In 1952 Beale Street was only a shell of its former self. It was seedy and run-down, primarily a gathering place for unemployed laborers attracted to its garish history. Elvis liked to hang out there, especially at Lanksy's, a clothing store that specialized in outrageous clothing; Scotty would not have been caught dead there.

Toward the end of the summer, Scotty's band started playing at Shadow Lawn, a honky tonk in Laconia, Tennessee. Sometime that fall Bobbie Walls went into the club with her two sisters, Janie and Alice. She lived in Memphis, but often went to Laconia to visit her parents and sisters. The club was just a joint, a bottle club where men and women could meet and dance, but it was the only nightspot for miles around and it was the place to go if you were young and single.

Bobbie and her sisters were regulars at the club. "One night Bill Black came into the club," says Bobbie. "He had his bass in the car and said he wanted to sit in with Scotty. He was sort of a clown, always cutting up and carrying on, hollering 'Sueee' and things like that. He was a card." Bobbie noticed Scotty, but that's as far as it went. "The first time I saw him, he didn't strike me much," she says. "After about the fourth time, I started to wonder about him. He didn't seem to associate with too many people."

One night she noticed he came with a "date." No one remembers for certain, but his "date" that night may have been Mary. In the early months, Mary accompanied Scotty on many of his gigs. That enabled her to get out of the house, but it did little to alleviate her homesickness or her inability to adjust to life in the South. She started working part-time in the dry cleaners selling head bands, but that, too, became a source of contention when she complained that Carney did not pay her as much as he paid the black employees. "We had a fight, so Scotty wouldn't let me go with him anymore when he played music," she says.

As his marriage disintegrated, Scotty turned inward, looking to his music as a release for emotions he little understood. Mary was right: music was becoming his life, though he never admitted that to himself or anyone else. Scotty never dreamed of obtaining worldly riches—and still doesn't—but he did dream of having control over his life. When he played music, he had that control, if only for the moment.

One day Mary accused him of seeing another woman.

"We had a big fight," says Mary. She blamed their troubles on his music. Honky tonks were no place for a married man, she reasoned. To make matters worse, she had gotten pregnant when they arrived in Memphis that spring. Her baby was due in December. She took out her frustration on what she saw as the source of their marital discord: his guitar. She lashed out, striking his Fender Esquire in a fit of anger. "That was a no no," she says. Scotty exploded. That guitar was more than an instrument of wood and metal; it was his life. He responded by slapping her across the face.

Normally, Scotty is reserved and soft-spoken. Mary had never seen him angry; she had never even seen him drink. That was important to her because both her mother and father were alcoholics. She had grown up in an atmosphere of alcoholism, with all the sudden mood swings that entails. In Scotty, she had found the opposite—or so she thought.

The fight over the guitar frightened her. She did what young women often do when things go awry in a marriage: she called her mother, who sent money for a ticket back to Bremington. "I was a mama's girl and I was homesick." she says. "The people were different [in Memphis], and I didn't know anybody." Mary took the gamble of her life. She packed up the baby and headed back to Bremington. Despite the fight, she loved Scotty. She didn't want to end the marriage. She wanted to get him away from the source of their problems: his music, and, of course, the other woman.

After she returned to Bremington, she gave birth on December 16, 1952, to a son she named Donald. Incredibly, both of Scotty's and her children shared the same birth date. She was certain Scotty would come to be at her side. His response was not what she expected: he sued for divorce. "I was shocked," she says today, looking back to the day it occurred. Even after all this time, her voice, emotional and tinged with regret, betrays her pain. In her early sixties, she is now in her third marriage. "Scotty's a sweet guy. I always thought we would get back together again." She pauses, sifting through nearly fifty years of memories. "If we had more time together, we might have made it," she says wistfully. "We had a crazy marriage, but I loved him and always will."

✳ ✳ ✳

One night Bobbie was in Shadow Lawn with her sisters when one of the guys in the band, Bud Deckelman, came over to their table and talked to Bobbie's sister. "I asked him about Scotty," Bobbie says. "He said, 'Do you want to meet him?' He brought him over and introduced us. He rode back to Memphis with us that night. I didn't think I would see him again for a while, but the next night my sister and I were driving down Getwell toward the VA hospital and we stopped at the light and there Scotty sat with Bud Deckelman. They had been playing at the VA hospital. They hollered at us and we went on Park Avenue to Berretta's, a drive-in, and got together. It seemed, after that, we were together almost every night."

Meanwhile, Elvis concentrated on graduating from high school. On a parallel course with Scotty, he experimented with his musical talents, trying to find a place to fit in. He learned to play guitar, though not very well. It was as much a prop as anything, something to hold onto while he sang. Jimmy Denson remembers how Elvis would sit on the steps of his family's apartment at night and perform for his friends. Invariably, he reached a point where his singing outran his guitar playing. If he lost his way, he threw up his hands in exasperation and said with a sheepish grin, "I forgot the chords." When he saw that got a laugh, he started doing it even when he knew the chords. Anything for a laugh. Music was a means to an end. It was attention he really wanted.

In the fall of 1952 Elvis and a friend, Ronald Smith, sang and played guitars in an amateur show at South Side High School. That December Elvis sang the dog-lover's tearjerker, "Old Shep," at a Christmas concert at Humes. January 1953 was an emotional month for him. First came Hank Williams's sudden death. Then he and his parents moved from Lauderdale Courts to an apartment at 398 Cypress Street, then to a house at 462 Alabama Street, located just across the street from the Courts. In the spring of 1953, as Elvis was approaching graduation, he sang in the Humes High Annual Minstrel Show and with the choir at East Trigg Baptist Church.

In March the big news, musically, was that Sam Phillips had recorded a hit record in his tiny studio on Union Avenue. The record, "Bear Cat," was a takeoff on Big Mama Thornton's "Hound Dog." Recorded by Rufus Thomas, a popular black disc jockey on radio station WDIA, the song gave Phillips the momentum he needed to get Sun Records off the ground. Later in the year, Phillips followed that success with a song called "Just Walkin' in the Rain." It was recorded by five inmates from the Tennessee State Penitentiary in Nashville who called themselves the Prisonaires. Phillips talked the prison warden into allowing the inmates to come to his studio in Memphis under armed guard to make the recording. The session attracted the attention of the afternoon newspaper, the *Memphis Press-Scimitar*, which reported on the session as though it was a major event. Tennessee governor Frank Clement was so impressed by the success of the song that he pardoned some of the inmates, proving that crime, when spiced with a dash of rehabilitation, could be made to pay.

In June Elvis was graduated from Hume High. He got a job as a truck driver at Crown Electric Company, but it didn't pay enough for him to leave home and get a place of his own. While he technically wasn't of age—in Tennessee the age of majority was twenty-one—he was in the eyes of most adults, himself included, now a man. Instead of parading up and down Beale Street, his ducktails plastered into place, he sought refuge in the neighborhood movie theaters.

Others have written that Elvis sampled the nightlife inside the clubs on Beale, sometimes sitting in with Johnny and Dorsey Burnette, two brothers he had met in the projects, but Scotty says that surprises him since he never heard Elvis or the Burnette brothers talk about it. Scotty performed with the Burnette brothers during that period, but he doesn't recall ever hearing Elvis's name mentioned. Once, when he was two players short for a booking at the Shadow Lawn, he asked the Burnette brothers to perform with him. In those days Johnny played bass and Dorsey played steel guitar. Before playing the date, he rehearsed with them at the dry cleaners. Musically, they clicked, so Scotty was confident everything would go smoothly. Was he ever wrong.

Shadow Lawn wasn't what you would call a high-class supper club. It was a roadhouse located on the side of the road off Highway 64 in the middle of nowhere between Memphis and Somerville. Most of the patrons were farmers and blue-collar workers who partied as hard on the weekends as they worked during the week. They liked their music hard driving one minute, and crying-in-your-beer, hold-your-honey-tight sweet the next.

All of the roadhouses in and around Memphis were almost identical. There was usually a front room that contained a bar (you had to bring your own hard liquor because by-the-drink sales were still illegal) and a back room where the band performed. "Some were more freshly painted than others, but most of them were alike," says Scotty. "The lights were always turned down low and you couldn't see a thing."

That night there was a mixed crowd, because several carloads of people had driven in from Memphis. For most of the evening, everything went smoothly. Then, for reasons no one recalls, all hell broke loose in the club. "Johnny and Dorsey were notorious fighters," says Scotty. "Both of them were Golden Gloves in Memphis. They were banned from all the Cotton Carnivals. That night we were playing and someone got into it and they emptied that place. I don't know how many the two of them were fighting—a bunch of them. Dorsey got stuck in his thigh with a knife. It wasn't a huge cut, but I'm sure it smarted a bit. I decided right then, 'Well, boys, I don't think we can book you again around here.'"

If Elvis ever heard Scotty and any of his bands, there is no record of it. He and Elvis just didn't move in the same circles. When Scotty wasn't working at the dry cleaners—or playing in honky tonks—he practiced on his guitar. It was about this time that he traded in his Fender Esquire for a Gibson ES 295, a cello-shaped, semiacoustic jazz guitar. The streamlined Fender just didn't feel right when he played it. "It probably had something to do with its shape," he says with a laugh. "The Gibson was more feminine. I could make out with the Gibson. I couldn't get it on with a Fender."

In June 1953 Scotty and Bobbie were married by a justice of the peace across the state line in Mississippi. Unlike Mary, Bobbie was a

Scotty and Bobbie, c. 1954 (Courtesy of Scotty Moore)

born-and-bred Southerner—and she owned a car, a 1952 Chevrolet. Bobbie didn't like to wear dresses and high heels any more than Mary did,
but Scotty never pressed the issue with her. One thing Bobbie did dif-
ferently was to encourage Scotty in his dream of becoming a professional
musician.

"I knew he didn't want to do anything else," says Bobbie. "He hated
working nine to five. Of course, if you marry a musician, you know you
are going to be separated a lot, but I wanted to see him do well. Scotty
tried to teach me how to play the guitar, but I didn't have an ear for it.
I guess opposites attract."

Bobbie felt the excitement of Scotty's music. She sat and watched
him practice for hours. "I liked what he played," she says. "Today, I can
even tell if he's playing on a record. I got to know his style of playing, I
guess. He admired people like Chet Atkins and Les Paul. He tried to be
like them. He was playing country music at the time, but he didn't really
like it. He wanted to play something else. He just didn't think he was
good enough."

Growing tired of his work as a hatter—and seeing little future as a
Saturday night, honky-tonk guitar picker—Scotty got serious about
putting together a first-rate band. "He was looking for someone who
would go on the road," says Bobbie. "Family men, like the ones he was
playing with, didn't want to give up their jobs to go on the road. Scotty
didn't have a good job, like at Firestone or something like that. He
thought that he could record and maybe make a living at it." What Scotty
needed were musicians who had the time and dedication to make the
Big Time. Married men were fine—if they were like him and had an
understanding wife—but single men were preferable, especially if they
were hungry for success.

Just as Scotty was beating the bushes to put together a band, Elvis strolled into Sam Phillips's studio to make a record. He said it was for his mother's birthday. Marion Keisker, Sam's secretary, told him it would cost $3.98, plus tax, to make a two-sided acetate. While he waited to make the record, he engaged Marion in conversation.

"If you know anyone that needs a singer . . ."

"What kind of a singer are you?" she asked.

"I sing all kinds."

"Who do you sound like?"

"I don't sound like nobody."

Elvis recorded two songs, "My Happiness" and "That's When Your Heartache Begins." He wasn't too pleased with the way he sounded, but Marion was impressed enough to ask him for his name and phone number in case Sam ever needed a singer and wanted to get in touch with him. Elvis took his time leaving the studio, and Marion surmised it was because he thought Sam might come out from the back to speak to him. After schmoozing with Marion for a while, Elvis stuck the acetate under his arm and left.

Convinced she had made a discovery, Marion told Sam about Elvis. Sam brushed her comments aside, which is not surprising. No self-respecting studio owner of that era would have entertained recommendations from a mere secretary.

In later years, as Sam began to take more credit for discovering Elvis, Marion wrote a letter to Elvis biographer Jerry Hopkins in which she complained about Sam's version of events. The way Sam tells it, he was searching for a way to merge black and white music when Elvis walked in the door. He worked with Elvis for several months, then introduced him to Scotty. In her letter, Marion took exception to Sam's version. She sent Hopkins a copy of an interview Sam did with a Memphis newspaper. "I can only say this ain't the way I remember the first visit of EP to our small shop," she wrote. "Perhaps he is actually recalling a later visit. Elvis did come by several times in the months between his first record and the time Sam actually started to work with him. I know that he came by at least once when I was out of the office, because—as I think I told you—I found a note in Sam's handwriting on my desk saying: 'Elvis Presley—good ballad singer, Save.' So I guess you just take your choice of authentic, genuine first-hand versions of what happened. I still have not seen the great SCP [Sam Phillips]. I understand he has bought a weekend place on Pickwick and spends a lot of time there. As for being 'disappointed' by him—well, Jerry, it's like eating at a restaurant where the service is consistently poor and the food always unpalatable. If you keep going back, you forfeit the right to complain."

Scotty also is mystified by the "official" version that has come to be accepted as fact. "Sam may have been talking about merging black and white music in those days, but he never talked about it to me," he says. Marion's version, that Elvis came in to do the vanity recording, then kept in touch with her over the next few months, is the version Scotty heard at the time. He was shocked in later years when Sam told interviewers he had worked with Elvis prior to the landmark July 1954 session. "It just doesn't jive," says Scotty. "When we went into the studio, Elvis acted like it was the first time he met Sam. I have often wondered why [Sam], if he had worked with him before, never mentioned it at the time."

In the ten months or so that elapsed between the time he first went into Sam's studio and did the July 5 audition with Scotty and Bill, nothing seemed to go right for Elvis. Various clubs in Memphis and across the river in West Memphis allowed him to take the stage on amateur night or during intermission, but for the most part his efforts to become a singer were ignored. He seriously considered a career as a gospel singer.

The Blackwood Brothers Quartet allowed him to hang out with them backstage and they encouraged him with his singing. On occasion they allowed him to sing, backing up his struggling solos with their own polished harmonies. When Cecil Blackwood, a cousin of the founding member of the quartet, formed a group called the Songfellows, Elvis tried out for a slot opened by a departing member. However, at the last minute the member decided to remain on board, and Elvis did not get the job. However, he continued to hang out with both groups.

Elvis kept in touch with Marion, who obviously had become smitten with his gentlemanly mannerisms and youthful good looks. "He always called me Marion, which was queer, because anybody two years older was mister or missus," she says. "Here is a young man so pure, so sweet, so wonderful, that he's unbelievable." For his part, Elvis must have been impressed with Marion's glamorous good looks and her reputation as "Miss Radio of Memphis." Before going to work for Sam, the former child actress had her own program called "Meet Kitty Kelly." The fifteen-minute show aired daily at 2 P.M. on WREC. The thirty-something Marion had a flair for the dramatic and that would have been exotically attractive to Elvis, who was himself experimenting with alternative personas.

The only thing going right for Elvis during that time was his personal life. He started dating Dixie Locke, a pretty, fifteen-year-old high school sophomore. She became his first serious girlfriend, and despite their age difference—and her father's opposition to his daughter dating an eighteen-year-old truck driver—they toyed with the idea of marriage.

That fall and winter Memphis was a hotbed of musical activity. Sam was scoring with his black artists. Memphis was becoming a secondary recording center—however small—to New York and Los Angeles. Black entertainers were making records in vacant rooms all over town. Black radio was vibrant, shaking the city to its foundations.

Caught up in the excitement of it all, Scotty put together his first real band, the Starlite Wranglers. To front the group and sing lead vocals, he recruited Doug Poindexter, a baker who had a Hank Williams type of voice. He added Bill Black on bass, Millard Yow on steel guitar, Clyde Rush on guitar, and Thomas Sealy on fiddle.

To cement the relationship, he had a lawyer draw up an ironclad contract that designated Scotty as the personal manager of the group. Each member of the group would receive 16 2/3 percent of the net proceeds, except for Scotty, who, as manager, would receive an additional 10 percent. Under the terms of the contract, Scotty would make all the business decisions and collect the money. The signees agreed to "abide by" Scotty's directions and to "carry out all engagements, appearances, and performances, faithfully and unless prevented by illness or good cause" and to appear "at all times promptly and faithfully for rehearsals under the direction of the manager." A contract like this was rare for groups in Memphis at the time.

In the five years that had elapsed since he left the farm to join the Navy, Scotty had become savvy to the ways of the world. The Starlite Wranglers contract offers a revealing glimpse of Scotty at that time. He wanted success—and all the trappings of success—but more than that he wanted control of his destiny. The best way to do that, in Scotty's mind, was to find people who were agreeable to "fronting" for his own ambitions. He was most comfortable when he was behind the scenes, pulling the strings that made the show work. The Starlite Wranglers were his creation. What did he care if people thought Doug Poindexter was calling the shots? More than glory, Scotty wanted anonymity.

Scotty booked the group at Shadow Lawn, then got bookings at various clubs around Memphis, including the Bon Air. Then he got the group on radio station KWEM in West Memphis. He dressed everyone in matching hats and shirts, and he constructed a large star out of Christmas lights and used it to illuminate the band's name.

Once he had all the pieces in place, he prepared for the final step. "I knew that to get better jobs, we had to put a record out," he says. "You had to have a record to get radio play and you had to have radio play to get bookings. I had that much figured out."

At that time, there were two record labels in town. Modern/RPM, a

West Coast label that had a branch office in Memphis on Chelsea Avenue, was operated by the Bihari brothers and specialized in blues recordings. Sun Records, a Memphis-owned label, was housed in Sam Phillips's Memphis Recording Service. Although both labels were targeting blues performers, Scotty decided to focus his attention on Sun Records. As Elvis was going in one door of the Union Avenue studio, Scotty must have been going out another. They never met during that time, but they were wooing Sam and Marion at about the same time. It took a while, but Scotty finally talked Sam into giving the Starlite Wranglers a chance. "Sam either came out to a club and saw us, or we went down to audition," recalls Scotty. "He finally agreed to put a record out on us."

The Starlite Wranglers went into the studio in May and recorded two sides, both written by Scotty. The A side was titled "My Kind of Carryin' On." Scotty gave the songwriter's credit for the B side, "Now She Cares No More for Me," to Poindexter because he was the singer, and he gave one-third to his brother Carney because he wrote out the lead sheet for them. The song was released in June. It got a little airplay on radio, but not enough to generate sales. "Of course, we didn't get anything to do the record," says Scotty.

Discouraged by the record's failure, but encouraged by the fact that, at last, he had broken the recording barrier, Scotty stopped by every day after work to talk to Sam about the future. He was hoping that Sam could give him work—any work—that would help him break into the music business. And that opportunity, it turns out, was just around the corner.

Starlite Wranglers. L to r: Scotty, Thomas Sealy, Doug Poindexter, Bill Black, Clyde Rush. Not pictured: Millard Yow (Courtesy of Scotty Moore)

MEMPHIS BAPTISM: LOST SOULS
ON THE ROAD TO NIRVANA

CHAPTER 4

JULY 1954:
THREE DAYS THAT SHOOK
THE WORLD

emphis in July is unbearable. On most days the temperature hits one hundred degrees. Drive ten miles in any direction, out into the rich farmland of north Mississippi, east Arkansas, or West Tennessee, and the temperature drops noticeably. Whether Memphis is a thermal hot spot because of the tons of concrete that surround it or because rising moisture from the Mississippi River envelops the city in a suffocating cover of humidity—or simply because the gods bear a grudge for some unpardonable sin anchored in the city's past—is really beside the point: July is the month Memphians dread the most. It is the make-or-break month in which temperatures and passions run the highest.

On the afternoon of July 3, 1954, Scotty, then twenty-two, stopped by Memphis Recording Service to chat with Sam Phillips. It had been two months since the release of "My Kind of Carryin' On." Scotty wasn't wedded to the music of the Starlite Wranglers, though the country band was his own creation. It bore Poindexter's name only because of Scotty's desire to stay in the background. Scotty liked to be in control of his surroundings, but he didn't like the spotlight; it is a characteristic that has stayed with him his entire life.

Scotty wasn't sure his future was in country music. He also liked to play blues and jazz. He made it clear to Sam that he was open to new musical styles. Scotty was a detail man. Give him a problem and he would solve it. Sam was also a detail man, although he approached problem solving from a different angle. He didn't always know what was wrong with a song, but he usually knew when something was wrong and—perhaps more important—he instinctively knew when something was right.

Sam had opened his recording studio in 1950, five years after moving to Memphis from Alabama to work at WREC, an AM radio station at 60 on the dial. Sam kept his job at the radio station while he worked to get his recording studio off the ground. Most of his business was vanity related—weddings, funerals, ordinary people who wanted to find out how they sounded singing their favorite songs—but he had some success with African-American entertainers, whose recordings he was able to sell to record labels in Chicago and Los Angeles. In 1951 Ike Turner recorded a song in Sam's studio that went to No. 1 on the national R&B charts. The song, "Rocket 88," featured Jackie Brenston, Turner's saxophonist, as the vocalist. Because it gave Chicago-based Chess Records its first No. 1 hit, it resulted in stiff competition for black talent in the Memphis area.

In the early fifties Sam discovered a number of major black artists, such as Chester Burnett, better known as Howlin' Wolf, but he couldn't hold onto them. After brief stints with Sam, they usually left for greener pastures.

Race relations were not good in Memphis in 1954. All the public facilities were segregated. There were signs everywhere that read "whites" and "colored." It was illegal for blacks to go into the public library, unless they had been invited there to do janitorial or repair work. That July, race relations worsened when five black students sought enrollment at Memphis State College, the largest state-supported institution of higher learning in West Tennessee. The state board of education in Nashville rejected their applications, but in the eyes of many whites, the city of Memphis compensated for that by erecting a thirty-foot memorial to Tom Lee, a black man who had saved the lives of thirty-two whites following a riverboat disaster in 1925. Interestingly, the memorial was built in the shape of a giant shaft.

On that July 3 the heat was suffocating. Since it was Saturday, many people sought refuge in the air-conditioned movie theaters. Memphis had dozens of theaters in those days. On that particular day, you could see Gary Cooper and Susan Hayward in *Garden of Evil*, Elizabeth Taylor and Dana Andrews in *Elephant Walk*, or if your tastes were more exotic, Lana Turner in *Flame and the Flesh*. The hottest movie in town would not be shown until after dark, when the Sunset Drive-In ran the steamy *Naughty New Orleans*, an uncensored look at New Orleans strippers.

Memphis Recording Service, home of the fledging Sun Records, was located at 706 Union Avenue, just a few blocks from the busy downtown district. Union Avenue was one of the main thoroughfares in the city. If the street today seems a little gritty, the result of urban wear and tear, fifty years ago it sparkled with promise as a major street in the Mid-South's largest city. In keeping with the custom of the day, Scotty would have put on a clean, neatly ironed short-sleeved shirt and worn his good shoes to go downtown to do business. To do otherwise would be to risk the wrath of the gatekeepers to the Big Time.

Memphis Recording Service was a five-room building, with an entrance at which the secretary, an affable blonde named Marion Keisker, sat at her desk and took care of the day-to-day business. Beyond the entrance and the studio itself was a partitioned control room. At the rear of the control room was a bathroom. Past that were two additional rooms, which no longer exist, that contained a warehouse and a room for the equipment used to cut the acetates.

The studio was not air-conditioned. The window units popular at that time were too noisy for use in a studio, and quietly efficient central air-conditioning systems were a rarity. On most days Sam would wear a necktie and dress shirt, and sometimes a sports coat, to work, depending on how hot it was outside; Marion would wear a dress, her well-groomed hair sometimes set off by large earrings. It was an age in which ambitious go-getters dressed up, not down, for success.

53

For weeks Scotty had been talking to Sam, trying to figure out where he was headed with his studio. Finally, after it became clear his subtle probes were getting nowhere, he asked Sam outright: "What exactly are you looking for?"

Sam said he wasn't sure. He would know it when he heard it. All he knew was that it wasn't the same old, same old everybody else was recording. Sam had a feel for music, but little technical understanding. He wasn't a professional musician. His experience was limited to what he had picked up on the tuba and the drums in his high school band.

At that point Marion joined in the conversation. "Sam, you remember that boy who came in to record that song for his mother's birthday about a year ago?'

"Yeah, I remember him," said Sam. "A dark-haired boy."

"Well, you said you thought he had a pretty good voice. Why don't you get him to come in and try it?"

"Yeah, I'll probably do that."

That was all Scotty needed to hear. For two weeks, he "worried Sam to death with the same question: 'Have you called that boy yet?'"

When Scotty arrived at the studio on Saturday, July 3, there were no customers, so the three of them went next door to Taylor's cafe for a cup of coffee. Scotty got right to the point.

"You called that boy yet?" he asked.

Finally, Sam gave in. He told Marion to dig out the boy's name and phone number and give it to Scotty. Later, when she gave Scotty his name, he was taken aback. "What kind of a name is this?" Scotty asked. He read the name over a second time—Elvis Presley.

"I don't know," answered Sam. "It's his name. Give him a call. Ask him to come over to your house and see what you think."

By the time Scotty got home it was late in the afternoon. He called Elvis that evening after dinner. Gladys Presley, his mother, said that he had gone to a movie. Scotty said he represented Sun Records and wanted to talk to Elvis about an audition. Gladys was polite. She said she would make sure Elvis returned his call.

**Scotty with Bill Black's children outside of his home on Belz Street.
The Chevy in the background was Bobbie's car, which Elvis and the
Blue Moon Boys used for their initial tours
(Courtesy of Bobbie Moore)**

Scotty and his wife of one year, Bobbie, were setting up house at 983 Belz Street in north Memphis. They had moved into the four-unit house in June after their friends Bill and Evelyn Black, who lived down the street, told them it was for rent. At night and on weekends, Bill played bass with the Starlite Wranglers; during the day he worked a few blocks away at Firestone Tire Company.

Belz was a quiet, family-friendly residential dead-end street. Children played in the streets and swung on the slender young trees that showed promise of one day becoming shade-bearing giants. The front door of Scotty's house opened into the living room. Past the living room was a hallway that led into the kitchen on the left and the bathroom on the right. The kitchen was large and had an adjoining dining area that opened into the bedroom.

When they got married in June 1953, Bobbie moved in with Scotty at his boardinghouse for a month for so, then they stayed with family members until they found the house on Belz. Although this was Scotty's second marriage, it was Bobbie's first, and she worked hard to make the house into a home. At twenty-two, she had been out on her own for several years, but she had met no one special until Scotty came along. She was a tall, leggy brunette who wore her hair cut fashionably short.

Dresses were still the accepted fashion of the day, but Bobbie liked to wear pants, especially "pedal pushers," tight-fitting slacks that ended past mid-calf. She didn't know it in 1954, but she was only three years away from turning prematurely gray. She was more outgoing than Scotty, who at times seemed painfully shy, and she was very attractive, a quality high on Scotty's wish list when it came to women.

Bobbie had just cleared away the dinner dishes when the phone rang. The caller said his name was Elvis Presley. He said he was returning Scotty's call. Scotty explained that he was working for Sam Phillips, helping him look for talent for Sun Records. Would Elvis be interested in coming over to the house for an informal audition?

"Well, I guess so," said Elvis.

"How about tomorrow?" asked Scotty. It was a holiday, the Fourth of July, but Scotty was never much for celebrations. Growing up, Christmas was the only holiday his family had observed, and even then festivities were held at a minimum. Scotty was eager to hear the youngster, because if it worked out, it would be his ticket back into Sam's studio.

"All right," said Elvis.

Scotty gave him directions to the house. They agreed to meet sometime after lunch.

On Sunday, July 4, 1954, Memphis sizzled. The temperature peaked at 100 degrees at 3:20 P.M. and didn't dip below 90 until 8 P.M. The humidity hung fast at 92 percent. The Fairgrounds Amusement Park opened at 2 P.M., offering cold watermelon and a concert by Slim Rhodes. There would be no fireworks on the Fourth that year—it would be sacrilegious to do that on Sunday—but the following day the skies over the fairgrounds would be ablaze with rockets' red glare.

To escape the day's heat, Scotty took refuge in the bedroom to play his guitar. Elvis arrived shortly after noon.

Bobbie saw him coming up the walk. He had on a white lacy shirt, pink pants with a black stripe down the legs, and white buck shoes. He was carrying a guitar.

"Is this the right place?" he said when Bobbie answered the door.

"Yeah, it's the right place. Come on in."

Bobbie left Elvis in the living room and went into the bedroom to tell Scotty.

"That guy's here," she said.

"What guy?" asked Scotty, who had lost track of the time.

"You know—the guy you invited over," she said.

After Scotty and Elvis exchanged pleasantries, Bobbie offered Elvis a Coke. "They sat around for a while talking," recalls Bobbie. "Then they started playing. Scotty asked me to go and ask Bill [Black] to come down and I did." Bill's bass was already there, propped in the corner of the living room. He kept it at Scotty's house because, with two children, he didn't have room for it at his own place.

As Scotty and Elvis went through Elvis's song list, Bill came over and sat down to listen. When he had heard enough, he got up and went home. Today Scotty remembers thinking how uncanny it was that Elvis knew so many songs—everything from Eddie Arnold to Billy Ekstine, "every damn song in the world."

An hour or two later, Bobbie returned. "He had his audience then," she recalls. "He was doing a lot of slow ballads. Everything had the word 'because' in it—'Because of You,' 'I Love You Because,' 'Because You Think You're So Pretty'— I don't think anyone was real impressed. He had a good voice and he could sing, but the type of stuff he was singing, he was just like everybody else."

Bobbie was impressed even less by his appearance. "He was still kind of a pimply faced kid, you know," she says. "He had his ducktail hair pulled back. He was kind of odd for that time."

When they ran out of songs to do, they put the guitars aside. "I'll talk to Sam, and we'll probably be in touch," said Scotty. It was his first time to use the "we'll be in touch" line, but it wouldn't be the last. Elvis left, and Bill came back to help critique the audition.

"What did you think?' asked Scotty.

"Well, he didn't impress me too damned much," said Bill. "How about you?"

"I thought he had good timing. A good voice. Nothing different jumped out from the material he was doing."

After Bill left, Scotty called Sam to give him a report. He was upbeat but not gushing in his assessment of Elvis's talents. He was surprised that Elvis knew so many rhythm and blues songs. Sam asked Scotty if he thought it would be worthwhile to audition him in the studio.

"Sure," said Scotty.

Based on Scotty's recommendation, Sam called Elvis later that afternoon and set up an audition for Monday night at the studio.

Scotty and Bobbie suffered through another stifling night. The temperature never went below 75 degrees. By the time they left for work Monday morning—Scotty to the dry cleaners and Bobbie to her job in the billing department at Sears—the temperature was already pushing 90 degrees. As usual, Scotty took his guitar with him to work. Most days Scotty practiced during his lunch hour. This day was no different.

In and out of the dry cleaners that day, as she was all summer, was twelve-year-old Mississippi transplant Wynette Pugh. Years later she would change her name to Tammy Wynette and become a superstar of country music, but for now she was like most girls her age and curious about the world around her. Because her mother worked in the office of the dry cleaners, she often stopped by to hang out—and to listen to Scotty's guitar picking. She was fascinated with guitars. Her father, William Hollis Pugh, who died when she was an infant, was a well-known guitarist in northern Mississippi. As a result, she had grown up in a home filled with musical instruments.

Nearly forty years later, Tammy Wynette would recall the experience with relish. "Oh, yes. I watched Scotty many times," she says. "There was this old black guy who worked in the back and Scotty would go back there with his guitar, and this old black man and him would talk back and forth about guitar licks." As the summer of '54 wore on, she was drawn inextricably to a series of practice sessions held upstairs over the dry cleaners—and to the mystery of the boy named Elvis.

Scotty didn't mind the young girl's curiosity. He had two children of his own from a previous marriage. Besides, he knew what it was like to be drawn to the sound of music. Perhaps he was a little more focused than usual on this day. It would be his second trip into the studio with

Sam. Scotty knew as well as anyone that the music business didn't always abide by the "three strikes—you're out" rule. Sometimes you got only two strikes. If Scotty struck out, it wouldn't be because he was caught flat-footed at the plate. He was determined to make it as a guitarist.

That night they all showed up at the studio around seven o'clock. Scotty had offered to bring the entire band, but Sam didn't want to make a big deal out of it. The idea was to see what Elvis could do, not to make a record. Scotty on guitar and Bill on bass would be enough. Sam wanted to keep it as simple as possible.

That was fine with Scotty, but it did put added pressure on him. On most nights the Starlite Wranglers were a six-piece group, with a fiddle, a standup bass, and three guitars, and, of course, the vocalist Doug Poindexter. With all those instruments in the fray, Scotty could play a little lead or play a little rhythm or simply fade into the background. Tonight, for all practical purposes, he was the entire band. If he felt the pressure, he never showed it.

First came the small talk. Complaints about the heat (the temperature was still hovering around 90 degrees). Then the inevitable, what songs do you know? Then, what songs do you know that I know? Finally, for starters, they picked "Harbor Lights," a song that had been a hit for Bing Crosby several years back. Then they did one of Elvis's "because" numbers, "I Love You Because," which had been a hit for Ernest Tubb on the country charts. They did both songs just like they had been recorded. When it became obvious they were not going to outshine the work Tubb and Crosby had done on their own songs, they moved on to something else.

They did one ballad after another. Musically, ballads were easier to play than uptempo numbers, but that wasn't where Scotty's heart lay, especially with the musical setup they had in the studio. He preferred uptempo tunes. With only three pieces, everything they did sounded naked to Scotty. During all of this, Sam sat in the control room, pressing the record button, then rewinding the tape to start over again on the next tune. As the night wore on, it became obvious they were going nowhere fast. Of course, no one wanted to give up, least of all Scotty.

Around midnight they took a break. It was late and they all had to go to work the next day. Maybe it was time to wrap it up. They could try again tomorrow. They had sort of lulled themselves into a post-session stupor when Elvis suddenly jumped up and started playing his guitar. Actually, as Scotty remembers it, he beat the hell out of the guitar. He started singing a blues song that had been recorded by Arthur "Big Boy" Crudup in 1940, "That's All Right, Mama."

Bill was sitting on his bass. When Elvis started singing, he leaped to his feet and began playing. Then Scotty joined in. The uptempo tune hit home with Scotty. Fast music was what he liked. For years he had been making up guitar licks for uptempo music, a combination of finger slides and bent-string pauses, but he had found nowhere to put them. It wasn't until Elvis was flailing away at his guitar that he suddenly knew where those licks belonged.

While they were playing, Scotty saw Sam's head perk up on the other side of the glass. He looked at them, then stuck his head out of the control room door. "What are ya'll doing?" he asked.

"Just foolin' around," Scotty said.

"Well, it didn't sound too bad. Try it again. Let me get in there and turn the mics on."

They played it several times, with Sam making some technical suggestions, telling Elvis to move closer to the microphone or farther away from it. Finally, Sam thought they were ready to run the tape. They played it through again, with the tape machine on, then Sam ran it back for them to hear.

"Man, that's good," he said. "It's different."

"Yeah, what is it?"

They looked at each other. That was a good question.

"Well, you said you were looking for something different," Scotty said.

"Damn, if we get that played, they might run us out of town," Bill said.

"Okay, we've got to get a back side," said Sam. "I just can't take one song down to the disc jockey." Exhausted, they called it a night at two o'clock in the morning. When Scotty got home, Bobbie was waiting up for him. He told her all about the session. He said they were tired and worn out but planned to return to the studio that night to pick up where they left off. He told her about "That's All Right, Mama," about how Sam finally heard something he liked.

When Scotty and Bobbie went to sleep that night, they had no way of knowing that the session had launched a revolution in American music. All they knew was that it had been a good day. Also unknown to them, Scotty had become a father that night. It would be six years before he would learn that Frankie Tucker, an aspiring nightclub singer he had met in West Memphis three months into his marriage with Bobbie, had given birth to his child, a bright-eyed girl she named Vicki.

59

Sam Phillips clowns with Elvis in Sun Studios control room,
December 4, 1956 (Courtesy of Colin Escott)

* * *

Two days later, on the evening of July 6, 1954, Scotty, Bill, and Elvis returned to Memphis Recording Service to pick up where they had left off after recording "That's All Right, Mama." They were pumped. Sam Phillips himself had told them they had a record. Well, half a record. All they had to do was come up with a B side. Sam said he would take care of the rest.

When they faced off in the tiny 18-by-32-foot studio, they weren't sure what to expect. "That's All Right, Mama" had been a fluke—and they understood that. If Sam thought they could do it again, then they probably could. At least, they convinced themselves of that. There was still a hour's daylight left when they began and the studio was stifling hot. They ran through a number of songs, including Billy Eckstine's 1949 hit "Blue Moon."

Nothing clicked.

"We were all below-average musicians," says Scotty. "Elvis didn't know all that many chords, but he had a great sense of rhythm. Sam used that. I don't think he did it consciously for effect. He treated Elvis as another instrument and he kept his voice closer to the music than was the norm at that time. If you listen to the records that were being played then, the singer's voice was way out front. If he left Elvis's voice way out front, it would have sounded empty because we only had three instruments. Elvis had great vocal control. He could do just about anything he wanted to. Sam mixed his voice closer to the music like it was an instrument."

After a series of duds, Sam suggested they take a couple of days off and then try again. He was upbeat. He told them he knew they could do it. What Sam's secretary, Marion, remembers most about the first week was how much fun everyone had. "One session had run on and on," she recalls. "Bill was on the floor and we couldn't get him up. Finally everybody else dropped [to the floor]. Suddenly, Bill leaped to his feet and said, 'Where's everybody? Where's everybody?' Sometimes Elvis would just roll on the floor, kicking his heels."

Despite his assurances that they would be able to get a B side, there seemed to be some doubt in Sam's mind as to whether they could. That night after everyone left, he called a local disc jockey, Dewey Phillips. The two men weren't related, but over the years they got into the habit of not correcting people who jumped to the conclusion that they were. Dewey had a daily nine-to-midnight show on radio station WHBQ, which broadcast from the downtown Hotel Chisca.

61

In 1954 Dewey was easily the most popular white disc jockey in Memphis, though none of his listeners, if pressed, would be able to explain exactly why. He was in the vanguard of America's shock-jock tradition, sort of a southern-fried Howard Stern. A moon-faced country boy from West Tennessee, he was decidedly unschooled in the radio tradition. He taunted his listeners with nonsensical exuberance and language that did not endear him to the parents of teenagers (he called people he didn't like "pissants" on the air until the station manager made him stop).

Sam told Dewey he had something he needed to hear. After Dewey put the wraps on his *Red, Hot and Blue* show that night, he stopped off at Sam's studio on his way home. Sam had a scheme going with Dewey: he would give him copies of tapes or acetates before they were released as records. If Dewey liked them—and played them on his show—Sam could judge by audience reaction how many records to press.

That night Sam played "That's All Right, Mama" for Dewey. For nearly two hours they drank beer and listened to that one record. Sam played it over and over again. Dewey sat and listened stone-faced. He left the studio without ever commenting on the record. Early the next morning he called Sam and told him it was the damnedest record he had ever heard. He asked for a copy to play on *Red, Hot and Blue*. Later that day Sam made an acetate and left it for Dewey at the radio station. Then he called Elvis and told him to be sure to listen to Dewey's show that night.

Elvis told Gladys and Vernon about the show, but he ducked out of the house and went to a movie before it aired. As expected, Dewey debuted "That's All right, Mama." He played it and he played it and he played it. When he liked a song he played it over and over again, back to back, without a break. Some say he played Elvis's song seven, ten, fourteen times in a row—then took a break, whooping it up, screaming this hoodoo jive he had made up himself—and started playing the record all over again. The phones rang off the hook. "That's All Right, Mama" was an instant hit. Dewey got Elvis's phone number from Sam and called him at home. Gladys said he had gone to the movies. Dewey told her to get her cotton-pickin' son down to the station.

Within minutes Gladys and Vernon rounded up Elvis and got him to the station. He was so nervous, he shook all over. In one of the last interviews before his death in 1968, Dewey told writer Stanley Booth that Elvis told him: "Mister Phillips, I don't know nothing about being interviewed." Dewey's advice was simple and to the point: "Just don't say nothin' dirty."

The notion that Elvis would say anything dirty—even think about saying anything dirty—struck Marion as absurd. "He's never said a wrong thing," she says. "He's been misquoted, but he's an innately fine person. It's not in him to do anything or say anything malicious. He didn't smoke. He didn't drink. I never even heard him say damn."

When Scotty, Bill, and Elvis returned to the studio on Thursday they were local celebrities, at least among Dewey Phillips's hip radio listeners. Sam had let the cat out of the bag. He really did have to get a B side now. "The reaction was fantastic," says Marion. "We were backordered 5,000 records on this brand new artist, this brand new type of thing, before we could get our mastering done. It was that immediate."

Over the next few days they had their work cut out for them. Not only did they have to come up with a B side, the group had to have a name, Marion had to draw up contracts for Sun Records, and Elvis, as the vocalist, had to find a manager. Marion did the Sun Records contracts herself, a fact that later became a source of contention between Sam and herself. "While our advisors thought it was perfectly legal, I don't think Sam had much trust in it," she recalls.

Because Elvis, at nineteen, was legally a minor, Vernon signed as his guardian. The contract was for three years. Scotty and Bill were not asked to sign contracts. They were told to make their own deal with Elvis. They agreed on a 50-25-25 split, with Elvis getting 50 percent because he was the vocalist. Nothing was ever put in writing.

❋ ❋ ❋

By the end of that first week it seemed like the world had been turned upside down. Within the space of four days, Elvis, Scotty, and Bill had recorded "That's All Right, Mama," Dewey Phillips had played it on the radio, creating a stampede to the stores—which placed orders for more than 5,000 records—and Sam had slapped a recording contract down in front of Elvis. Add to that Scotty's need to get a contract drawn up between himself and Elvis, and you understand how hectic it all became. "Don't feel pressured or anything," Sam told them, "but we got to have a B side by tomorrow."

Twenty-four years after the fact, Sam looked back to that week, telling a reporter for Memphis's The Commercial Appeal that he thought one of the key ingredients for the success that followed was a spirit of teamwork. "I think my biggest contribution was to let these people [the musicians] know that I wasn't a record executive. Never was and never would be . . . so instead of a big producer behind the glass window, looking onto a group of people in the [studio], saying 'Man, you got to do this, you got to do that,' I was one of them. We all had the same goal in mind . . . . At that time, I did not see one person in there thinking in terms of 'Man, I'm gonna be a superstar.' It was 'Isn't there some way we can say what we want to say through music?'"

If the trio had a weakness, it was their inability to compose original songs. There wasn't a penny's worth of songwriting talent among the three of them. That meant they had to work their magic with songs written by other people. That's what happened with "That's All Right, Mama." What they tried to do over that three-day period—Friday, Saturday, and Sunday—was find another song they could breathe fire into. Sam made suggestions; so did Scotty, Elvis, and Bill.

"We went through song after song, just running through them," says Scotty. "I don't think any of them were ever put on tape."

Nothing seemed to work out.

Then they got lucky again. "Blue Moon of Kentucky" was a beautiful waltz that Bill Monroe had scored a hit with in 1946. Since then it had become a classic country tune, revered by the Grand Ole Opry and handled with kid gloves by country and bluegrass musicians, who had anointed it with magical properties. No one told Bill Black the song wasn't fair game.

"He jumped up and grabbed his bass and started slapping it, singing 'Blue Moon of Kentucky' in a high falsetto voice," says Scotty. It was Bill doing what Bill did best. The song was recorded as a ballad, but Bill sang it uptempo, his bass lines thumping at a feverish pace. Elvis loved it. He jumped up and started singing along with Bill. Scotty joined in right behind them.

Suddenly, Sam stuck his head out the door. "Hey, that's the one!" he shouted. On the final take, Sam was jubilant: "Hell, that's fine. That's different. That's a pop song now."

With "That's All Right, Mama," Elvis took a blues song and sang it white. With "Blue Moon of Kentucky" he did the opposite: he took a country song and gave it a bluesy spin. On paper it probably wouldn't have worked, but in the laid-back, anything goes atmosphere of Sam's studio, it seemed perfect. "It had the same sort of feel as 'That's All Right, Mama,'" says Scotty. "After that, we sort of had our direction."

Sam didn't need a direction. He was running straight ahead as fast as he could. Over the weekend, he made two-sided dubs of the songs and distributed them to all the disc jockeys in Memphis. Dewey Phillips had lost his exclusive. Getting acetates this go-around were Bob Neal, a popular early-morning country DJ at WMPS, Dick Stuart at KWEM in West Memphis, and Sleepy Eyed John, a country announcer at WHHM. By

Monday, both songs were getting airplay. As Dewey was going crazy over "That's All Right, Mama," Sleepy Eyed John, who had a country band of his own and booked bands for a local country-music club, the Eagle Nest, was talking up "Blue Moon of Kentucky."

Jack Clement remembers hearing "Blue Moon of Kentucky" on Sleepy Eyed John's show. Jack went on to become Sam Phillips's engineer—and right-hand man—and a highly regarded producer in his own right, but at that time he was trying to get his own band off the ground. Sleepy Eyed John had booked Jack's band at the Eagle's Nest, and whether out of a sense of loyalty or a desire to monitor his bosses' musical tastes, Jack listened to his show on a regular basis.

One morning Jack awoke and turned on the radio by his bed. Sleepy Eyed John was doing his regular country show. As Jack rubbed the sleep from his eyes, Sleepy Eyed John said, "Here's the record everyone is screaming about." Then he played "Blue Moon of Kentucky." The song left Clement dazed. He had never heard anything like it. No one had.

By today's standards, "That's All Right, Mama" and "Blue Moon of Kentucky" seem more like country music than rock 'n' roll, but that's because over the years country music has changed, incorporating many of the innovations introduced by rock 'n' roll in its infancy. At the time they were released, "That's All Right, Mama" and "Blue Moon of Kentucky" were raw, irreverent, and bristling with energy. Those were the elements that made it rock 'n' roll. The elements that define rock music today—the blistering electric guitar solos, the pounding drums, the omnipotent bass—were added in later years by musicians to duplicate electronically what Elvis, Scotty, and Bill accomplished with little more than raw talent.

"Blue Moon of Kentucky" gave them more than a B side, it ultimately gave them a name: the Blue Moon Boys. On the first two records, they were identified simply as "Elvis, Scotty, and Bill." By the third record, they had started going by the name "Elvis and the Blue Moon Boys," an obvious outgrowth of Scotty's Navy band, the Happy Valley Boys.

In the beginning, they were a group. They thought as one, created as one, performed as one. David Briggs, a prominent Nashville producer, who—as a member of the Muscle Shoals rhythm section—opened for the Beatles when they first came to America, views the Blue Moon Boys as a band that succeeded not just because of Elvis's star power, but because of their ability to work together as a unit. "Everyone gives the Beatles credit for being the first group to make history," says Briggs. "My point is that they weren't the first white group. The first was Bill, Scotty, and Elvis. Although Elvis was the star and eventually outshone them,

WHEREAS, W. S. Moore, III, is a band leader and a booking agent, and Elvis Presley, a minor, age 19 years, is a singer of reputation and renown, and possesses bright promises of large success, it is the desire of both parties to enter into this personal management contract for the best interests of both parties.

This contract is joined in and approved by the Father and Mother of Elvis Presley, *Vernon Presley* and *Mrs Vernon Presley* Presley.

IT IS AGREED that W. S. Moore, III, will take over the complete management of the professional affairs of the said Elvis Presley, book him professionally for all appearances that can be secured for him, and to promote him, generally, in his professional endeavors. The said W. S. Moore, III, is to receive, as his compensation for his services, ten (10%) percent of all earnings from engagements, appearances, and bookings made by him for Elvis Presley.

IT IS UNDERSTOOD AND AGREED that this is an exclusive contract and the said Elvis Presley agrees not to sign any other contract pertaining to his professional work nor make any appearances at any time for any other person or manager or booking agent, for a period of one (1) year.

Now, we, *Vernon Presley* and *Mrs Vernon Presley*, father and mother of Elvis Presley, join in this contract for and in his behalf, confirm and approve all of its terms and his execution of same and our signatures are affixed thereto.

The said W. S. Moore, III, agrees to give his best efforts to the promotion and success of the said Elvis Presley professionally.

SIGNED AND EXECUTED on this *12th* day of *July* 1954.

_____
W. S. Moore, III

_____
Elvis Presley

_____
Father of Elvis Presley

_____
Mother of Elvis Presley

Original management contract between Scotty and Elvis,
July 12, 1954 (Courtesy of Scotty Moore)

they were a group. They were the first [group] to make number-one records."

❖ ❖ ❖

At some point during those first few days, they were sitting around the studio, throwing out "what if's." Someone (Scotty doesn't remember who) asked what they were going to do if some jerk of a disc jockey or wannabe booker pressured Elvis into signing a management contract. Unsigned, Elvis was a target for unscrupulous disc jockeys and bookers who might demand a piece of the action in return for playing his records. The best way to avoid those problems was to get Elvis locked into a contract with a "safe" manager. Sam and Scotty decided it would be to everyone's advantage if Scotty became Elvis's personal manager.

The contract between Scotty and Elvis was similar to the contract Scotty had drawn up for the Starlite Wranglers, but it was done by a lawyer, not Marion. Sam was several years Scotty's senior, but it was the sailor from Shanghai who, at age twenty-two, better understood the machinations of an imperfect world. Over the years, Scotty found it advantageous to assume the role of the shy, quiet second fiddle, the farm boy who made good. If Sam, Elvis, or anyone else wanted to take credit for something he did, that was fine with him. All he asked in return was that the spotlight not shine on him.

67

On July 12, 1954, one week to the day after their first session, Scotty got the managerial contract back from his lawyer. It identified W. S. Moore III as a "band leader and a booking agent" and Elvis Presley as a "singer of reputation and renown" who possessed "bright promises of large success." The agreement allowed Scotty to "take over the complete management of the professional affairs of the said Elvis Presley, book him professionally for all appearances that can be secured for him, and to promote him, generally, in his professional endeavors." As compensation, Scotty was to receive 10 percent of "all earnings from engagements, appearances, and bookings made by him." The agreement prohibited Elvis from signing any other contract pertaining to his professional work for a period of one year.

That day, Scotty took the contract to Vernon and Gladys Presley to sign as Elvis's guardians. With his short, neatly trimmed hair and slender, boyish good looks, Scotty made a good impression. Elvis didn't smoke, drink, or use profanity. He went to church and had a deep spiritual center. Vernon and Gladys wouldn't sign their son over to just anyone. They didn't know much about Scotty (Elvis had only known him for little over a week), but he looked like a nice clean-cut young man and they knew all about Sam Phillips because his name was in the newspapers and Elvis had been talking about him for about a year. If Sam said Scotty was all right, then he must be all right. The four of them signed the contract and dated it. After the signing, Gladys told Scotty she expected him to look after her son. It was an obligation Scotty took seriously.

As Sam got ready for the record's release, Scotty got busy being Elvis's manager. Because they only had one record with two sides to play, the best way to introduce them to the public, he figured, was to incorporate them into the Starlite Wranglers act as "special guests." The band was booked that weekend at the Bon Air Club, a bar on the outer rim of the city limits. Scotty asked Sam to bring Elvis to the club that night to sit in with the band.

The next step for Elvis and the Blue Moon Boys was to learn enough songs to perform on their own. Carney told Scotty he could use the room up over the dry cleaners as a practice hall. Late in the afternoon or early in the evening, or whenever they could all three get off work together, Scotty, Bill, and Elvis met at the dry cleaners to build up a playlist.

Tammy Wynette remembers the rehearsals with fondness. Just getting to the dry cleaners from her house or from school was always an adventure in itself. Because the zoo was located nearby, she often was greeted by a cacophony of grunts, groans, and hair-raising bellows from the always hungry caged animals. The noise frightened her sometimes, but once she got to the dry cleaners, she always had fun. Carney, Auzella, and Scotty would take turns pushing her around the shop in a clothes cart. Of course, when the Blue Moon Boys were upstairs, rocking and rolling, there was no better place in the world to be.

"The day I remember the most was the one when they were coming down the stairs and Auzella looked up and said, 'My, my, my. Look at the stars,'" says Tammy.

"Elvis was nothing then, but he looked at her with that little smile of his and he said, 'Auzella, one of these days I'll wrap you up in hundred dollar bills.'"

✳ ✳ ✳

That Saturday night Sam took Elvis to the Bon Air as planned. When the time came, the Starlite Wranglers, with the exception of Scotty and Bill, stepped down—and Elvis took the stage. They performed their two songs and Elvis sat down. The reaction was polite but not wildly enthusiastic. Elvis felt dejected. Sam agreed it wasn't a great reception, but he told Elvis he had given a solid performance. He told him better days were ahead.

Starlite Wranglers, c. 1953. L to r: Bill Black (in "hayseed"
costume), Tommy Sealey, Doug Poindexter (at microphone),
Millard Yow (steel guitar), Clyde Rush (guitar), and Scotty
(Courtesy of Colin Escott)

After Sam and Elvis left, Scotty realized all was not well with the
Starlite Wranglers. Doug Poindexter considered himself a local star of
serious magnitude. He and the others were miffed that Scotty and Bill
had not included them on the recording session with Elvis. Quickly, it
became apparent to Scotty that his idea of making the Blue Moon Boys
part of the Starlite Wranglers show was not going to work. Egos aside,
there was a contractual problem. The Starlite Wranglers contract clearly
stated that "any and all compositions and songs, or productions, com-
posed or written by any member of the group, or in conjunction with,
or with the aid of any member or members of the group, will be considered by all parties as community property, owned by the group, and
any and all monies received from sales, recordings, or royalties, from
said compositions, shall be community property and divided among the
members."

Where did the Starlite Wranglers end and the Blue Moon Boys begin?
The Starlite Wranglers wanted answers. Were they entitled to a share of
the earnings from the Blue Moon Boys? Scotty's earlier desire to control

the destiny of the Starlite Wranglers came back to haunt him. That tightly drawn contract now had the potential to control him. Was that the reason Sam did not include Scotty and Bill in his contract with Elvis? No one seems to remember today, but it is interesting that Doug Poindexter was asked to play guitar on a couple of tracks with Elvis. On one song, "Just Because," Poindexter put paper through his guitar strings and made it sound like a washboard. On another song, "I Don't Care If the Sun Don't Shine," singer Buddy Cunningham was in the studio. "Wait a minute," he said, and went into the back room. He returned with two or three different sized boxes, which he taped together into a bongo-drum configuration. His box-playing rhythms can clearly be heard on the record.

On top of the loyalty issue, Elvis's exotic appearance did not go over well with the more conservative Starlite Wranglers. They didn't like the way he looked, his attitude, or—indeed—anything about him. After that night it was obvious that while its contract ran until March 1955, the Starlite Wranglers were finished as a group. They parted on good terms, and Scotty and Bill gave their full attention to Elvis and the Blue Moon Boys.

On Monday, July 19, Sam released "That's All Right, Mama" and "Blue Moon of Kentucky." By that time the record had already generated over 6,000 orders from local record stores. Sam's radio blitz was paying off. After the disappointing showing at the Bon Air, Sam called disc jockey Bob Neal, who was putting together a hillbilly show for later that month at the Overton Park Shell, an amphitheater located adjacent to the city zoo. Sam asked Neal if he would book Elvis for the show. The headliner was Slim Whitman. Sam thought the family-oriented audience he would attract would be more receptive to Elvis than the hard-drinking crowd at the Bon Air. Neal agreed to add Elvis to the bill on the condition that Sam get Elvis and the Blue Moon Boys signed up with the local musicians union.

Scotty continued to hustle club bookings for the group. He asked Sleepy Eyed John to book them at the Eagle's Nest as the floor show with the eight-piece swing band fronted by Jack Clement.

"I had to bring him on and then I had to follow him," says Clement. "When he came on—just the three of them, with Scotty on electric guitar and Bill slapping that bass—it was magic."

Elvis and the Blue Moon Boys performed there three weekends in a row, with the club packed each night. On July 27, three days before the concert at the Shell, Sam asked Marion to take Elvis to the newsroom of the *Memphis Press-Scimitar* for an interview with entertainment writer

Edwin Howard. They went during Elvis's lunch-hour break at Crown Electric. It was Elvis's first newspaper interview and he was scared to death. He wore a bow tie, with his greasy hair slicked back into duck-tails. His sideburns were long and scraggly. Howard tried to interview him, but all he could get were "yes sirs" and "no sirs." Marion did all of the talking. "The odd thing about it," Marion said in the interview, "is that both sides seem to be equally popular on pop, folk, and race record programs. This boy has something that seems to appeal to everybody."

Howard's story, which ran the next day, touted the record as show-ing promise of becoming "the biggest hit Sun has ever pressed." He dutifully plugged Elvis's upcoming appearance at the Shell. Interest-ingly, he never quoted Elvis in the story—with his "yes sirs" and "no sirs," he surely must have been the toughest subject he had ever inter-viewed—and he never mentioned the Blue Moon Boys or Scotty and Bill. Whenever Sam booked them or promoted the record, it was always as "Elvis." When Scotty did the bookings and promotions, it was always as Elvis and the Blue Moon Boys. The records themselves gave them equal billing.

On July 30, the day of their scheduled performance at the Shell, the trio realized they had forgotten to join the musicians union. Amid the hurly burly surrounding their first big public performance, they scraped together the money they needed and completed the necessary paperwork to become members of the American Federation of Musicians, Local No. 71. It was not the largest chapter in the country, but it was on its way to becoming one of the most important. In time, its membership read like a *Who's Who* of American music. Bluesman B. B. King joined in the early 1950s and is today still a member in good standing, as is Scotty.

That night, when the show began at eight o'clock, Elvis was a ner-vous wreck. He was so jumpy that Scotty was surprised he couldn't hear his knees knocking. The stars of the show, Slim Whitman and Billy Walk-er, had a loyal fan base. Elvis wasn't sure they would like him. Sam, who was there with Marion and Elvis's girlfriend, Dixie, reassured him: "You're going to be great."

When the time came, Bob Neal did the introduction. From the audience the stage at the Shell doesn't appear all that large, but if you are on the stage, looking out at the audience, it seems enormous. When they heard their names, Elvis, Scotty, and Bill took the stage, facing row after row of waiting fans who had no idea what to expect. They felt dwarfed by the conical shape of the backdrop. "We were scared to death," says Scotty. "All those people—and us with these three little funky instruments."

SCOTTY and BILL   SUN Records 706 Union Ave.,Memphis,Tenn.

Scotty and Bill's first publicity photo, which they sold
when touring with Elvis (Courtesy of Scotty Moore)

THAT'S ALRIGHT, ELVIS

They started out with "That's All Right, Mama." Elvis was so nervous that he raised up on the balls of his feet and shook his leg in time with the music, a move he sometimes used in the studio. To his shock—and horror—the young girls in the audience went crazy, yelling and applauding. He couldn't see what the audience saw. Because he was wearing baggy pants that were pleated in the front, his attempt to keep time with the music created a wild gyrating effect with his pants' legs. From the audience's angle those movements seemed exaggerated against the backdrop of the Shell, which had a tendency to amplify whatever was on stage, visually as well as acoustically.

"We didn't know what was going on when all those people started screaming and hollering," says Scotty. Next they did "Blue Moon of Kentucky." When they got offstage, Elvis asked why people were yelling at him. Someone told him it was because he was shaking his leg.

Later in the show, they returned to the stage and repeated the same two songs. Marion remembers that they also did a new song they were working on, "I'll Never Let You Go (Little Darlin')." Elvis looked at her when he sang it. "Now I'm a restrained person, in public anyway, and I heard somebody screaming, and I discovered it was me—the staid mother of a young son," she says. "I was standing out there screeching like I'd lost my total stupid mind. The rest of the audience reacted the same way."

Sam couldn't believe what he was seeing—and hearing. In August he loaded up his car with records and hit the road, preaching the gospel of Elvis to every promoter, local distributor, and disc jockey in the South. Many nights he slept in his car. As Sam was taking care of business, spreading the word about Elvis, Scotty continued to book them in every Memphis venue he could find.

In early September they performed at a Katz Drug Store opening. The store was located in a shopping center at 2256 Lamar Avenue. They set up on the back of a flat-bed truck that was parked in front of the store. Attending that performance were Johnny Cash, a newcomer to Memphis, and John Evans, who later achieved fame as the keyboardist on the first Memphis pop record to go to No. 1: the Box Tops' "The Letter."

Evans was a Dewey Phillips fan and had been listening to him plug "That's All Right, Mama." "My dad had wired our house so that we had an intercom running through the house," says Evans. "That way the radio could be heard throughout the house. We listened to Dewey Phillips that way. He played that song all the time. Those were magic moments in broadcasting history."

When Evans, who was about six, and his brother heard on the radio that Elvis would be performing at the shopping center, they went to watch since it was just a short distance from their home. "People came from all over the neighborhood and swarmed down on the place," he says. "My brother held me up to where I could see. I remember they were dressed like real weird country musicians. Elvis was wearing pink and gray. I was struck by that. They had a big string bass and the guy would twirl it around. There was only one amp and it was sitting on a chair. There was a little guy playing a big guitar."

Encouraged by his reception at the Shell, Elvis repeated his leg-shaking movements at the shopping center. Says Scotty: "He just started adding a little more to it and made it into a fine art. But it was a natural thing for him to do."

Ralph Moore, supportive of his brother's sudden success, was also at the shopping center that day. What struck him was the fact that it was a racially mixed audience. "The coloreds were dancing and they'd get up on these barrels and they would fall off," he says. That was the first time he met Elvis, and he walked away that day carrying an impression of the man that stuck with him over the years. "He was a plain ole country boy—very polite," he says. "It was 'yes sir' and 'yes m'am.'"

❊ ❊ ❊

In September, Elvis, Scotty, and Bill returned to the studio. They were solid hits in Memphis, but they hadn't broken out of the city, with the exception of a *Billboard* review that had praised their single in the magazine's "Spotlight" section. It was beginning to dawn on them that they were on the verge of something. Of what, they weren't sure.

"Bill, myself, and Sam, our feelings were, 'Hey, this guy is going to be big,' but none of us felt it was going to be as big as it was as fast as it was," says Scotty. "We weren't in any rush. It busted loose so fast we didn't really have time to think about it."

In the studio Sam gently nudged them as he had done before. "He was like one of the guys," says Scotty. "He would have made a great preacher. You can get him started on any subject. Sometimes we'd get to drinking and he would get off on a tangent. Him and me would argue like you would not believe—really get into each other's face—but we were having fun with it. He had his own set of beliefs on everything. He was a taskmaster when we were working, pushing everybody to the limit—and he was right on a lot of it. 'Let's do it one more time,' he would say. He couldn't tell you what he wanted, but he would suggest you try something. He wanted it loose. We couldn't have taken direction even if he had known what he wanted."

Performing with Elvis was a joy, but working with him in the studio was sometimes difficult because he never came prepared. Choosing the songs they recorded was a trial-and-error process. In later years, Sam would see the value in having a publishing company and recording original material, but in the early days of Elvis's career no one brought original material to the sessions.

It was during this time that Scotty really developed the guitar style that stayed with him the rest of his life. "Although a song might be like something we did before, it made no sense to play what I played earlier," he says. "I tried to come up with something different. I tried to play around the singer. If Elvis was singing a song a certain way, there was no point in me trying to top him on what he just did. The idea was to play something that went the other way—a counterpoint. Sometimes it got pretty rough. A few times it was just pure anger and I got frustrated."

They recorded a number of songs during the September session, but the two that made the next single were "Good Rockin' Tonight" and "I Don't Care If the Sun Don't Shine." Marion took a special interest in the latter. "Elvis came up with just one verse—that's all he knew," she says. "So we took a break and I wrote the second one. We recorded it and Sam took the only dub to a record convention. He called back and says, 'Everybody loves it . . . taking orders like mad.' Then I got a call from New York, from a music firm, and they said we understand you're releasing a record of 'I Don't Care If the Sun Don't Shine.' They said, well, Mack David wrote that song and he's very particular about what you do with his songs and he reserves the right to hear the material before you release it."

Marion told Sam and he sent the record airmail to the publisher the next day. When Marion heard back from the publisher, he was ecstatic. David walked into his office while he was playing the record. "He thinks it's great—go ahead," said the publisher. "But I noticed you added a verse and I'm sending you some disclaimers that say whoever wrote the verse can't put their name on the label, can't collect any royalties and so on."

"I said, okay," recalls Marion. "I just wanted to get the record out . . . [but] every time I turned the radio on, I'd hear [Elvis] singing my lyrics."

"Good Rockin' Tonight" and "I Don't Care If the Sun Don't Shine" were released in late September. By that time, Elvis was becoming a regular visitor at the Moore household. One day Bobbie and Scotty were home alone when Scotty decided to go to the store to get some cigarettes. He left the front door unlocked. "I was standing in the bathroom combing my hair," says Bobbie. "Somebody opened the front door and I thought it was Scotty."

She heard footsteps in the living room. Then she looked up and saw Elvis standing in the bathroom door. "Where's Scotty?" he asked.

75

Startled, Bobbie said he had gone for cigarettes. "He'll be back in a minute," she said.

"Uh, I'll be back," Elvis mumbled, and left.

When Scotty returned, Bobbie told him about the unexpected visit. Although Elvis said he would return, he did not. They never did find out why he stopped by the house. He was unpredictable in some ways, but in other ways they always knew what to expect. "He liked to walk, walk, walk," says Bobbie of his nervous energy. "He paced the floor. He couldn't be still." Sometimes he roamed nonstop through the house, "looking in the refrigerator . . . making himself at home."

Once, after they came in late from a performance or rehearsal, Elvis decided to spend the night. Bobbie was shocked. "He had said something about his mother never going to sleep until he got home, and I wondered if she was going to sleep that night," says Bobbie. Their sofa made into a bed, so they flipped it out for Elvis and gave him some clean sheets. The next morning, while Bobbie was cooking breakfast, Scotty told her Elvis liked his eggs fried real hard. She cooked them to specifications and put them on Elvis's plate.

"He looked at me and said, 'Could you cook this a little more?' and I put them back in the skillet and cooked them some more." Bobbie laughs when she thinks about it. "He still didn't eat but a couple of bites. He ate the bacon and toast. I like mine well done, too, but . . .'"

Elvis was still dating Dixie at that time and they often "double dated" with Scotty and Bobbie. One of the places they went was a drive-in on Park Avenue where they could sit outside and eat watermelon. "Elvis and Scotty would start spitting seeds to see who could spit them the furthest," says Bobbie. After shows, they often went out together to eat. Usually Bobbie was the only one who had any money. Her 9-to-5 at Sears wasn't glamorous, but it did pay on a regular basis.

"When they played at the Eagle's Nest, they didn't get paid until they went to the union," she says. "Elvis never had any money. We'd go out to eat and we had to buy his burger and milkshake. One night he wanted another milkshake. He asked Scotty if he could have one. Scotty said he would have to ask me. I was the only one who got paid."

Once Elvis had cleaned his plate, he had a tendency to munch off the plates of those around him. It was Evelyn Black who discovered, quite by accident, the secret to protecting her meal from Elvis's wandering fingers. "We stopped once to get a sandwich and some french fries, and I put ketchup on my potatoes—you know so I could dip them," says Evelyn. "Elvis would get a potato off of my plate, and I noticed he always got one that didn't have ketchup on it. From then on, I learned to put ketchup on my fries or else Elvis would eat them all."

Besides his voracious appetite for burgers and shakes, one of the things Bobbie remembers most about their outings with Elvis was his refusal to dance with her. She kidded him about it. The more she urged him to dance with her, the more adamant he became not to dance. Bobbie was mystified. "He danced on stage, but he never danced on the floor," she says.

Once she asked him to autograph a photograph. On the back he wrote: "No, I will never dance." He signed it "Elvis Q-Ball Presley."

❊ ❊ ❊

In August Sam Phillips called Jim Denny, manager of the Grand Ole Opry, and talked to him about booking Elvis for the show. Denny told him that he had heard Elvis's record and—while it wasn't exactly his cup of tea—he would keep an open mind and if there was ever an opening he would give him a call. Meanwhile, Nashville buzzed over "Blue Moon of Kentucky." Record executives weren't sure they liked it, but they were sure of one thing: it was a hit.

Elvis introduces Bill Black onstage. Scotty is in the right background (Courtesy of Scotty Moore)

Sam pressured Denny until he finally agreed to let Elvis and the boys play the Opry. But there were conditions: they couldn't do an entire segment, but they could do one song—"Blue Moon of Kentucky"— during Hank Snow's segment.

Sam was elated. So were Elvis, Scotty, and Bill. In those days, playing the Opry was the pinnacle of success; there just wasn't anything bigger. On Saturday, October 2, they loaded up Sam's big black Cadillac, strapping Bill's bass to the roof, and drove the 200 miles to Nashville. Marion closed the studio and took a bus. Elvis didn't own a suitcase, so Marion loaned him hers. He packed most of his wardrobe into the suitcase.

When they arrived, Elvis wandered about the Ryman Auditorium. It was unpainted and had a homey feel to it. Elvis was disappointed. He expected it to look a little fancier. "You mean this is what I've been dreaming about all these years?" Elvis asked Marion. The disappointment was mutual. When Denny saw Elvis, Scotty, and Bill walk in he was shocked. "I wanted the full band that's on the record," he said, counting a singer and two musicians. "Our agreement was we were gonna have the performance just like it is on the record."

Denny expected a big band to go along with the big sound he heard on the record. They explained that it was only the three of them on the record. He was amazed. He sent them backstage to get ready for the show. Marion sat out in the audience. "Who'd you come to see?" she asked a woman next to her. "Marty Robbins," the woman said. "I never miss Marty Robbins. Who'd you come to hear?"

"Elvis Presley," Marion said.

"Who?"

"After this show, you won't ask me again," she told the woman.

Unknown to Scotty and Bill, their wives had disobeyed their orders to stay at home. "After they left [Memphis], Evelyn came by the house and said, 'Let's go,'" says Bobbie. "We didn't get there until about eight o'clock, but we got some good seats down front. Bill stuck his head out from backstage and saw us and they took us backstage. Scotty was kind of mad, but he got over it."

Before they went on stage, Hank Snow turned to Elvis and asked him his name.

"Elvis Presley."

"I mean, what's the name you sing under?" he asked.

When Elvis and the Blue Moon Boys took the stage, they didn't know what to expect. They played their song the way they had recorded it. "They applauded, but they didn't go wild," says Scotty of the audience's reaction. "There wasn't any booing or hissing. Just polite applause. It wasn't as bad as people have written it up to be. It was after we did the song and went offstage that Jim Denny, according to Sam and Elvis, made the comment, 'You'd better keep driving the truck.'"

Scotty and Bobbie both dispute accounts that Elvis cried after the show. "He seemed pretty happy to me," says Bobbie. The fact that the audience was polite—and not wildly enthusiastic like they were in Memphis—was disappointing, says Scotty, but not ego shattering: "It didn't take long to get over it."

Scotty, Bobbie, Evelyn, and Bill drove back to Memphis that night. Sam wanted to listen to a piano player who had been recommended to him, so he got rooms at a motel for himself, Marion, and Elvis so they could spend the night. Elvis went into the club with them to hear the piano player, but quickly turned around and went back outside. Marion followed after him and asked why he had left. He told her it wasn't the type of place his parents would want him to be. He told them to go ahead and have a good time. He would wait outside on the sidewalk.

"It was unthinkable to him that everyone didn't love their parents—didn't want to do everything for their parents," says Marion. On the way back to Memphis the next day, Elvis took Marion's suitcase into a service station bathroom. Not until they got home did they realize they didn't have the suitcase. It took three or four days for them to retrieve the suitcase, which contained Elvis's entire wardrobe, from the service station.

That November Bob Neal took Sam aside and asked him if he could take over Elvis's management contract. Sam told him they couldn't make any changes right then—Scotty's contract with Elvis still had five months to go—but he authorized Neal to arrange bookings for the band. Everyone, including Scotty, liked Neal. "He was a good man," says Scotty. "He was straight as an arrow." The squeeze play was on for Scotty, but he didn't realize it at the time.

By the end of 1954, Sun Records had released four records of Elvis and the Blue Moon Boys. Sales were brisk, but because Scotty wasn't under contract—and, in fact, was receiving nothing from record sales—his only income from music was from performance fees. His share of that was 25 percent. Tax records show that Scotty's total income for 1954, from all sources, including his job at the dry cleaners, was $2,249.49. Of that, only $139.25 was derived from his performances with Elvis.

ON THE ROAD
WITH THE BLUE MOON
BOYS

Sam had been sparring with the Louisiana Hayride for several weeks over booking Elvis for its weekly, Saturday-night radio program. Broadcast on KWKH, a 50,000-watt station in Shreveport, it was second only to the Opry in influence with country-music audiences. In some ways, the six-year-old program had eclipsed the Opry in importance, especially when it came to discovering new talent. While the Opry boosted the careers of big-name artists, the Hayride, perhaps feeling it had more to gain by banking on long shots, took a chance on new talent such as Hank Williams, Jim Reeves, Kitty Wells, and Faron Young.

Pappy Covington, the booking agent for the Hayride, had heard "That's All Right, Mama" and "Blue Moon of Kentucky." In the latter part of September 1954, he told Sam he wanted to book Elvis and the Blue Moon Boys for the show. Sam put him off, saying he didn't want to make any commitments until after the Opry performance. He thought Elvis would be a sensation at the Opry, so he didn't want to do anything contractually that would limit his ability to make Elvis available for future performances at the Ryman. The smattering of polite applause received by them from the Opry audience brought Sam back to reality. The day after they returned to Memphis, Sam got Covington on the telephone . . . "yes, yes, Elvis will be delighted to perform at the Hayride."

The first performance was booked for October 16. A couple of days before the show, D. J. Fontana was asked to stop by the Hayride's office to listen to Elvis's records. On weekdays, D. J. played drums on the cocktail and strip-joint circuit with Hoot and Curley, a popular Shreveport trio, and other groups in the city. On Saturday nights he was the staff drummer at the Hayride. That meant that whenever visiting artists wanted to beef up their act with drums, D. J. made himself available. He always played behind the curtain, so he could not be seen by the audience. In those days, drums were considered a musical sacrilege to country-music fans.

"Good Rockin' Tonight" had been released in September and was doing well in Arkansas, Mississippi, and Alabama. That day in the office, D. J. listened to the record with great interest.

"That's a good record," he said. He commented on the echo effect. He had never heard anything quite like it. "How many musicians they got? Five? Six?"

When he was told there were only three people in the band, it floored him. "I had never heard anything like that," says D. J. "I said, 'Boy, that's good.'"

Early Saturday morning, after they wrapped up their Friday night gig at the Eagle's Nest, Scotty, Bill, Elvis, and Sam loaded up two cars and struck out for Shreveport, a drive of about seven hours. It was their second big road trip. Awaiting them was the Louisiana Hayride, broadcast each Saturday night from the Shreveport Municipal Auditorium. The sturdy, brick and concrete building, located at Grand Avenue and Milam Street, on the fringe of the city's business district, boasted a large stage and a seating capacity of 3,800. The three-hour Hayride was broadcast in its entirety over a twenty-eight-state area; curtain time was 8 P.M.

When they arrived at the auditorium, they went backstage to meet with the announcer, Frank Page, D. J., and others on the Hayride staff. Page gave them a rundown on how the show operated. "They all seemed nervous, being on a big show like this," says Page. "They knew how many people had become stars by being on the Hayride. I talked to Elvis. He was a little discouraged by the things that had happened so far, about being turned down by the Opry, about not getting kick-started like he wanted to be. I encouraged him and told him to just do his thing."

After the meeting, Elvis, Scotty, and D. J. went to the dressing room so D. J. could listen to the records again. They had never performed with a drummer and were looking forward to it, particularly after their reception at the Opry. D. J. listened to the songs, asking questions about what they wanted him to do, offering his ideas. "I figured the best thing for these guys was to stay out of the way," says D. J. "Why would I clutter it up with cymbals? I'll just play the back beat and stay out of their way. They already had the good sound."

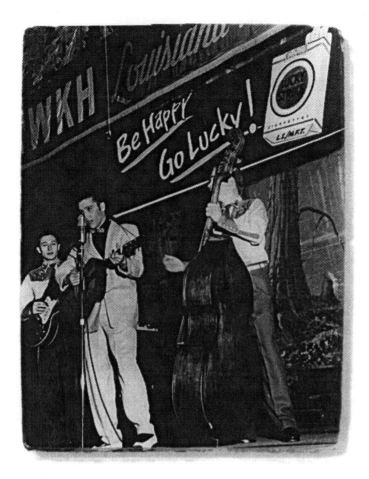

Performing on the Louisiana Hayride, c. 1954 (Courtesy of Showtime Archives [Toronto] and Colin Escott/Langston McEachern)

D. J. noticed that Elvis looked to Scotty for guidance. "Scotty was acting road manager and took care of the business end," says D. J. "He was like the buffer zone. Elvis would agree to anything. If someone said, 'Would you work this free?' he'd say, 'Well, yeah.' Rather than Elvis being the bad guy, it was Scotty. He'd just say, 'We can't do it.'"

That night, Page introduced Elvis and the Blue Moon Boys. With Elvis, Scotty, and Bill standing onstage in front of the backdrop, a thin curtain on which was painted a barn, a wagon, trees, and moss, Page tried to engage Elvis in conversation.

"Well, I'd like to say how happy we are to be here," said Elvis. "It's a real honor for us to—get a chance to appear on the Louisiana Hayride. And we're going to do a song for you."

Self-consciously, Elvis ended his onstage banter with Page by asking a question. "You got anything else to say, sir?"

"No, I'm ready," said Page, who knew he had squeezed every ounce of conversation he could out of Elvis. He turned the show over to him and left the stage.

With D. J. hidden behind the curtain, Elvis launched into "That's All Right, Mama." Elvis didn't have a monitor, so he couldn't hear himself. D. J. could hear the music, but he couldn't see any of the other players. Standing offstage, Page couldn't help but notice how nervous they all looked. Elvis seemed ill at ease and Scotty struggled with his guitar solo. The audience was polite, but there was no screaming or dancing in the aisles. They did two songs, then left the stage.

They were scheduled to return later in the show to repeat the first set. Backstage, Sam gave Elvis a pep talk. He told him to just relax and do it the way he did it in Memphis. If these people didn't like that . . . well, to hell with them.

During the performance, Page had watched the audience with interest. "The audience was a little shocked," he later recalled. "Scotty's guitar, of course, was different and had a unique sound—one the audience was not quite ready for at the time."

When they returned for the second set, the audience had changed somewhat. This time there were more students in the crowd. As they repeated the same two songs, Sam, who sat in the audience, noticed a marked difference in the crowd's reaction. This time the students were shouting and clapping. While it wasn't exactly on the level Sam had seen in Memphis, it confirmed his belief that Elvis was on the right track.

The Hayride felt the same way. They invited Elvis and the Blue Moon Boys back for a return engagement. "Elvis didn't really take off until two or three weeks after that," says Page. "The young ladies started showing up. Elvis wiggled his leg a bit, snarled a bit, and let his hair hang down. The audience changed as the demeanor of the act changed."

Three weeks later, Elvis returned to Shreveport with his parents to sign a twelve-month contract with the Hayride. Under the terms of the contract, they would be paid basic union scale—$18 to Elvis as the bandleader, and $12 each to Scotty and Bill. They were expected to perform for fifty-two consecutive weeks, with occasional absences permitted with adequate notice.

❄ ❄ ❄

That November, after Sam gave Bob Neal permission to do bookings for Elvis, it became obvious that Scotty and Bill were in a precarious

Letter from Tom Diskin turning down Elvis Presley,
January 13, 1955 (Courtesy of Scotty Moore)

contractual position. Neither had a contract with Sam. The Hayride
contract included them only if Elvis took them along as his musicians.
Scotty was Elvis's manager, but it was an uncompensated position,
unless he obtained bookings for the group. Scotty had always been
ambivalent about the contract, but now, with Neal usurping some of his
responsibilities as manager, he put extra effort into trying to get bookings with big-time promoters.

One of the promoters he approached, Colonel Tom Parker, was based
in Madison, Tennessee, but had an office in Chicago that operated under
the name Jamboree Attractions. The company's slogan was "We cover the
nation." Scotty thought that had a nice ring to it. He wrote the office in
Chicago, asking if they could book Elvis and the Blue Moon Boys in or
around Chicago. Maybe Scotty didn't want to be Elvis's manager, but
neither did he want the contract snatched away . If he could be the first
to book a big-time performance outside of the South, he knew his value
to the group would increase. It took a while for Jamboree Attractions to

respond, but on January 13, 1955, Parker's assistant, Tom Diskin, sent Scotty a letter that curtly informed him that there were few outlets for hillbilly entertainers in Chicago. Said Diskin: "While we are a booking and promotion agency I don't have anything at present where I could place your artist."

✻ ✻ ✻

One evening Scotty and Elvis sat out on the steps of Elvis's house on Alabama Street. Elvis could see that Scotty and Bill were being squeezed out of the picture. That troubled him. Under their agreement, they had a 50-25-25 split, with expenses coming off the top, but that was for performances only. Scotty and Bill didn't make a penny off the records. Further highlighting those inequities was the fact that their touring car, a '54 Bel Air Chevy, had been purchased by Bobbie, who alone was making the payments and taking care of repairs.

Elvis told Scotty he thought it was only fair they split record royalties the same way they split performance fees. Scotty told him that wouldn't work. "If we do that, you'll start resenting that later when you learn more about the business," Scotty said.

"But you guys need to share in this," he answered.

Elvis was adamant they needed to do something. They talked about it a while longer. Finally, seeing that Elvis was determined to find a solution, Scotty offered an alternative he thought was fair. "I said, 'Give Bill and I each one-quarter of one percent.'" Scotty knew Elvis was getting three percent. "That would have cut him to two and a half. In my mind, I thought that was fair. From what I knew about the business, I knew it would turn sour down the road if we did it his way. He said, 'OK, fine—I understand.'" They left it at that; nothing was ever put down in writing.

In December, Scotty, Bill, and Elvis returned to the studio in between performances at the Hayride and an occasional appearance at the Eagle's Nest. They recorded "Milkcow Blues Boogie" and "You're a Heartbreaker," which were released in January 1955. With Bob Neal doing more of the booking, they started performing in Texas, Arkansas, Alabama, and Mississippi. Sometime in January, Neal officially took over Elvis's management. "We worked out a simple thing without consulting attorneys, just a simple management-type contract," Neal told writer Jerry Hopkins in 1970. "I think the terms were fifteen percent. I set up a little office over there on Union, right across from the Peabody Hotel."

Scotty began the new year with high hopes, not paying particular attention to the fact that he had relinquished all contractual ties to Elvis and Sun Records. From that point on, he and Bill would remain members of the team only at the pleasure of management. Scotty reminded Neal of Elvis's offer to include him and Bill on the royalties received from record sales.

"Oh, yeah, we need to do that," said Neal.

Today, in retrospect, Scotty wishes he had been more aggressive in pursuing the matter. "I should have gone the next day and gotten it drawn up and signed, but I kept putting it off," he says. "Whether Elvis talked to Neal or his mama or daddy [or later to Parker] I don't have any idea. I told Bobbie about it, and Bill, and I can almost hear myself telling Sam. There were just the three of us. We were a group. Elvis was the main guy and I said the main guy always gets paid more, but that doesn't keep the main man from helping out the other guys a little bit."

Scotty didn't make an issue of it. The band was just getting off the ground. He didn't want to cause trouble. Elvis said he would cut them in on record royalties, and Scotty had no reason to doubt him.

On February 6, 1955, a meeting took place that sealed the fate of the band. After a Sunday performance at Ellis Auditorium in Memphis, Scotty, Bill, and Elvis went across the street to a cafe, where they met Sam and Neal; also there was Colonel Tom Parker and his assistant, Tom Diskin. In his new capacity as manager, Neal had set up the meeting to introduce Sam and the boys to Parker, who had recently taken over the management of Hank Snow, one of the Grand Ole Opry's most popular members. Parker's booking agency, which had been formed in partnership with Snow, was making a name for itself at the national level. As a country music disc jockey, Neal knew how important a good booking and promotions man could be to an artist's career.

After a few minutes of banter, Bill got up and returned to the auditorium. Scotty had only received the letter from Diskin the week before informing him that Jamboree Attractions was not interested in booking a hillbilly performer like Elvis in Chicago. Now Diskin and Parker were making a spiel to Elvis and Sam about how much they could help Elvis's career. Scotty didn't say anything about the letter. Mostly, he sat and listened, watching the show.

Parker and Neal could not have been more different. Neal was an affable man who didn't have an enemy in the world. In his mid-forties, he had a son about Elvis's age, and perhaps because of that he developed a paternal approach to dealing with all the boys in the band. "We all liked Bob," says Scotty. "He was a big ole bearlike guy—real easygoing."

Parker was equally gregarious, also in his mid-forties, but there was something about his demeanor that bothered Scotty. At the time, he

Scotty, Elvis, D. J., and Bill onstage
(Photo © 1996 EPE, Inc.)

couldn't put his finger on it. The more Parker talked, the less Scotty trusted him. At first glance, Parker seemed just what they needed to get them over the hump. He had what they needed most: connections. In addition to Snow, he was booking Minnie Pearl, Mother Maybelle and the Carter Sisters, and Slim Whitman. Scotty didn't know enough about Parker to dislike him. His reaction was instinctive, colored perhaps by his dealings with club owners and by his experiences in the Navy.

No one knew it at the time, but Parker was an illegal alien. Born Andreas Cornelius van Kuijk in Holland, he had entered the United States under mysterious circumstances in the late '20s. After a stint in the Army—he had changed his name and birthplace in order to enlist— he went to work for a carnival in Florida. For twenty years, he worked as a carnie, learning the trade as an advance man and two-bit huckster.

From the Hank Snow Show Souvenir Photo Album produced for the jamboree tour featuring Elvis (Courtesy of Scotty Moore)

In the mid-'40s he found a home in country music by becoming the personal manager of Eddy Arnold, a new RCA artist who was quickly making a name for himself. It was because of that association that he picked up the title of "Colonel." In the South at that time, it was customary for governors to anoint their campaign supporters with the honorary title of Colonel. It was used as a signal to law-enforcement officials, particularly highway patrolmen, that the bearer had once done a favor for the governor. Parker received his title from Louisiana governor Jimmie Davis, himself a former country-music performer.

The Colonel, as he liked to be called, was a boisterous, cigar-chomping braggart, and he rubbed Scotty and Sam the wrong way, but Neal had known him since the mid-'40s, when he first came to town with Eddy Arnold—and if he said the Colonel was the real thing, they felt they had to respect his judgment. When the meeting ended, Parker agreed to put Elvis and the Blue Moon Boys on the bill with Hank Snow. Even so, Scotty left the meeting with a sinking feeling in the pit of his stomach. Elvis, Scotty, and Bill—as a band—were about to become history.

With the last single doing poorly on the charts, the boys returned to the studio to record the electrifying "Baby, Let's Play House." Before they could nail anything down for the B side, they went back out on the road, with performances booked by Neal in New Mexico and Texas. On February 16 they joined the Hank Snow jamboree in Odessa, Texas. Also on the bill were Hank's nineteen-year-old son, Jimmie Rodgers Snow, and Whitey Ford, a popular comedian and instrumentalist, who performed under the name "The Duke of Paducah." It was the first stop on a five-day tour booked by Parker.

To Snow's displeasure, the audiences, one by one, began to show a vociferous preference for Elvis. Snow may have been the star, but it was the youngster from Memphis who made the crowds scream for more. "I felt sorry for Hank," says Scotty. "It didn't matter whether Elvis was on first or last, the reaction was always the same."

Neal noticed that audience reaction depended on whether they were within range of KWKH in Shreveport. "In towns where he'd had radio exposure, it was a very frenzied type of reaction," he says. "The girls were screaming, jumping up and down and passing out. The reaction was negative with the boys. A great many resented it."

In the midst of all the excitement over their first tour, Scotty noticed things going on behind the scenes. "The Colonel started sabotaging Neal's relationship with Elvis," he says. "Bob tried to go on the road with us, but it had a toll on him. He got tired, especially under the stress of the other Elvis stuff coming along." With Neal wavering under the pressure of a heavy touring schedule, Parker promoted himself with Elvis, telling him he deserved better than what he was getting.

Once he felt he had Elvis's confidence, he took aim at his next target: the Blue Moon Boys. Scotty got the news from Hank Snow's band. They told him Parker had approached them about backing Elvis. Parker told them he wanted to ditch Scotty and Bill.

"Elvis absolutely refused," says Scotty. "Hank's band didn't want it either. They blew up when they heard about it. Hank had a great band, but they didn't play the type of music we played. Most of them were older. We knew from day one the Colonel didn't want us around. It became more obvious as it went along. I had Elvis's ear, and he didn't like Elvis's friends being around."

After completing the tour with Snow, they went to Cleveland, Ohio, to perform on a country show broadcast from the Circle Theater by radio station WERE. It was their first trip out of the South. Neal went along because he thought it would be helpful if he did promotions with the radio stations. When they returned to Memphis, they went back into the studio to do the B side for "Baby, Let's Play House." They chose a song cowritten by Memphians Bill Taylor and Stan Kesler, a steel guitarist who had been hanging around Sam's studio, trying to do what he could to break into the business. The song, "I'm Left, You're Right, She's Gone," was Sam's first attempt to tap into the local talent pool.

With a bluesy introduction borrowed from the Mississippi Delta and cutesy lyrics of the type that were popular with country fans, the song gave Elvis an opportunity to do a vocal that ran counter to Scotty's guitar. It also gave Sam an opportunity to add a new element to their sound: drums. For that, he used a local drummer, a high school student named James Lott.

As Sam prepared "Baby, Let's Play House" for an April release, Neal took Elvis and the Blue Moon Boys to New York to audition for a popular television show, *Arthur Godfrey's Talent Scouts*. Neal had been to New York before, but none of the boys had. The trip took on added significance when it was learned that neither Bill nor Elvis had ever flown. Neal had to scrape together the money for the trip, but he was convinced television was the key to breaking them to a national audience.

Once they arrived, they took in the sights; then, with Bill acting the clown, cracking jokes, making faces, and poking fun at the bustling crowds of city folks around them, they rode the subway to the television studio, where they performed live for the show's talent scouts. The reaction was not what they hoped for: "Don't call us, we'll call you," they were told.

Elvis didn't take the rejection well. A new side to his personality was beginning to emerge. The youthful, super-polite teenager they had started out with was beginning to display signs of developing an ego. He was still playful and self-effacing, but for the first time it was becoming apparent that he really did care what people thought about him. Scotty wasn't as bothered by the rejection. "I wasn't too impressed with any of it, to tell you the truth," he says. "None of us ever liked television. That eye is so unforgiving."

Back in Memphis, they awaited the release of their next single and got ready to go back out on the road. With its odometer spun around three times, Bobbie's '54 Chevy had made its last trip with the band. Elvis bought a 1951 Lincoln for them to tour in and painted the words "Elvis Presley—Sun Records" on the door. Over the years, it would be a source of mystery—and consternation—to Bobbie as to why Elvis never replaced the car she had purchased herself and freely loaned to the band for their road trips. In later years, when she read stories about Elvis giving new cars to perfect strangers, she wondered if he would remember to replace her 1954 Chevy. He never did.

Scotty and Bill sat in the lobby of the Shreveport hotel. They couldn't afford more than one room on what they were being paid to perform on the Hayride, so they rented a room with two beds and tried to stay out of each other's way as much as possible. That night Elvis was using the room to have sex with a girl he had met earlier in the day. The more Scotty thinks about it today, the more convinced he is that it was Elvis's first time.

Time spent waiting in a hotel lobby, especially at two or three in the morning, is never time well spent—not when you're waiting for someone who is in the process of losing his virginity.

Finally, Scotty looked up and saw Elvis coming down the stairs with the girl at his side. After a moment of confusion, he left her at one end of the lobby and walked over to where Scotty and Bill were sitting. They could tell from his face that something was wrong.

Scotty, Elvis, and Bill onstage (Photo © 1996 EPE, Inc.)

"The rubber busted," said Elvis. "What do I do now?"

Bill laughed. "I think you had better marry her—or get the hell out of town."

Scotty and Bill had no pearls of wisdom to offer, so they went upstairs to the room and went to sleep, leaving Elvis in the lobby to deal with the problem himself. At least they had cautioned him about disease and getting girls pregnant. Short of putting the condom on him and monitoring its condition during the experience, what more could they do?

The next morning they asked Elvis how he had handled the crisis.

"Oh, I took her to the emergency room at the hospital," he said nonchalantly.

"The emergency room!"

"Yeah, I got them to give her a douche."

Scotty looked at Bill. "I didn't know they did that," he said.

Whenever Scotty went by to pick up Elvis for a road trip, Gladys always took him aside and admonished him to "take care of my boy." Although Scotty had brothers, they were so much older than he was he never had the day-to-day experience of being someone's brother. Out on the road, Elvis became the younger brother he never had. In time Elvis started calling him "The Old Man," a reference not only to his paternal attitude, but to his fastidiousness.

In the beginning, they shared their rooms the same way they split the paycheck: Elvis took one bed; Scotty and Bill took the other. Scotty was appalled at Elvis's grooming habits. "We had to ease him into more hygienic methods of living," he says. "It was the way he was raised. People didn't take a bath every day back then. We all sweated like hogs. We had to coach him, without being insulting, you know, to take a bath. Later his buddies would say he would get home and when you opened his suitcase all his dirty clothes would just be piled in there and would be all smelly. At home he probably threw his dirty socks into the corner and his mama picked them up. I had been in the Navy, and you couldn't do that. As time went by, he got more and more in tune with the norm. He just wasn't used to being closed up with other people. He didn't stink to high heaven, but in a closed car, any odor—however slight—gets blown out of proportion. In the Navy, you learned those things pretty quick."

Marshall Grant, who traveled with Elvis and the band on occasion while working as Johnny Cash's bass player, noticed the lifestyle differences between Elvis and Scotty with amusement. Watching them pack their suitcases was always entertaining. Elvis would toss his things into his suitcase and slam the lid shut. Says Grant: "Scotty would take a shirt, and he would straighten the collar and he would take the sleeve and he would work with it and he would take the other sleeve and do the same thing. When he got through folding them, they looked just like they came out of the laundry."

Scotty paid the same attention to detail when he was loading the car. His amplifier was the first thing that went into the trunk. Once he had it in place, he padded it with foam rubber, then he loaded his guitar into the car. "Scotty was one of those immaculate type of people. He treated everything with kid gloves," says Grant. "When they got to the next stage, his amplifier would always work. It was a delicate piece of machinery and it was only because of the care he gave it that he could make it work. Everyone else would throw theirs into the trunk and when they got down the road the next day, they wouldn't work."

Scotty and Bill decided the best way to get Elvis to take better care of himself was to make a joke out of it. Some mornings they would rise before Elvis and threaten to throw water on him if he didn't get up and hit the shower. Once, while driving along in the car, they smelled an awful odor. They pulled off the road and made a big deal out of searching for the source of the bad odor. It turned out to be Elvis's shoes, which he had taken off and slid beneath the seat. They got back in the car, but when they passed over the next bridge they grabbed his shoes and threw them into the river. After that, it got to be a game. Without warning, Elvis would throw their clothing, or the car keys, out the window.

"Elvis liked to do pranks—just kid stuff," says Scotty. "We used to do all kind of silly stuff out of boredom. Sometimes we'd get into arguments and be ready to kill each other. It might be me and Elvis, or me and Bill, any combination. We'd jump out of the car, running around—just normal stuff, when you're cooped up like that."

Actually, it was their game of throwing things out the car window that evolved into Elvis's habit in later years of throwing scarves to the audience. Says Scotty: "We'd be playing something and Bill would walk over to Elvis and whisper in his ear and say something like, 'Take off your belt and throw it out into the audience'—and he would do it. We did that for several weeks. He would do it to me, too. I would be taking a solo and he would take my belt off or my tie off and throw it out into the audience. Then one day in Texarkana, Elvis took off his shoe and threw it out into the audience and it hit some old lady in the head. After that, we figured we'd better stop before somebody got hurt."

To combat boredom on the road, they developed a game in which a tap on the forehead was used as a signal. "It was just this silly thing we did," says Scotty. "Whoever was talking or doing something, someone else would reach over and tap him on the forehead. Then you automatically did an 180-degrees on whatever you were saying or doing." Sometimes they would do that on stage. Bill would walk over and tap Elvis on the forehead and he would stop whatever he was doing and start doing something else. Kid stuff, sure, but it helped with the monotony—and it helped channel Elvis's nervous energy. "He was always keyed up," says Scotty. "There was many a night when we would stop fifty miles down the road from leaving a town and either Bill or I would get out and start walking Elvis around, trying to get him calmed down so we would be able to sleep to get to where we were going." It was Elvis's hyperactivity, not his sexual exploits, that was the main reason they started getting two rooms as soon as they could afford it. "We would want to go to sleep. Elvis was so full of energy he wanted to stay up and talk all night."

In the early days Elvis was like a "young stud at a rodeo" when it came to girls, says Scotty. "I didn't blame him for trying. I think he later came to think that was expected of him. If he didn't give her a peck on the cheek, show some kind of interest, then people would be disappointed—it was part of the act. But I've always told people, 'Put yourself in his shoes.' You've got all these girls chasing you and they aren't camp followers. They're all nice girls, well scrubbed, well dressed. They weren't groupies. Who could hold up under that? I once read where Bill and I had pillows in the back of the car and would run the girls in one side and out the other. That's a bunch of bull."

Rumors in later years that Elvis was bisexual or homosexual astound Scotty. "That's a bunch of horseshit," says Scotty. "They could have nicknamed him Man o' War. He'd have been the first one to lay someone out if a man made an advance on him, I can tell you that. If he was prejudiced about anything, that was it." Scotty attributes the rumors of homosexuality to the fact that Elvis wore eye makeup. "Let's face it, the man was damned near too pretty to be a man. He had those Roman chiseled features. He found out by watching movies that Tony Curtis wore mascara so that when they took pictures his eyes would be more defined, so he started doing it when he performed. Later on, he got to where he just wore it all the time. Why not? Every time he stuck his head out the door, someone took his picture. Actors have been wearing make-up for as long as there have been actors."

Once a day—sometimes twice a day—Elvis would want to stop so that he could call his mother. He kept her updated on where they were going and what they were doing. He called his girlfriend, Dixie, a lot, too, in the beginning. "As his roving eye kept getting bigger, those calls ended," says Scotty. "Dixie was a nice little gal. I liked her. He wasn't prepared for all that was happening and she wasn't either—all that adoration. Looking back, he stayed in trouble all the time."

✻ ✻ ✻

Lovesick fans weren't the biggest problems they faced on the road. Automobile accidents became their constant—and most unwelcome—companion. Only a month or so after Elvis purchased the Lincoln, they loaded up the car in Memphis, with Bill's bass in its protective cover strapped to the roof in a canvas bag, and headed out for a performance in Texas.

With Bill at the wheel, somewhere near Carlisle, Arkansas, a truck pulled out in front of them from a side road. Bill slammed on the brakes and hit the tail end of the truck, sending his bass careening off into the dark. As Scotty and Elvis assessed the damage to the car, Bill went to get his bass. Soon the thump, thump, thump rhythm of the bass filtered out of the darkness, back up to the accident site. "It had landed perfectly," says Scotty. "It didn't hurt it one bit."

Later in the year, while in the 1955 Cadillac Elvis purchased to replace the Lincoln, they were leaving New Orleans when a pickup truck turned in front of them near Texarkana. This time Scotty was at the wheel. "We were late, as usual, heading north," says Scotty. "The law was that if you made a left turn onto private property, you had to pull off on the shoulder, stop, and make sure the traffic was clear before you turned. Well, this guy made the signal and pulled over, but he immediately turned in front of us."

Damage to the Cadillac was estimated at $1,000, and the accident made news because Scotty picked up a speeding ticket. Subsequent published stories that Elvis was the driver, with Scotty and Bill traveling in a separate car, were untrue, according to Scotty, who has a vivid recollection of the accident.

Not all of their road difficulties were the result of accidents. Sometimes they were waylaid by mechanical troubles. Once their car broke down in Forest City, Arkansas, just outside of Memphis. They called Bobbie and asked her to come pick them up. "Elvis rode back with us," Bobbie says. "We put him in the back seat. He sat there leaning over the seat, talking to us. He liked to talk, that's for sure." Bobbie, who was wearing shorts, commented on Elvis being so friendly. Scotty knew the reason why Elvis was leaning over the seat talking so much. "He's just looking at your legs," he said.

In the years after Elvis's death, journalists wrote stories galore about the eccentricities of his living habits, creating minor mysteries for the faithful to ponder. Many of those stories have left Scotty scratching his head. One common myth, for example, has been perpetuated that Elvis carryied his own knife and fork out on the road so that he would not have to use restaurant utensils. "If he did, he was the quickest sleight of hand person I have ever seen," says Scotty. "I never saw him do that. I don't understand why people would say that. All the time we spent together, I think I would have noticed it. Maybe it was something he did as a child, and he stopped doing it by the time I met him."

Then there is the matter of Elvis's sleepwalking. A number of his close associates, including his former wife, Priscilla, have made a big deal of Elvis's sleepwalking. Scotty never saw him do that. He never even heard it discussed. Says Scotty: "His mother never mentioned anything about him sleepwalking. You would think she would have if he was that bad. She always called me over to the side and said, 'Take care of my boy and make sure he gets his rest.' She never said a word about sleep-walking and he never did it when I was around him." Scotty doesn't know which bothers him more: the fact that people would make up stories like that or the possibility that he was a sleepwalker and no one told him. "I was supposed to be the father protector," says Scotty. "I would have felt terrible if the boy had walked out of the room into the highway and got run over."

As the excitement built over the spring and summer, Bobbie and Evelyn got more involved, doing what they could to promote the records, and traveling with their husbands whenever possible. Once Bobbie and her sister Alice loaded up the battered 1954 Chevy with records and drove to Biloxi, Mississippi, a distance of about 300 miles, to work the radio station there.

"The disc jockey took us back in the office and played both sides and asked us a lot of questions," she says. "He did like the record. It was interesting to watch the reactions of people to the records." Before heading back to Memphis, they circled around through New Orleans and stopped at a radio station there. The reaction wasn't as hospitable. "The guy there took the record and kind of pushed the door shut on us."

Bobbie always got a kick out of watching the way the young girls reacted to Elvis. "After shows, they would come backstage and they'd go back to the dressing room with him," she says. "Elvis would come out, saying, 'It's dark back there. I'm not sure who I'm kissing.'" Sometimes he would talk to Bobbie about certain girls. "When he'd see a girl, he'd say, 'She's fine,' or 'Oh, she don't show me much.'"

The irony wasn't lost on Bobbie, especially when she and Scotty were out with Elvis and Dixie. "Elvis would pout when he didn't get his way," she says. "One night he and Dixie were arguing about something in the back seat. Someone had seen her with another guy, in a park or something. She [thought] he was probably going with other [girls]. He said, 'That guy's too old for you anyway.' She answered, 'What am I supposed to do?' I guess he expected her to just wait for him." Of course, to keep Elvis's relationship with Dixie in perspective, it should be remembered that she was only fifteen—not yet old enough for a driver's license.

What Evelyn remembers most about traveling with them was how crazy the fans sometimes got. "They were as wild as can be," she says. "One time Bobbie and I were sitting on the steps that led to the dressing room. I had never seen so many kids. This guy said, 'When they hit that last note, you had better scatter because they're coming down these steps.' Boy, we liked not to have gotten down the steps in time. We were lucky to find an open place where we could get out of the way. You had to be careful or they would run over you. They were just wild—out of their head. [But] I never got scared for my own safety. It was fun."

One time that was not so much fun was when Evelyn and Bobbie went with the boys on a tour that took them through North Carolina. They had reservations at the Robert E. Lee Hotel, a decent place to stay, but there was a convention in town and when they didn't claim their rooms before midnight the hotel gave them to someone else. The only place they could find rooms was at a three-dollar-a-night hotel named the Ambassador. "It was a fleabag hotel," says Bobbie. They were assigned rooms on the second floor, but to get there they had to dodge a phalanx of winos wandering the hallway. "There was one bathroom for the whole floor, and I don't think any of us used it."

Not long after they went to sleep, Scotty and Bobbie were awakened by a loud bang. It came from across the hall, where Bill and Evelyn were staying. Scotty hurried to the door and peered out into the hallway. Just as he did, Bill opened his door.

"Damn," said Bill. "The bed fell down."

Scotty and Bobbie went back to sleep. Bill and Evelyn didn't. "After the bed broke, we went out to the car," says Evelyn. "We couldn't stand the smell."

Early that morning, about five o'clock, Scotty and Bobbie hopped up, washed in the sink that was in the room, and left before anyone could see them. Neither of them had enough nerve to visit the bathroom. Bill and Evelyn were already waiting for them in the car, but it would be forty years before Scotty learned they had spent the night in the car rather than sleep in the hotel. "It was a place to stay, but that was about all," said Bobbie. "I'll never forget the name of that hotel."

By 1955 Bill and Evelyn had been married nine years. At age twenty-eight, Bill already had a good sense of who he was and what he wanted out of life. They had met in her home state of Virginia when she was fifteen. Her father and brother had a country band that played for the USO. She sometimes performed with them, singing duets with her brother. Once, when they showed up for a USO show, they discovered they were short a bass player. Bill, who was stationed with the Army in Virginia, volunteered to sit in with them. Sparks didn't fly musicially that day, but it was love at first sight for Bill and Evelyn. They were married the next year, when she turned sixteen. After his discharge later that year, Bill returned to Memphis.

"I didn't want to leave home," says Evelyn. It was her brother who finally convinced her she should join her husband in Memphis. "He said, 'I'll go just go down there with you.' We went down on a Greyhound bus and got off somewhere on the other side of Nashville. We were sitting there, eating, when a bus pulled up that had Richmond written on it. We both got on that bus and went back home. Bill had a hissy. He didn't know where we were. I finally had to break down [and move to Memphis]."

❊ ❊ ❊

Sometimes the trajectory of Elvis and the Blue Moon Boys carried them through Crockett County. A couple of times they spent the night with Scotty's parents. Mattie was proud of her youngest son, a fact made evident by the photographs of Scotty, Bill, and Elvis that adorned her bedroom wall. After a home-cooked meal, she'd send them on their way.

Scotty didn't see much of his parents after the wild ride with Elvis began. His father died of leukemia in 1963, thirteen days before his seventy-third birthday. Scotty wasn't there when it happened, but his friend James Lewis did what he could to make the old man comfortable. "I remember him getting on the floor and being unable to get back up on the bed," says James. "We had to roll him back up on the sheet and two or three of us picked him up on the sheet. He was in so much pain he couldn't bear for anyone to touch him."

"James, is there bugs crawling on me?" he asked.

"No, Mr. Scott, it's just the medicine they're giving you."

James thought nothing about being there for Scott Moore's passing. "You try to help your neighbors," says James, reflecting a generations-old custom, still strong at that time in Crockett County, of maintaining deathbed vigils for friends and neighbors.

The summer of 1955 was in many ways the most eventful of their careers. It began with Elvis and the Blue Moon Boys developing their skills as stage performers and experiencing the first wave of fan hysteria. As the summer progressed, it would become even more eventful. Back in Memphis after a twenty-one-day tour with the Hank Snow Jamboree that had taken them across the Southeast—and spawned a pattern of fan reaction that would at times leave Elvis shaken and stripped of some of his clothes—they played dates in Arkansas and Mississippi and got ready for another session in Sam's studio that July. They had no way of knowing it would be their last session for Sun Records.

On July 7, four days before the session was scheduled to begin, Scotty traded in his Gibson ES 295 for a Gibson L5. In May he had purchased a new amplifier, one that would duplicate the echo effect heard on their records. He first heard the amplifier, called an Echosonic, on one of Chet Atkins's records. It had been custom built by a radio repairman, Ray Butts, who operated a music store in Cairo, Illinois.

Scotty tracked Butts down and gave him a call. He agreed to make an amplifier for Scotty, but would not let him buy it on an installment plan (the only way Scotty could afford the $495 price tag). They worked out a deal in which the O.K. Houck Piano Company in Memphis bought the amplifier from Butts, then sold it on an installment plan to Scotty. He got a $65 trade-in allowance for his Fender Deluxe amplifier, made a down payment of $25, and agreed to pay Houck $26.54 a month until the Echosonic was paid for. Any analysis of the development of rock 'n' roll would have to include Butts's Echosonic. His amplifier defined the fledging art form by allowing it to project a raw, full-bodied sound that set it apart from any other music being created at the time.

Bob Neal was getting offers for Elvis's contract on a regular basis. He told Elvis about some of them; others he kept to himself. For his part, Sam Phillips said he would consider selling his contract if the price— and the buyer—suited him, but he never sat down and talked seriously with anyone about it. The July session was no different than the others, except that Sam had asked Johnny Bernero, a local drummer, to be there in case he was needed. The first song was "I Forgot to Remember to Forget," another Stan Kesler composition.

Elvis didn't particularly like the song at first, but they experimented with the drums, adding a rim shot on the offbeat and—by the time they finished—Elvis was high on the song. Next they tried a song that Little Junior Parker and the Blue Flames had recorded for Sam two years earlier. "Mystery Train" was the same type of blues number that had brought them their first success. They started playing around with the song without the drummer, much as they had done with "That's All Right, Mama," when they suddenly discovered the defining lick in the song. The rhythm of Elvis's voice fed an extra bar of rhythm into the song that Scotty says today he couldn't duplicate if his life depended on it. "At the time, with him singing, it just felt natural," he says. They wrapped up the session with "Trying to Get to You," a rhythm and blues tune they had failed to nail down earlier in the year. This time they got it. For the next single release, Sam paired "Mystery Train" with "I Forgot to Remember to Forget." It was released in August.

With "Mystery Train," Scotty's style was cemented into place. His idea of using his guitar to provide counterpoint to the vocalist was a radical concept in popular recording at that time, especially when he used that same counterpoint rhythm as a foundation for his sparse, but often breathless, solos that cried out with a voice of their own. Intuitively, his guitar became the anti-Elvis component of the music.

Before heading out on the road again, they took a few days off to relax. Elvis used the time to visit with Dixie and to be seen about town in local clubs. Colonel Tom Parker used the time to politick with Vernon and Gladys Presley. Scotty and Bill liked the way the drummers had worked out on the last couple of sessions. Now that their records included a drummer, they wondered if their touring band shouldn't also have one. Scotty, in particular, was in favor of it because it would help fill out the sound. Just how much music could one guitar produce? When Nashville producer David Briggs listens to their early material he is amazed. "Scotty was the whole deal," he says. "He made it all work. Listen to it. It's all guitar. People still try to copy what he played forty years ago."

When Scotty and Bill suggested to Elvis that he needed a drummer, he agreed with them, but said he couldn't afford to hire one. Scotty and Bill talked it over. If Elvis would hire D. J. to tour with them, they would share the cost of his $100-a-week salary. D. J. already was performing with them every week at the Hayride (after their first appearance, he was allowed to come out from behind the curtain and be seen by the audience), and they all liked him. That December, D. J. officially joined the band, although he had been performing with them on and off since August.

Scotty and Bill were elated. They didn't mind helping with D. J.'s salary. The music was the thing . . . you know. Unfortunately, their elation was short-lived. That same month, after a conference with Elvis,

Scotty and Elvis onstage (Photo © 1996 EPE, Inc.)

Bob Neal told them it had been decided that their old verbal agreement, whereby Elvis received 50 percent and Scotty and Bill each received 25 percent, was no longer acceptable.

"It became obvious this wasn't fair, because Elvis was the star, regardless of the fact they contributed largely to it," Neal explained to Jerry Hopkins. "So we had a crisis and I had to handle that, announcing to Scotty and Bill we were no longer going to operate like that, but that they would receive a fee we would all agree on."

Scotty and Bill were devastated. It was the end of the Blue Moon Boys. They had begun with Elvis as partners. Now they were nothing more than salaried sidemen. They never had a written contract, so they didn't have a legal leg to stand on. They threatened to quit, in a quiet sort of way, but Neal was adamant: take it or leave it. Scotty and Bill blamed it on Parker, but Neal told them it was not Parker's doing, a story he has stuck to over the years. Despite Neal's protestations that it was not Parker—and evidence that the decision was indeed made by Elvis— to this day Scotty refuses to believe Elvis would betray him.

Scotty and Bill agreed to go on salary. Henceforth, they would receive weekly paychecks of $200 if they were working and $100 if they were not working. Says Scotty: "It looked like we would make at least as much as if we were blocking hats or making tires. It was a bird in the hand situation. That may not have been a decent salary for what we were doing, but at that time it was for the guy on the street. The problem was, the guy on the street didn't have all the responsibilities we had. We bought our own food and our own stage clothes, plus paid all the incidentals. Elvis didn't know about money. I think his daddy looked at it like the guy on the street. He was probably thinking: 'Those guys are making $200 a week. I never made over $30 or $50.' I can understand that mindset. But that still doesn't make it right."

Neal was clearly uncomfortable about what happened, but he viewed it as part of his job. "My contract was with Elvis, not with Scotty and Bill," he explained later. "They weren't contracted to me—or to Sun."

Later that month, Scotty and Bill got more bad news. Parker, having convinced Vernon and Gladys that he—and only he—could navigate Elvis's career through the musical minefield ahead, took over his contract from Neal. Oddly, Neal turned it over without a whimper. Just as things were beginning to happen, he stepped aside, keeping nothing for himself. Strange things were beginning to happen in Elvis's career.

Parker was now top dog; Scotty and Bill knew what that meant. "We knew he didn't want us around," says Scotty. "Elvis was being brainwashed. We'd be traveling together in the same car, and Elvis would bring up something—'The Colonel said so and so'—I'd say, 'Elvis, you have to stand up and speak your mind. There's nothing wrong with you arguing about something.' He'd say, 'Ah, well, I made a deal with him—I'd do the singing and he'd take care of the business.' He'd mumble and grumble about it for a day or two and that'd be it. He'd go ahead and do whatever it was he didn't want to do."

But it was more than the way Elvis was being manipulated that bothered Scotty and Bill—it was the Colonel himself. "We had heard in the very early days, probably from Hank Snow's band, that he was really here illegally," says Scotty. "Of course, we never paid any attention to it. It was never any deep, deep secret. In later years, when Parker wouldn't let Elvis tour Europe, we wondered if there wasn't more to the story. Why, after Elvis got so big—and this is the part that puzzles me—wouldn't he go to Germany? I believe they had enough pull they could have gotten [Parker] a waiver of some kind. The Tennessee senators would probably have done something for him. So I maintain there is something even more mysterious about why he wouldn't leave [the country]. It's not logical. He tried to beat Elvis down on European tours. He told him all kinds of stuff—except that he didn't want to leave the country."

Before they went out on tour again—this time with D. J.—Parker got in another dig at the former Blue Moon Boys. From the beginning, Bill had been in charge of the group's concessions, which at that time were confined to photographs. Says Scotty: "Bill was selling pictures for twenty-five and fifty cents and keeping a nickel for himself and doing good. That was when a nickel was a nickel. As soon as Parker got control, he took away the concessions. He offered Bill some pittance so he could keep selling the pictures, but Bill turned it down and I don't blame him."

Scotty and Bill didn't dwell on their troubles. They had shows to do, and regardless of what was happening with Elvis and his management, they were too busy to be distracted for long by Parker's not-so-subtle machinations. The Colonel's biggest coup of all was in the works, but they knew nothing about that when they set out from Memphis in August for performances in Texas and beyond. D. J. didn't have the same Memphis cultural nexus shared by Scotty, Bill, and Elvis, but his Louisiana bayou ways endeared him to them and allowed him to slip right into the groove.

The addition of D. J. also meant they had another driver. In those days, they took turns behind the wheel. That usually worked out fine, except when Elvis was driving. He was a good driver, but he didn't pay attention to where he was going. The others were afraid to go to sleep when he was driving because, without someone acting as navigator, Elvis was certain to miss the scheduled turnoffs. Sometimes his oversights would take them miles out of their way. Says Scotty: "Several times we went 100 miles out of the way and had to double back." If Elvis was behind the wheel, the only way they could be certain of getting to their destination was to stay awake and watch his every move. "We'd let him drive during daylight hours," says D. J. "They'd let me drive if it was a straight shot to El Paso or something." It got to be a big joke with them.

Late one night, as they were driving through St. Louis, Scotty pulled off the road and gave the wheel to D. J. Confident they were in good hands, Scotty, Bill, and Elvis curled up as best as they could on the car seats and went to sleep. Hours later, Scotty was awakened at sunrise as the car filled with sunlight.

"Where are we?" he asked. He sat up and looked around. The car was pulled off on the side of the road. That was the question D. J. had been dreading for hours.

"Hell, we're still in St. Louis," D. J. said.

Scotty looked at him in disbelief.

"I got lost," D. J. said. He explained that he had been driving in circles for hours trying to find a way out of St. Louis. "I didn't want to wake you up."

Scotty was refreshed after a good night's sleep. He told him not to worry about it. He got behind the wheel and drove them to the next stop. In retrospect, D. J. figures he should have awakened them, but when you're the new guy, you naturally want to make as few waves as possible. Besides, he says, "I just knew I'd get out of there any second."

Life on the road for rock 'n' roll's first touring band bore little resemblance to today's mammoth undertakings. A typical Rolling Stones or Bruce Springsteen concert requires a caravan of trucks, hundreds of support personnel, and a logistical organization capable of dealing with mind-boggling detail. For Elvis and the Blue Moon Boys, it was a matter of loading up the car, piling in on top of each other, and striking out for the next town. The trick was to keep the floorboard clear of soft drink and beer bottles, and to keep unwrapped candy bars off the seat.

In the beginning, Elvis was filled with questions. He had never been out of Memphis. He wanted to know what was out there. Scotty had been all over the Far East. Elvis asked him lots of questions about the Navy, about where he had been and what he had seen. "Pretty soon he knew more than you did," Scotty laughs. "But he had a good mind. He was fresh out of high school, so he was inquisitive—mainly about girls. You let him out of the chute, and there he went. We might be going down the road after a show and he would say, 'What did you think of so and so?'" They were the same type of questions he asked Bobbie. Girls were new to him. How could he possibly know what he thought until he knew what others thought? He approached dating like he approached buying a new car. How much mileage does it get? How fast does it go?

Scotty tried to get them to hold rehearsals while they were on the road. They would all tell him what a good idea it was, but they always found excuses not to do it. "I wanted to work up something new or different; I hated playing the same songs every night," says Scotty. "I guess that's one of the things I feel cheated about—well, not really cheated—but when I started playing with Elvis I was extremely interested in learning to play other things. Once we got on the road and got into a rut, doing all those one-nighters, I was too tired to think about it. Everything becomes very focused. You play the same things day in and day out, then you go into the studio and cut some more, which I really loved doing, then you start all over again, except then you have some new material. But then you get in another rut again until you get back in the studio."

Food was a constant problem on the road. Because of the hours they kept—if they had asked the promoter the name of the nearest caterer, they would have been slapped silly—finding a decent restaurant that would fry up a late-night order of burger and fries was always a challenge. Because fast food restaurants had not yet been invented, they learned to rely on truck stops. In those days truck stops had higher standards than they have today. "Now they are into selling souvenirs, while back then it was magazines, but food—and getting it to you fast—was the thing," says Scotty. Sometimes they would get lucky and the local promoter would take them home for a meal with his family. If it were not for the kindness of strangers—and the "all for one" and "one for all" attitude they honed into a loosely defined brotherhood—they would never have survived the rigors of life on the road. There was nothing "fun" about long trips and long hours. What made it fun was what they did once they stepped up on the stage.

Suddenly, amid the screams and shouts of fans, they were transformed from road-warrior vagabonds into cheerleaders for a phenomenon they neither saw coming nor understood. They knew something was happening, but they were far too busy acting it out to spend time thinking about what it was. When they first started out, their shows lasted only ten or fifteen minutes. Concerts in those days were multientertainment programs, with each act performing only its own records. The music business was built on singles—albums weren't important in popular music until much later—and most recording acts were lucky to have released enough singles to fill fifteen minutes onstage.

L to r: Bill, Scotty, unidentified woman, D. J. (Photo © 1996 EPE, Inc.)

For several months "That's All Right, Mama" and "Blue Moon of Kentucky" were their only hits. Scotty remembers working up several songs recorded by other artists so they would have enough music to fill fifteen minutes. "We worked up a couple of Chuck Berry's songs," he says. "And we did 'Tweedle Dee'—six, eight, maybe ten songs like that—uptempo things that fit the rhythm of the first two songs we cut. As soon as we cut more songs, we'd drop the others off."

Looking back on those early performances, Scotty and D. J. today are amazed at what they were able to do under such primitive conditions. Usually they had only two microphones: one for Elvis and one for Bill's bass. Scotty's amplifier rested on a chair behind him. He usually stood to Elvis's right, with Bill on his left and D. J. directly behind him. The only time they could hear Elvis's voice was when he was announcing a song. Once the music began—and the cheering from the audience reached a fever pitch—they played by sight alone. "The only way I could describe the sound is that it was like, you know, if you dive into a swimming pool—that rush of noise that you get," says Scotty. "In audio terms, it would be like phasing—phew!—it would be so loud that all you could hear in your ears was that sound."

Elvis didn't have a monitor, so he couldn't hear himself or the music. Once they started a song, they all watched Elvis, measuring the progress of the song by his movements. Says D. J.: "Elvis would never miss, even though he couldn't hear. I never saw him break meter. He always came right back in there. How he didn't get lost is beyond me. Scotty, Bill, and

I just used eye movements to communicate with each other. We could tell by Elvis's arm and leg movements which part of the song he was in." Scotty once told a reporter they were the only band in the world directed by an ass. "I thought that poor guy was going to faint—he took it literally," says Scotty.

Marshall Grant watched a lot of those shows. "Bill and Elvis were the show," he says. "All Scotty did was stand alongside Elvis and play his guitar. He duplicated what you heard on the record. He's a perfectionist. He let Bill and Elvis do their thing, and he just did what he did best—play his guitar."

Elvis and Bill had a regular act. For years, it was standard practice in country music for the bass player to be the comedian. Bill was a natural at it. He taunted Elvis, yelled at him, and cracked jokes. Grant recalls one of their routines:

Bill walks over to Elvis's microphone.

"Roses are red and violets are pink," Bill says.

"No—roses are red and violets are blue," Elvis corrected.

"No, no, man. Roses are red and violets are pink."

"Naw, you're wrong, Bill."

"I know Violet's are pink," he says, at which point he yanks a pair of pink panties from his back pocket and holds them up for the crowd to see. "I know Violet's are pink 'cause I got them right here."

Scotty recalls one of the few skits in which he participated. "Bill would say something about me playing checkers. Elvis would say, 'He doesn't play checkers.' Then Bill would say, 'No, I was out in the parking lot and I heard someone say to him, 'No, it's your move'—so he must be playing checkers." Scotty credits Bill with much of their early success. "Elvis wasn't a great MC—I think everyone agrees on that," says Scotty. "If it hadn't been for Bill, there were a bunch of shows where we would have died on the vine. Elvis picked up a few corny lines that he would use in between songs. All he wanted to do was go out there and sing."

Sometimes their comedy routine was upstaged by acts that preceded them. June Carter Cash, who as a member of the Carter Sisters was also managed by Colonel Parker, sometimes found herself on the same bill with Elvis. "I used to do a little comedy act in the beginning and do my little set and then [they] would go on," she says. Before and after the shows, they would sometimes all go to a cafe. She remembers Elvis playing Johnny Cash's record, "Cry, Cry, Cry" on the jukeboxes.

Often Elvis used the song to tune his guitar. "Red West was with him at the time and that was about the only way we could get Elvis's guitar tuned [using 'Cry, Cry, Cry']," says June. Red West was a Humes

High senior, a star football player, who later became one of Elvis's body-guards. "Red and I used to sit backstage and try to change those strings because Elvis kept breaking them all the time. We spent all our time stringing that guitar and keeping it in tune."

✳ ✳ ✳

While Elvis and the Blue Moon Boys were out on the road that November, Sam Phillips was wheeling and dealing, expanding his financial base in a business partnership with Kemmons Wilson, a Memphis entrepreneur who recently had constructed the first units in a hotel chain named Holiday Inn. The previous month, using money received from Wilson, he made history by starting up the nation's first all-female radio station. He gave it the call letters WHER.

After conducting secret auditions that fall at Memphis Recording Service, Sam hired a female broadcaster, Dotty Abbott, to run the station. Next he hired his wife, Becky, with whom he had worked at a radio station in Alabama, as an announcer. Marion Keisker was the next hired. Sam moved her from her all-important post at the studio—she was in many ways the foundation of the business end of Sun Records—and put her on the air at WHER as an announcer and news reporter. Marion cleaned out her desk at the studio and moved over to the radio station office, located in a Holiday Inn on Third Street south of Crump Boulevard.

On November 21 Sam announced that he had sold Elvis's recording contract to RCA Records. With great ceremony, Elvis, Sam, Colonel Parker, Hank Snow, and representatives from RCA gathered at the studio to sign the contracts. Scotty and Bill were stunned; D. J. was so new to the group he didn't know what to think. Marion was gone. Jack Clement had become Sam's right-hand man in the studio. Even though he was signing new artists to Sun Records—Johnny Cash had already released "Cry, Cry, Cry"; Jerry Lee Lewis was cutting some hot tracks; and Carl Perkins was only a couple of months away from recording "Blue Suede Shoes," Sun's first record to break the Top 10 on the pop charts—Sam was building radio stations and looking and talking more like a businessman than a record executive.

The deal with RCA Records—Colonel Parker's biggest coup to date—called for Sam to receive $35,000 and Elvis to receive a signing bonus of $5,000. Later, when asked why he had sold Elvis's contract, Sam said it was an offer he couldn't turn down. Still later he explained that by saying he was having financial difficulties and needed the money. It was a curious explanation: then and now.

"Mystery Train," released that August, had gone to No. 1 on the country charts, giving Elvis and the Blue Moon Boys their first chart-topper. Their records were selling like gangbusters. On top of the success being enjoyed by Sun, Sam's new partnership with Wilson had put him on a financial fast track.

In view of the way Elvis's records were selling—and the ease with which he was entering into new ventures with Wilson—Sam's explanation for why he sold Elvis's contract may have been unconvincing; Scotty simply figured that Sam had his reasons. Besides, by not signing Scotty and Bill to Sun, Sam had effectively blocked them from benefiting financially from whatever success Elvis's records achieved.

Apart from sentiment for the tiny studio itself, Scotty and Bill had no reason to want Elvis to remain with Sun Records. There was nothing in it for them. Because Elvis himself had only recently severed their partnership, putting them on salary, there was now a ceiling on their expectations. No matter how successful Elvis became, no matter how many hit records they recorded with him, they were nothing more than employees. Of course, they had every reason to think they would benefit in some way. Says Scotty: "I figured the salary would get bigger as we went along. If he made more, we would be compensated more. I never begrudged him his success. In fact I told him so, that he should make more because he was the star, but I always figured I would share in it somehow."

Sam told Memphis's *Press-Scimitar* he thought Elvis was one of the most talented "youngsters" in the country: "By releasing his contract to RCA-Victor we will give him the opportunity of entering the largest organization of its kind in the world, so his talents can be given the fullest opportunity." As Sam was stepping out of Elvis's life, others were stepping into his life. On that same day, Parker and Bob Neal agreed to evenly split their combined 40 percent commission on Elvis's earnings until March 15, 1956, at which time Neal would step out of the picture and Parker would become Elvis's sole manager.

Marion Keisker kept quiet at the time, but years later she was not hesitant about expressing her unhappiness over Parker's relationship with Elvis. "Colonel Tom had been working on the family at least a year—in the most polished and Machiavellian way," she says. "You couldn't believe it. Mrs. Presley, God rest her soul, she was just a mother, was what she was, you know. The Colonel'd go to her and say, 'You got the finest boy in the world and it's terrible the way they're making him work.' Sam might deny this, but I think it's the only thing Elvis ever did against the advice of Sam."

For his part, Bob Neal was content to move out of Parker's way. "My contract was going to expire, and I simply let it go," he says. "I [didn't] ask for anything and [didn't] try to negotiate anything. I could have, but I didn't try to." Realizing he was no match for Parker, he opened a record store on Main Street in Memphis and extended his management arm by becoming Johnny Cash's manager.

D. J. had watched Parker long enough to know he didn't want to get any closer to the man than he had to. "Oh, yeah, you had to watch him," says D. J. "He didn't want us as the band. He'd say, 'Don't pay the boys, they'll just want more money. We can get more guys.' That was his theory. I didn't let him bother me. We'd all get mad at him, but we didn't have to deal with him. Elvis paid us. We didn't care what the Colonel thought."

With RCA Records stepping into the breach, Scotty knew the pace was going to pick up—and fast. Their first session was set for January. Their new producer, Steve Sholes, would work with them at the RCA studio in Nashville. At year's end, Scotty's financial situation had improved. His income, for the year, from Elvis amounted to $8,052.24. He didn't know it at the time, but it was the second best year he would ever have with Elvis.

That Christmas, as Scotty and Bobbie celebrated their apparent good fortune, Auzella Moore asked thirteen-year-old Tammy Wynette if she wanted to go with her to take some Christmas presents by Elvis's house. That April Elvis had purchased a three-bedroom house at 1034 Audubon Drive for himself and his parents. Tammy thought she had died and gone to heaven. When she returned home, she couldn't wait to tell her mother about the visit. "I said, 'Mother, that rug that you walk on, it comes up around your ankles'—it was white carpet."

6

LIGHTS, CAMERA, ACTION: THE MOVIE YEARS

B y the time Elvis arrived in Nashville on January 10, 1956, with Scotty, Bill, and D. J., for his first recording session with RCA Records, the record label already had released their previous records under its own imprint; as part of the deal with Sun, the company had acquired all of Elvis's previous masters. RCA's first release was the last single issued by Sun Records, "I Forgot to Remember to Forget." It stayed on the country charts for weeks, but not surprisingly did not make it onto the pop charts. Four additional Sun singles were rereleased two weeks before the Nashville session began.

RCA didn't expect the earlier singles to reappear on the charts. They rereleased them to have records with their imprint to cover back orders, and to "brand" their new artist with their logo as a means of severing ties with Sun in the minds of radio DJs and retailers. For his part, Colonel Parker printed up new souvenir booklets that proclaimed Elvis to be RCA's "sensational, new singing star." In small print, the booklet announced that he was performing with the Blue Moon Boys.

Within weeks RCA dropped the band's name from its materials—and Colonel Parker soon followed suit—although Elvis and others continued to use the name when introducing Scotty, Bill, and D. J. The new promotional booklet—and all the others that followed—did not contain photographs of the backup musicians. It was a transparent ploy by Colonel Parker to disassociate Elvis from his former partners.

In the months that followed, as fan magazines clamored to turn out special issues on Elvis, Parker monitored the reportage with an iron hand. Under no circumstances, he told the magazines, were they to publish photographs of Scotty and Bill. Most of the magazines did as they were told. Those who ignored Parker's instructions experienced the wrath of the Colonel, who was not shy about administering tongue lashings.

Typical of the special Elvis publications flooding the newsstands in 1956 was one titled "The Amazing Elvis Presley." It contained fifty pages of text and photographs, including four shots of a teddy bear collection said to belong to Elvis, but there were no photographs in the magazine of Scotty and only one of Bill (a long shot in which his hand covers his face). However, Elvis did mention Scotty and Bill in the text in a Q&A in which he was asked about them by a reporter.

For the Nashville session, Steve Sholes decided to augment the sound that had been successful at Sun. Sholes was more than just a producer at RCA. As head of A&R, he was, in fact, the label's top executive in Nashville. In addition to Scotty, Bill, and D. J., he booked for the session Marvin Hughes on piano and Chet Atkins on guitar. At that time, Atkins was already a guitar legend, with many hit records to his credit, but he was more than that to RCA, which had hired him as a staff guitarist and consultant. He was the foundation on which the label would build its roster in the late '50s and early '60s. Sholes put Atkins in charge of the session.

When Atkins asked Elvis who he wanted for background singers, he asked for the Jordanaires, a popular gospel quartet that had been touring with Eddy Arnold. Elvis had met them in Memphis at Ellis Auditorium at one of the many gospel concerts he attended. However, RCA had just signed a new gospel quartet called the Speer Family. For Elvis's session, Atkins constructed a trio of his own making. He booked two members of the Speer Family—Ben and Brock Speer—and added Gordon Stoker of the Jordanaires. Stoker didn't much like the idea of performing without the other members of his group, but Atkins told him he couldn't use the entire quartet and needed to use some of the Speers because they were new to the label. Stoker was taken aback by Atkins's attitude toward Elvis. Recalls Stoker: "He didn't think Elvis would be around long. He said, 'You know, we've signed this kid from Memphis, but—you know—he's a passing fad.'"

When they arrived at the studio, Elvis, Scotty, Bill, and D. J. didn't know Atkins had reservations about Elvis's talent, nor did they know Sholes was antsy about RCA's investment in Elvis. It was the first time RCA had ever bought out a contract, along with previously produced masters. Sholes's job was on the line, and he knew it.

The session itself went smoothly enough, although it took the Memphis boys a while to adjust to the more structured Nashville way of doing things. Instead of Sam sticking his head out the control room door, yelling "Hey, how about doing it again," they had a seasoned engineer, Bob Ferris, calling outtake numbers. Scotty felt the pressure, but he was excited about working with one of his heroes, Chet Atkins. He knew Chet was there to do what he could to help.

At one point, Scotty, who was working on a guitar part, paused to ask Chet what he thought about what he was playing. Chet, who was also working on a guitar part, looked up at him and smiled. "Man, I'm just playing rhythm," he said. "Just keep doing what you've been doing."

Elvis was unhappy that Atkins had not booked the Jordanaires, but he did not make a big deal out of it. Instead, he called Stoker aside and told him that he would see to it that all four Jordanaires were at the next session.

Over a two-day period, they cut five songs: Ray Charles's "I've Got a Woman," along with "I Was the One," "Money Honey," "I'm Counting on You," and "Heartbreak Hotel," a song cowritten by Mae Axton, a Floridian who did promotional work for Colonel Parker. What Stoker remembers about Scotty at the session was how "cool and collected" he was: "He always seemed to know what he was doing."

Scotty was amused at the lengths to which Ferris and Atkins went to copy the echo effect Sam had captured in Memphis. For "Heartbreak Hotel" they added slapback—or delay as it is called today—to Elvis's vocal, then rerecorded the song in a hallway of the studio. "They had a speaker set up at one end of this long hallway and a microphone at the other end," Scotty says. "They had a sign on the door that said, 'Don't open the door when the red light is on.'"

After the session they returned to Memphis, then left for Shreveport to perform their weekly show at the Hayride. From there they went to Texas for a series of one-nighters; then, at the end of the month, it was on to New York for their first appearance on a nationally broadcast television program, *Stage Show*. While they were out on the road, Sholes took the five cuts to New York to play for his bosses at RCA. To his horror, they hated all five. They told him to head straight back to Nashville and record something that sounded like what Elvis had recorded at Sun. Sholes told them it had taken him two days to get those five songs. He didn't think it would do any good to rush back into the studio to do more. Elvis was going to be in New York at the end of the month to do the television show. Why not do more recordings in New York? The RCA executives agreed to set up a session for the week following their appearance on *Stage Show*.

LIGHTS, CAMERA, ACTION:
THE MOVIE YEARS

Despite Elvis's early rejection following his audition for the *Arthur Godfrey Show*, Colonel Parker felt Elvis was perfect for television. The contract with RCA gave him added ammunition, because it helped dispel criticism that Elvis was nothing more than a regional success. Finally, his efforts paid off when Jack Philbin, executive producer of *Stage Show*, saw a picture of Elvis and commented, "This kid is a guitar-playing Marlon Brando." Elvis was booked for four consecutive performances on the weekly, Saturday-night show, beginning on January 28. He would be paid $1,250 per show.

Stage Show was a musician's dream. Produced by Jackie Gleason, it was hosted by Tommy and Jimmy Dorsey, two of the biggest names in big-band music. The contract was dutifully reported in Memphis's *Press-Scimitar* by television reporter Robert Johnson: "Events are spinning faster than his records for the Memphis youngster . . . ," he wrote, concluding with a bit of advice: "Don't let your head spin with them, Elvis!"

Three days before they flew to New York to do the show, Scotty purchased a pair of tuxedo trousers for $21.12 from Wolf the Tailor in Memphis. The Blue Moon Boys had come a long way since the days of matching western shirts. Whatever the big time was, they were about to

Scotty and Bill, Tulsa, OK (Courtesy of Scotty Moore)

enter it. The executives at RCA in New York weren't sure about the material they had recorded in Nashville, but they decided it would be foolish not to release a single to coincide with Elvis's appearance on *Stage Show*. On January 27, the day before the show, they released "Heartbreak Hotel," with "I Was the One" on the flip side. Steve Sholes went to New York so that he would be there the following Monday to begin production on the second recording session. If things didn't work out, he knew his career with RCA was probably over. He had the uneasy feeling "Heartbreak Hotel" could be his swan song.

Stage Show was broadcast from CBS's Studio 50, a theater located between 53rd and 54th Streets. When Elvis was introduced, he ran out on stage like he had been shot out of a cannon; then, with barely a glance at Scotty and Bill, launched into a song they had not yet recorded, "Shake, Rattle and Roll." Elvis would eventually play his new RCA single "Heartbreak Hotel" on his third appearance on the show, but the performance would be marred somewhat by a trumpet solo from the Dorsey Brothers band. The solo was solid musically, but ran counter to the guitar sound Scotty had developed for the song. Even so, Elvis and the band were happy with the treatment they received on the show.

"They were super nice to us," says Scotty. "They had such a great band. Louis Bellson was playing drums and D. J. was a big fan of his and they got to be pals. I don't remember any problems with Tommy or Jimmy, either one. I'm sure they were looking down their noses at what we were doing. Our three pieces sounded so empty out there on their stage. They tried to do things with us—like adding a big crescendo ending—but the sound was bad in that theater and the engineers didn't know how the record was cut."

All the television executives cared about, says D. J., was how the band looked. "We were just out there," he says. "But those guys had a good band, and the Dorsey brothers were nice guys. I knew Louis Bellson, the drummer, from way back. He sounded like thunder back then, with those bass drums. They knew they had a job to do. They played chasers and stingers for us. That was what they got paid for."

Back home, Memphis watched in awe and held its breath.

❊ ❊ ❊

The week after the first *Stage Show*, the group gathered at the RCA studios on East 24th Street. Steve Sholes hired a honky-tonk piano player, Shorty Long, who specialized in Broadway musicals, to sit in with the band. To Elvis's disappointment, the Jordanaires were not booked for the session. Elvis was polite, but distant. He said "no sir," and "yes sir." Sholes wasn't connecting with him and he knew it. For their first song, Sholes chose Carl Perkins's "Blue Suede Shoes," the latest single from Sun Records. The song was going great guns up the charts. As a courtesy, Sholes called Sam Phillips and told him they were recording the song. He promised Sam it wouldn't be released as a single.

After more than a dozen takes of "Blue Suede Shoes," Elvis begged off, saying he really didn't think they could improve on the original. After all, it was Carl's song. Elvis wanted to record "My Baby Left Me," a blues song written by Arthur Crudup, who had penned his first hit, "That's All Right, Mama." It was the kind of music Elvis preferred. Perhaps because it was the kind of music the boys in the band felt, the song went effortlessly to tape. For the first time since the addition of D. J. on drums, they clicked as a band. Sholes was afraid it wasn't the pop sound his bosses wanted to hear. By trying to make Elvis conform to his vision of what he thought RCA wanted to hear, Sholes was making a classic mistake: he was thinking the music, instead of feeling it. For all his success as a music executive, he didn't seem to understand that Southern boys invented music better than they copied it.

Elvis recorded another Crudup number, "So Glad You're Mine," and Sholes persuaded him to do one of the honky-tonk numbers he had brought, "One Sided Love." It went back and forth like that all week. Sholes wanted to get enough songs so that RCA could release an album. He didn't come right out and say, "If you do one of mine, I'll do one of yours," but that is what it amounted to. When they had time off, Elvis went sightseeing, but the band members hung close to the Warwick Hotel, where they were staying. When they got paid, they took the cash across the street to a bar. Says D. J.: "We had a couple of hundred dollars apiece, and we'd spread it out across the table, like a big deal. We got to know the bartender. We said, 'When this runs out, throw us out.' The bartender bought us drinks. We bought him drinks. I think the name of the place was Jerry's Bar. When we were in New York, that's where we stayed. We had a good time there."

They wrapped up the session that week, did the second *Stage Show*, then hit the road. "Heartbreak Hotel" was soaring on the charts, but the band had no idea how well it was doing. They didn't have time to read newspapers and the only time they were near a radio was late at night when they were traveling. In those days few radio stations broadcast after midnight and the ones that did tended to play old standards. For the next several weeks, they stayed on the road, returning to New York each weekend to appear on *Stage Show*. The original four performances were extended to six, with the last show scheduled for March 24. After four consecutive shows, they took time off to meet their Saturday night obligations to the Hayride.

As March began, "Heartbreak Hotel" hit No. 14 on the pop charts. It was the first time Elvis had broken the Top 20 on the pop charts. Just ahead of "Heartbreak Hotel" at No. 13 was Carl Perkins's "Blue Suede Shoes." Fiercely competitive, Sam Phillips arranged for Perkins to receive a gold record on the *Perry Como Show*, which aired opposite *Stage Show*.

On the way to New York, Perkins and his band were involved in an automobile accident in Delaware. Perkins was seriously injured and missed the show. Scotty, Bill, and D. J. heard about the accident on the radio as they drove to New York to do *Stage Show*. When they passed through Delaware, they stopped by the hospital to visit Perkins. "It was in the wee hours of the morning," Perkins later said of the visit. "That was one of my darkest hours . . . and I remember so well when I looked up and saw [them]." Elvis was already in New York, but he sent a telegram to Perkins wishing him a quick recovery.

Ironically, as Perkins languished in the hospital, "Heartbreak Hotel" overtook "Blue Suede Shoes" on the charts. By May, Elvis's song was No. 1 and Perkins's song had stalled at No. 3. Perkins recovered from his injuries, but his career never fully recovered from the bad timing of the accident. For the rest of his life, he would wonder how different his career might have been had he received that gold record on the *Perry Como Show*.

On March 13 Elvis's first LP was released. It contained seven songs recorded in January in New York and Nashville, and five previously unreleased songs gleaned from the Sun Records masters. With "Heartbreak Hotel" racing to the top of the charts, there was little suspense about how the self-titled album would do: by March 1, RCA already had received 362,000 advance orders.

Bob Neal watched from the sidelines. Colonel Parker had been running things for months. When Neal's contract formally ran out on March 14, he quietly stepped out of the picture. One of the first things Parker did as Elvis's manager was to get him released from his contract with the Hayride. A country-music venue was hardly appropriate for the nation's new king of pop. To get it done, according to Neal, Parker agreed to allow Elvis to do a benefit at the Shreveport Coliseum, with the proceeds going to the Hayride.

Elvis's next television appearance was scheduled for April 3 on the *Milton Berle Show*. It was to be broadcast from the deck of the aircraft carrier USS *Hancock*, which was docked in San Diego. Elvis's appearance was vintage slapstick. Berle played the part of "Melvin," Elvis Presley's twin brother. Elvis sang three songs, including "Heartbreak Hotel," and—perhaps with his thoughts on his fledging movie career—didn't protest playing opposite "Melvin." Scotty felt right at home on the carrier deck. He was the only member of the entourage who had been on a ship. "We had a ball," he says. "Uncle Miltie was great. He did the wig thing with Elvis and busted up a guitar. He did all kinds of goofy stuff. It was funny."

Prior to appearing with Berle, Elvis made a screen test with movie producer Hal Wallis. The test went well, and Wallis, who was famous for films such as *Casablanca* and *The Maltese Falcon*, was impressed enough to offer Elvis a role in an upcoming movie named *The Rainmaker*. However, Parker would not allow him to accept that role. He asked Wallis to find Elvis another movie. By the end of the week, Elvis had signed a seven-year, three-picture contract with Paramount.

For two nights following the Berle show, the boys performed at the San Diego Arena, drawing 11,250 screaming fans to both shows. Back in San Diego for the first time since his release from the Navy, Scotty tracked down John Bankson, who was still in the Navy. Luckily, he was in port. Bankson's wife, Analee, recalls Scotty phoning when he got to town. "He invited my husband down to see the first performance," says Analee. "He was backstage with Elvis and Scotty. When he got home, he told me he had helped Elvis tune his guitar. I said, 'Oh, you did.' Of course, we didn't know who Elvis was at that time. Scotty came out to the house and they played until one or two in the morning. I went to bed. That was the last time I saw Scotty." A decade later, Bankson would see service in the Mekong Delta in Vietnam before succumbing to the cancer caused by his exposure to radiation during the nuclear testing that took place during the 1950s. "If he had lived, he would really have loved all this with Scotty," says Analee today. "He really thought a lot of Scotty." With that trip to San Diego, Scotty closed the door on his Navy past.

After leaving San Diego, the group worked in more concerts, then headed for Nashville on April 14, where they were booked for another recording session. Because they were behind schedule, they chartered a twin-engine plane in Wichita Falls, Texas. The flight plan called for them to stop in Little Rock to refuel, then proceed straight to Nashville. While they were still en route to Little Rock, the pilot realized they were running low on fuel. He told the passengers he needed to land and asked them to help him look for landmarks. When they spotted an emergency landing strip near Hot Springs, he took the plane down so that he could refuel.

"Daylight was just breaking," says Scotty. "This police car drove up and the officer asked us who we were and why we had landed. When we told him, he took us to an all-night diner so that we could get something to eat. The attendant was supposed to fill the gas tanks while we were gone."

Scotty sat in the copilot's seat when they took off. The plane ascended to 1,500 or 2,000 feet and leveled off. "The pilot turned to me and said, 'Here, hold the wheel while I get the maps out from under the seat,'" says Scotty. "I said, 'I don't know how to fly a plane.' He said, 'Just hold it a minute.' Just as I put my hands on the wheel, both engines sputtered and quit. Soon as that happened the pilot reached over and threw a switch, then took over the wheel. Both engines restarted, but it was enough to shake everybody a little bit. The only thing that I can figure is that he forgot to switch back to the main tanks before we took off. After we crossed the Mississippi River, we hit a bunch of turbulence. Bill turned white and put his coat over his head. I think he would have jumped if he could have gotten out. When we got to Nashville, Elvis eased up to us and said, 'We're though with this guy.'"

When they arrived at the studio, Elvis saw that the entire Jordanaires quartet had not been hired as he had requested. He was presented with the same configuration: two Speers and one Jordanaire. Hired to play piano was Marvin Hughes. The music didn't sound right to Elvis. They ended up recording only one song, a ballad titled "I Want You, I Need You, I Love You." It was a song Sholes had brought to the session.

Elvis was polite, as were the band members, but it was apparent to them that Sholes just didn't get it. The song Sholes had balked at recording at the last Nashville session, "Heartbreak Hotel," had gone to No. 1 on the pop charts. Why didn't he understand that the best way to get records out of these Southern boys was simply to turn them loose and let them play what they felt? After the session they returned to Memphis that same day. This time they took a regularly scheduled commercial flight.

✻ ✻ ✻

While Elvis and the band were on the West Coast, Parker booked them for a two-week engagement at the New Frontier Hotel in Las Vegas. It was a gamble to book Elvis in a venue accustomed to older, less frolicsome entertainers, but Parker was on a roll.

The flyer for the New Frontier Hotel advertised Freddy Martin and his orchestra, who were scheduled to do a stage show version of the Broadway musical *Oklahoma!* Also on the bill were comedian Shecky

**D. J., Scotty, Bill, and Elvis lounge by the pool in Las Vegas,
April 25, 1956 (Courtesy of Showtime Archives [Toronto])**

Greene—and as an added attraction, the "Atomic Power singer," Elvis
Presley. Since Nevada was the site of atomic testing, Parker thought the
name would be catchy. What Parker hadn't figured on was how an older, more sedate nightclub crowd would react to Elvis.

After the first performance, at which the audience politely applauded, but showed none of the wild enthusiasm to which they were
accustomed, Scotty, Bill, and D. J. knew they were in for a long two
weeks. Says D. J.: "I don't think the people there were ready for Elvis.
He was mostly for teenagers, kids. We worked with [Freddie Martin's
orchestra] on *Oklahoma!*, and here we were three little pieces making all
that noise, and they were eating $50 and $60 steaks. We tried everything
we knew. Usually Elvis could get them on his side. It didn't work that
time. The Colonel did a show for teenagers on Saturday, and it was just
jam-packed, with everybody screaming and hollering."

On their off hours, the band members did pretty much what they did in any town: they hung out in the bar. None of them were interested in the casinos. One night they all went to check out the other acts on the strip. Performing at the Sahara lounge were Freddie Bell and the Bellboys. They had a hit in 1953 with a song titled "Hound Dog" that also had been a hit for R&B singer Big Mama Thornton. When they heard them perform that night, they thought the song would be a good one for them to do as comic relief.

"We loved the way they did it," says Scotty. "They had a piano player who stood up and played—and the way he did his legs, they looked like rubber bands bending back and forth. Jerry Leiber and Mike Stoller wrote the song for Big Mama Thorton, but Freddie and the Bellboys had a different set of lyrics. Elvis got his lyrics from those guys. He knew the original lyrics, but he didn't use them."

Somehow they survived their two-week stint in Vegas. When it ended, they returned to Memphis and took a couple of weeks off before heading out on the road again. At a concert at the Municipal Auditorium Arena in Kansas City, Missouri, they performed in the round surrounded by the audience. When they started playing, the crowd surged forward, as everyone tried to get closer to the stage. Twenty minutes into the set, the crowd broke past the police barricade and stormed the stage. "Elvis took off," says Scotty. "I remember I just turned round with my back to the crowd and turned my guitar up out of the way. We looked out into the crowd and saw Bill's bass going across the room, then D. J.'s bass drum. We thought people were trying to steal them, but it was the people who worked there trying to help us get the stuff off the stage. They were holding the instruments up over their heads and it looked like the bass was just floating out of the room. Same thing for the drum. I don't think we ever played another concert in the round."

Whatever momentum they lost in Vegas, they picked up in the heartland, drawing record crowds. In June they returned to Los Angeles to appear on Milton Berle's last show of the season. With the Jordanaires backing him, Elvis did a sedate performance of "I Want You, I Need You, I Love You." Then, perhaps inspired by Berle's patented turned-foot walk, Elvis shocked a national television audience by gyrating with wild abandon as he sang their newly worked up version of "Hound Dog." In the days that followed, the network was bombarded with protests from people who called Elvis's performance obscene and vulgar. Elvis's unrepentant response was to the point: "You have to give them a show, something to talk about."

By the time Elvis and the band arrived in New York on July 1 for a

Elvis on the *Steve Allen Show*, July 1, 1956. L to r: Andy Griffith, Imogene Coca (partially obscured), Elvis, Steve Allen (Courtesy of Showtime Archives [Toronto] and Pictorial Press)

performance on television's *Steve Allen Show*, the host was gunning for him. Several weeks earlier, Allen told his audience that he had received requests to cancel Elvis Presley's upcoming visit as a result of the protests that followed his performance on the *Milton Berle Show*. "As of now he is still booked . . . but I have not come to a final decision on his appearance," said Allen. "If he does appear, you can rest assured that I will not allow him to do anything that will offend anyone."

Allen's solution was to have Elvis, dressed in a tuxedo, sing "Hound Dog" to a basset hound. The way Allen figured it, Elvis could hardly gyrate his pelvis if his audience was a dog. Elvis gamely went along, giving what certainly had to be one of the most excruciating performances of his career. Later in the summer, Allen came to Elvis's defense in an interview with *TV Guide*: "Opinions may vary as to the scope of his talent and the duration of his popularity, but I happen to think that he is a very solid performer, and will be around a lot longer than his detractors think."

After his performance on the *Steve Allen Show*, Elvis went backstage for a live interview with Hy Gardner, who had his own show on a local television station. Gardner asked him if he bore any animosity toward critics who criticized his style of "gyrating."

"Well, not really," answered Elvis. "Those people have a job to do and they do it."

"Do you think you have learned anything from the criticism leveled at you?" Gardner asked.

"No, I haven't. Because I don't feel I'm doing anything wrong."

"Do you read the reviews or comments concerning you?"

"Not if I can help it."

The next day they went to the RCA building for their second New York session. They had been playing "Hound Dog" for weeks in their live performance, so they felt they pretty well had it nailed down. It was the first time they had ever gone into a session with a song they knew they would record. Also, it was the first time all four Jordanaires were booked for a session with them.

Recording "Hound Dog," July 2, 1956. D. J. (back to camera),
Jordanaires, Scotty (on chair), Elvis, and Steve Sholes
(Photo by "Popsie" Randolph, © 1984, Frank Driggs Collection)

Unfortunately, their familiarity with "Hound Dog" did not make it an easy song for them to record. For some reason, they couldn't get the song down on tape the way they performed it live. They did take after take. Sometimes D. J.'s drums were off. Sometimes Scotty was off on his solo. At one point, Shorty Long, who was playing piano, had to leave to keep another appointment. He was replaced on piano by Gordon Stoker. Finally, on the twenty-sixth take, Sholes said he thought they had it. Not satisfied himself, Elvis said he thought they could do better. Not until the thirty-first take did they get a keeper.

One of the highlights of the song was Scotty's blistering guitar solo. Looking back on it today, he says it was the result of frustration. "To me, it was an angry song," he says. "People used to ask me if I was mad at someone. I'd say, 'Yeah, I was.' It was a rough, grunting song and that's what I tried to portray."

For their second song, they chose one sent by Elvis's publisher, Hill and Range. The publisher had sent a stack of demos with lead sheets and Elvis had listened to them, one by one, as Sholes played them over the studio speaker. When Elvis heard, "Don't Be Cruel," he asked Sholes to play it again. It was written by Otis "Bumps" Blackwell, a rhythm and blues singer.

Elvis was hooked. The song had that Memphis feel.

For Scotty, the song was a breeze. "I played the intro, but didn't hit another note until the end, when I played the last chord," he says. "It just didn't need more, not with the Jordanaires doing the rhythm behind it."

Scotty learned a lot from that day's session. He squirreled away that knowledge and used it later as a producer himself. "It used to be that a producer hired seven or eight guys for a session," he says. "He wanted to look out into the studio and see all of them playing all of the time, which was dumb. You hire a guy to play a certain instrument. If he's a good musician, he'll usually come up with something neat." The difference between a good studio musician and a good concert musician, Scotty learned, is that the good studio musician plays only when he thinks he can make a difference.

When they left New York the next day on the train to Memphis, they left with more than just a pair of hit singles. They left with definite idea of how they wanted to structure their future sessions. Over the years, they pretty much stuck to that format. Typically, Elvis would stand with his back to the wall, facing the band. The Jordanaires would stand next to him. He wasn't overly concerned about mistakes, unless he made them in a vocal. If the band made a mistake—and the music still felt right— he would leave it in. How each musician played was up to the individual, but he would sometimes make suggestions by asking, "Can you do this?" If the answer was no, he would say, "Do the best you can."

"Scotty did a lot of creating on the session," said Gordon Stoker. "All those guitar licks, like on 'Heartbreak Hotel,' that was all Scotty and D. J. working things out together. When we started doing backgrounds with Elvis, we found out he wanted suggestions. We would come up with all kinds of ideas and 90 percent of the time he would keep them."

When sidemen were hired for sessions, Elvis was usually more reserved in the studio. "If there was a strange musician there, he wouldn't talk as much," says Gordon. Unless he knew you, says Neal Matthews, Elvis wouldn't let his hair down: "He was very shy. He couldn't look you straight in the eye. Most of the time he looked down when he talked to you."

What Gordon noticed most about Elvis and Scotty together in the studio was the way they inspired each other. "I never heard Scotty be rude to a singer or musician on a session, and Elvis was the same way," he says. In Ray Walter's eyes, Scotty was more protective of Elvis than the Colonel was: "It was like Scotty was a speedboat and Elvis skied in the smooth water behind the speedboat. That's the way it had to be. Elvis trusted him for that. The first thing I heard about Scotty was that they had nicknamed him the 'old man.' Scotty told me they didn't do that for nothing. Scotty would meet the challenge and Elvis wouldn't.

"Elvis would let people walk right through him at times, but Scotty wouldn't. He knew where to draw the line. You can go a little way, but don't step or spit across the line. Scotty would cut people short because he could recognize someone who was going to take advantage quicker than Elvis could. Even when Elvis recognized it, he didn't have the heart to do anything about it."

Back in Memphis, they did a benefit concert for the *Press-Scimitar's* annual milk-fund event. They performed "Hound Dog," with Elvis announcing to the outdoor crowd of 6,100 that the song would be his next single. After the show, he told the band members he was going to take the remainder of July off so he could indulge himself with a little rest and relaxation. That meant, of course, that Scotty's salary dropped from $200 a week to $100 a week.

The next day sheriff's deputies showed up at Scotty's home at 1716 Tutwiler and took him off to jail. They had a warrant sworn out by his ex-wife, Mary—she had since married an Air Force officer named Vernon Cortez—that accused Scotty of being delinquent in his child-support payments for his two children. The deputies allowed him to call his lawyer before they took him downtown, but it was a humiliating experience for him. The warrant accused him of being six payments—or $240—delinquent.

Obviously, Mary had seen Scotty on television and convinced herself that anyone who was touring with Elvis Presley and appearing on network television certainly had the money to pay his child support. What Mary, or anyone else, didn't know was that Scotty and the other band members were not sharing in the wealth.

As a result of the child-support incident, Scotty went by O. K. Houck Piano Company on July 15 and asked if they would refinance his guitar and amplifier. With an unpaid balance of $445.20, they agreed to lower his monthly payments to $34.60.

❊ ❊ ❊

After cooling his heels in Memphis for nearly a month, his salary reduced to $100 a week during the down time, Scotty headed to Florida the first week in August with Elvis. Their first stop was Miami, where Elvis told reporters he was tired of being called the "Pelvis." He had picked up the hip-slinging moniker earlier in the summer from Pinckney Keel, a reporter with the *Clarion-Ledger*, a Jackson, Mississippi, morning newspaper. Keel had done a fifteen-minute interview with Elvis and was headed back to the newsroom when the phrase "Elvis the Pelvis" popped in his mind. To Elvis's displeasure, the tag stuck.

Everyone in the show was on edge, but just how much did not become evident until they moved on to a concert in Daytona. They arrived at the hotel after driving all night, and Scotty and Bill got into a fist fight in the parking lot.

"It was one of those godawful, all-night rides and everyone was ill," recalls Scotty. "We came in at three or four in the morning—and they didn't have any rooms ready for us or we didn't have any reservations. We went to two or three different motels and there were no rooms. Bill popped off something and we went to blows. All I remember is that it had something to do with a motel. Whatever it was over, it pushed my button."

The Jordanaires were traveling with them. "It was a pretty good fight," recalls Neal Matthews. "It didn't last very long. Scotty was a pretty good fighter."

"Yeah," says Gordon Stoker. "And Bill was bigger than Scotty. A whole lot bigger."

They moved on to Jacksonville, where they were scheduled to play six shows over a two-day period at the Florida Theatre. When they arrived they were greeted by unsigned warrants prepared by Juvenile

Court Judge Marion Gooding charging Elvis with impairing the morals of minors. The judge told them he was upset over what had happened during their last visit (hysterical fans nearly ripped Elvis's clothes off) and he wanted to prevent a recurrence. If Elvis did those hip-gyrating movements for which he was famous, Gooding warned, he would sign the warrants and Elvis would be taken straight to jail. In the days before Elvis's arrival, Gooding used the threat as if it were a platform in a political campaign. He was photographed at the Optimist Club, holding up a magazine with Elvis's image on the cover. He wanted voters to know he was taking a stand against the evils of rock 'n' roll.

When they did the concerts, the police were out in force, armed with movie cameras. Elvis did as he was told, but all that hip-swinging, nervous energy had to come out in some way. "That's where the curled lip and the little finger thing really got started," says Scotty. "He stood there flat-footed and did the whole show." The judge was delighted with the performance. Later, Elvis told reporters he was unhappy about the controversy. "I don't do no dirty body movements," he told a reporter.

Scotty was surprised by the criticism. "We weren't doing anything compared to what was going on five years later," he says. "We were clean cut. We wore jackets and ties on stage and had neat haircuts. We took baths. I never understood what people were upset about."

After Alan Freed was credited with coining the phrase "rock 'n' roll," there was a raging controversy among religious fundamentalists over use of the term. That didn't surprise Scotty. Any homegrown Southerner knew the phrase had been used by blacks for years as a code phrase for sexual intercourse. Blues singers used the phrase long before Alan Freed ever did. "I got tickled when some of the preachers got up and made statements about 'This rock 'n' roll has got to go,'" says Scotty. "What were they saying? Did they even know what it meant?"

Looking back on it now, the odd thing to Scotty is that despite all the hoopla over Elvis's stage movements, it failed to generate a single new dance step among the fans. When the fans danced at their concerts, they did the jitterbug, the dance perfected by their parents. "Chubby Checker came up with the Twist later," says Scotty, "but with all that commotion over our music, the kids were dancing just like their parents did."

After a concert in New Orleans—and a couple of days rest in Memphis—the group converged on Hollywood. Elvis had accepted a role in the David Weisbart movie *Love Me Tender*. Costarring with Elvis were Richard Egan and Debra Paget. Although Elvis had signed with Hal Wallis at Paramount, they had a loan-out agreement with Twentieth Century-Fox, which was producing *Love Me Tender*. Steve Sholes wanted

On the set of *Love Me Tender*. L to r: Scotty, Elvis, Neil Matthews, Richard Egan, Bill Black, D. J. Fontana, Gordon Stoker, Hoyt Hawkins, Hugh Jarrett (Photo © 1996 EPE, Inc.)

to use that opportunity to get more recordings for RCA, so Scotty and the other band members assumed they would have plenty of work. Initially, Elvis was told he wouldn't be asked to sing in the movie. After several songs were added to the script, Scotty and the other band members were taken over to Twentieth Century-Fox to audition.

"They took us out into a little bungalow," says Scotty. "No one told us it was going to be a western movie with hillbilly songs. Elvis didn't know either. So we did our regular act. They said, 'No, that's not what we're looking for.' But it was all politics. They were going through the motions to pacify Elvis."

Scotty was furious, not because they were turned down, but because no one told them at the audition they wanted country music. Scotty and Bill had been charter members of the Starlite Wranglers, for heaven's sake. They had been weaned on country music. It had been a setup from the beginning. Ken Darby, the movie's musical director, had his own singing trio and musicians he wanted to use. He never had any intention of using the Blue Moon Boys.

Colonel Parker was tickled pink. His boy would record with these new pickers and he would see for himself that he didn't really need the

Blue Moon Boys. Elvis told Scotty he was sorry, but for them not to worry about it. He would see to it that they were involved with his next motion picture.

It was sometime around this time that Arlene Camacho of Pleasant Hill, California, started up the first Scotty Moore fan club. "Hi. I would like to start a fan club for the coolest of the guitar players, Scotty Moore," she explained to would-be members in a small magazine ad. "For those who don't know, Scotty is the 'git' man with Elvis Presley. If you would like to join, make with the pencils and pens." Scotty was never told about the fan club. In fact, it was not until 1996, when the ad was brought to his attention, that he learned of its existence.

Sholes booked time at Radio Recorders, an independent recording studio, so Elvis could record new sides for RCA when he had time off from shooting the movie. "Don't Be Cruel"/"Hound Dog" was on its way that month to the No. 1 slot on the charts. Once it got there on August 18, it would remain there for eleven weeks. RCA needed a follow-up single, plus material for a new album. Elvis recorded a number of songs, including "Love Me," "Old Shep," "Too Much," and "Anyplace Is Paradise." RCA earmarked "Love Me Tender" for upcoming release as a single.

"Too Much" gave Scotty fits in the studio. It was in A-flat, an unusual key for them to play. "We did several takes, but on this particular one, I just got lost," says Scotty. "I just kept chunking away. I didn't make any mistakes, but it wasn't the same solo I played on the other takes. Somehow I came out of it exactly where I was supposed to be."

When the song was over, Elvis raised his hand—his method of calling for a playback. As he listened, he leaned over on the speaker with his head down so that the sound was hitting him full blast. When the guitar solo came on, he twisted his head and looked at Scotty with a shit-eating grin. "He knew I had gotten lost, but he loved the way it turned out," says Scotty. "When the song ended, he raised up and said, 'That's it,' and he did it for damned meanness. He knew I had gotten lost and he knew damned well I would have to live with it."

In between working on the album—and sitting on their backsides while Elvis filmed the movie—Scotty, Bill, and D. J. made a September 9 appearance with Elvis on the *Ed Sullivan Show*. It was Sullivan's premier show of the season, but he did not host the show because he was recuperating from an automobile accident. That night the guest host was actor Charles Laughton. The show was broadcast from New York, but they performed their segment from the CBS studio in Los Angeles. They opened with "Don't Be Cruel," then did "Love Me Tender," which Elvis explained was from his upcoming movie. Elvis was paid $50,000 for three appearances on the show; Scotty, Bill, and D. J. each received $78.23 per show from Sullivan.

Scotty and the band followed Elvis back to Memphis, after which they performed in Tupelo, Mississippi, and did some concerts in Texas. Tensions were still running high between Elvis and the band. They were happy to get the session work, but union scale at that time amounted to just $75 per three-hour session. That meant they could go to California for two weeks with Elvis, play eight or ten concerts coming and going, record a song or two, and their income for the two weeks would be less than $600—and out of that had to come their living expenses. From that they had to glean money to send back for their families' living expenses. For the same work, Elvis literally received hundreds of thousands of dollars. They discussed the situation among themselves, but not with Elvis. Even so, he began to feel the tension, however subtle.

During one of the *Love Me Tender* downtimes, Scotty went out on the road with Jerry Lee Lewis for a two-week tour of Arkansas and Texas. Lewis hadn't yet scored a hit for Sun Records, but his career was in high gear at that point. Everything went smoothly until they reached New Orleans. It was their last stop on the tour. That night, they sat around Scotty's hotel room, drinking. Suddenly, Lewis jumped up on the bed and started preaching.

"We were having a normal conversation about something, then all of a sudden he flipped over into hellfire and brimstone," says Scotty. "I said, 'I don't want to hear that,' but he went on and on. We were fixing to get with it, but his daddy-in-law got him quieted down. I made up my mind then [about Lewis]. There's the old saying, 'Cold ass me—and you is through.'"

In October, Elvis pulled into a Memphis service station to get gas for his new Mark II Continental. He politely asked the manager, Ed Hopper, to check his gas tank for leaks. As his car was being serviced, a crowd gathered. Elvis took time to sign autographs and chat with his fans. When he finished servicing the car, Hopper told Elvis his fans were blocking traffic and he asked him to leave. Elvis said he would, but continued signing autographs. With that, Hopper slapped Elvis across the back of head with an admonition to "move on."

Elvis leaped out of the car and punched Hopper, inflicting a half-inch gash at the corner of his left eye. When one of Hopper's employees, a six-four, 220-pounder, ran out of the office to help Hopper, he was also punched by Elvis after he pulled a knife on the singer. Before the fight could escalate further, it was broken up by a cop and a bystander.

"I'll take ridicule and slander, but when a guy hits me, that's too much," Elvis told the cop. When the arresting officer asked him his name, he said, "Well, maybe you'd better put down Carl Perkins." When the case went to court the following week, Elvis went without an attorney and answered all the judge's questions with a "yes sir" or "no sir." The judge dismissed all charges against Elvis and the service station attendants were fined $25 and $15. The judge's decision was greeted with applause by the packed courtroom.

On October 26 Scotty and the others went with Elvis by train from Memphis to New York for their second appearance on the *Ed Sullivan Show*. The trip took two days. This time Sullivan was there and engaged in onstage banter with Elvis. The next day RCA Records announced they had concluded a new, long-term contact with Elvis. *Variety* declared him a millionaire, and RCA proudly announced he had sold well over ten million singles. That translated to an income from records of about a half-million dollars for Elvis. Scotty couldn't help but wonder what his and Bill's share would be if Elvis had stood by his offer to give them a percentage of the royalties.

After taking a few weeks off, the band went out on a four-day tour that began in Louisville, Kentucky, and then moved on to Todelo, Ohio, where they did two shows in the Sports Arena. After the show, they went to the bar of the Commodore Perry Hotel to relax. As Elvis, Scotty, Bill, D. J., and Oscar Davis, Parker's assistant, sat together, talking, they were accosted by a nineteen-year-old man, who said he was angry because his wife carried a picture of Elvis in her wallet.

"He drew back like he was going to throw a shot and I jumped on his back," says Scotty. "There was a railing there—one of those things they put besides steps—and he tried to roll me over his back onto the railing. He actually threw me over the railing. But by that time, Elvis was absolutely using him as a punching bag. He was real fast. Quick as lightning with his hands. He would have made a good fighter, but that would have messed up his face."

When the police arrived to break up the fight, six teenage girls who had been watching from the lobby rushed up and gave their names as witnesses. The police officers took the man off to jail and didn't file charges against Elvis. Contacted later by a newspaper reporter, one of the police officers said, "Presley's no slouch. He was really working that guy over."

Later the man told reporters that he was hired by Elvis to stage the fight. He said Elvis still owed him his $200. "I read where Presley takes $16,000 out of Toledo for them two shows at the arena," he said. "Sixteen grand and he's too cheap to pay me my lousy $200." When he was

Bill, Scotty, and D. J. hold a guitar-shaped cake celebrating
Love Me Tender **(Courtesy of Scotty Moore)**

asked if the fight had been staged, Colonel Parker screamed out angry denials at reporters, then—after thinking about it a while—he calmed down and said, "Anyway, they've got Elvis's name spelled right." Scotty says if the man was hired to start a fight it wasn't by Elvis—and "it damn sure wasn't me."

As the November 16 release date for *Love Me Tender* drew near, Elvis took time off to go to Las Vegas for a minivacation. "Love Me Tender," the song, had gone to No. 1, with "Don't Be Cruel"/"Hound Dog" in the No. 2 slot. For the first time since *Billboard* began compiling its charts, the No. 1 and No. 2 positions were held by the same artist. "Love Me Tender" also had another distinction: it was the first song Elvis record-ed that didn't include the Blue Moon Boys.

When *Love Me Tender* was released, that, too, set a record with the release of 550 prints by Twentieth Century-Fox, the largest release of a film ever issued. As Elvis basked in the glow of having both hit records and a Hollywood movie, Scotty, back in Memphis on $100-a-week down-time, took stock of the year. In 1956 he had earned $8,193.58 from his

work with Elvis. That was a decent enough income for a working stiff—
it sure beat being a hatter—but with all his expenses, he was quickly
going into debt.

❊ ❊ ❊

On January 4, 1957, after Elvis completed his preinduction physical
at the Selective Service headquarters in Memphis, Scotty and the others
boarded a train with him for New York, where they were scheduled to
do their third—and final—appearance on the *Ed Sullivan Show*. It was
a long trip, with a train switch in Washington, DC. The possibility of
Elvis being drafted had never entered Scotty's mind. On the train to New
York, Scotty thought about it a lot, both in terms of what Elvis would
have to go through—for all his frustrations over the money issue, Elvis
was like a brother to him, and he felt protective toward him—and in
terms of what it would mean for his career as a musician. The more he
thought about it, the more he convinced himself Parker would never allow "his boy" to be drafted. All it took to beat the draft was a little pull,
a commodity Parker had in an ample supply.

They arrived in New York early Saturday morning and went by the
Maxine Elliot Theater later in the day for a rehearsal. Years later, the
theater would be refurbished for the *David Letterman Show*. They
returned to the theater the next day for another rehearsal before showtime.

That night, during the actual show, Sullivan pulled out all the stops.
In three separate appearances, they performed seven songs, including
"Heartbreak Hotel," "Love Me Tender," and "Too Much," their latest
single release. To accommodate critics, cameramen had orders to provide
shots of Elvis from the waist up whenever it appeared he might swivel
his hips or shake his leg. Also on the show that day was comedienne
Carol Burnett, who was just beginning her career.

Watching the show back in Crockett Country were James and Evelyn
Lewis. "There's Winfield," James said whenever the camera got a shot
of his old friend. He couldn't pass up the opportunity to kid his wife,
Evelyn: "See, if you had encouraged me, I would be picking somewhere,
too, making lots of money [like Scotty]."

When they returned to Memphis, Scotty contacted the Chicago
Musical Instrument Company and made arrangements to trade in his
Gibson L5 for a Gibson S 400, the so-called "blond" model with which
he is most identified. The guitar and a case were shipped to O.K. Houck
Piano Company in Memphis and sold to Scotty on the installment plan
for $735 ($675 for the guitar and $60 for the case). Their first week back,

the draft board announced that Elvis had passed his physical and would be classified 1-A. The board told reporters it was just a matter of time before Elvis received his draft notice. Contacted by the same reporters, Elvis said he would be honored to serve his country.

By mid-January they were again in Hollywood to do another recording session for RCA Records, and then to start filming on Elvis's next movie. The critics had panned Elvis's performance in *Love Me Tender*. Elvis was devastated by the criticism. He told friends he thought he had done a terrible job of acting. He was hopeful that he would be given better material for his next film outing.

Steve Sholes was greatly relieved to get Elvis in the studio again. He had been begging Colonel Parker for months for studio time. Parker had deliberately held him at arm's length. "Parker would keep Elvis on the road, anything to keep him out of the studio," says Scotty. "He didn't want them to get a backlog of material. He milked it as close as he possibly could."

Parker begrudgingly gave Sholes two weekends at Radio Recorders, but there was a condition attached: if the movie studio decided to alter its start-up date, then Sholes would be out of luck. Elvis was somewhat distracted during the sessions, but Sholes was able to get two No. 1 singles, "All Shook Up" and "Teddy Bear," plus additional material to squirrel away for the next album.

Poster for *Loving You* with the band in Western gear

True to his word, Elvis got Scotty and the others hired for the next movie. *Loving You* was a departure from the first movie in that it cast Elvis as a singer out on the road trying to make it to the "Big Time." Elvis would have plenty of dramatic scenes, but he also would sing and . . . well, be Elvis. Scotty, Bill, and D. J. were hired to play on the soundtrack and to play the roles of his band members in the movie. They would be paid $285 a week.

For Paramount's first picture with Elvis, Hal Wallis chose a director he thought would be perfect. Hal Kanter had never directed a movie, but he was from Savannah, Georgia, and had written the screenplay for Tennessee Williams's *Rose Tattoo*. Perhaps Kanter could talk to Elvis in his own language. Before they started filming, Kanter went to Memphis to get acquainted with Elvis. He even went with him to Shreveport for his farewell "benefit" performance for the Hayride. Unfortunately for Kanter, the visit didn't have the desired effect—Elvis told friends he thought Kanter was a little strange—but they got along well enough.

Elvis was relaxed and enthusiastic when they began shooting the movie. "It was all new to me, so it was a learning experience," says Scotty. "What Bill, D. J., and I didn't like was the waiting. You might wait around all day and then it would take thirty minutes for you to do what they wanted. I was always more interested in the audio side of it. I would go into the control room. It amazed me how different it sounded in the control room."

After they began work, Scotty, Bill, and D. J. were told they would be paid as extras, not as actors. The pay for extras was only about $100 a day, and they knew they could expect only a day or two of work a week, if that much.

"We knew we were going to be out there four or five weeks, so we went over to Wallis on the set and told him we were going home—we weren't getting paid enough," says Scotty. Wallis was over a barrel—and he knew it. Scotty and the others already had appeared in several scenes with Elvis; if they went home, Wallis would have to reshoot the scenes. "His money guy told him we could work so many weeks as actors on the musicians card, so he let us do that," says Scotty. "That was damned good, considering what Elvis was paying us. At least we would have enough to send more money back home."

✳ ✳ ✳

When it came time to do the dance segments on *Loving You*, Scotty was disappointed at how "exaggerated" the choreographer, Charles O'Kern, had arranged them. Says Scotty: "Look at any Broadway play or movie, anyone who does a country show, and notice how exaggerated all the dancers are. That always irritated me. It's so hokey. It's like they think everyone down South does a buck dance."

Scotty took his guitar and amplifier to the set each day. "Elvis got the electricians to get power for my amp, so in between takes we would jam," says Scotty. "It would make the director mad because the crew would gather around to listen."

Wallis didn't want Scotty and the others in the band playing on the sound track, but Elvis insisted and they were allowed to play, although Charles O'Kern hired a piano player, Dudley Brooks, and a second guitarist, "Tiny" Timbrell, to work on the session with them. They tried to record the songs on the Paramount soundstage, but they all felt uncomfortable there and couldn't really get into a groove. "We were used to recording in smaller rooms," says Scotty. The studio tried to accommodate them by putting up fifteen- or twenty-foot baffles around them, in effect creating a smaller separate room on the soundstage. When that didn't work, they packed up and went to Radio Recorders so they could do their recordings in a more comfortable atmosphere. Accompanying them was the union representative for the studio.

Everyone, including Elvis, was happier at Radio Recorders, where they worked with Thorn Nogar, the chief engineer, and his backup engineer, Bones Howe. What they couldn't get used to was the union representative, who stood up every hour on the hour and clapped his hands—a signal that it was time for them to take a ten-minute break. It didn't matter to the union man whether the band was in a groove or not. Rules were rules. Every hour on the hour: clap, clap, clap.

"I could see it was really beginning to irritate Elvis," says Scotty. "Finally, we were in the middle of something—I mean, we just about had it nailed—and we stopped to listen to the playback. Elvis said, 'Let's try it one more time.' At that precise moment, there it came: clap, clap, clap. Elvis turned around and looked at everybody. You could see by the look on his face that he had enough. He told the control room, 'Roll it.' He just ignored the union man. The guy never said another word. He was a nice old gentleman; his job was to hire the orchestra and be the timekeeper. He was into a different thing, and we were, too—but he got the message."

Two or three weeks into the filming, Gladys and Vernon Presley arrived in Hollywood for a visit. Elvis showed them around the set and took them to a movie theater to see *The Ten Commandments*. During that time, Bobbie Moore decided that she, too, wanted a glimpse of Scotty's glamorous new world. "I wanted to see as much as I could," she says.

"Scotty tried to talk me out of it. He said, 'Why don't you wait and we'll come back out by ourselves.' I said, 'No, it'll never happen. I'm going. I may not see you, but I'm going.'" After Bobbie arrived, Elvis asked Scotty if they would mind taking Gladys and Vernon to Burbank to see the Tennessee Ernie Ford show. With Scotty behind the wheel of Elvis's new white Cadillac, the four of them drove to Burbank to see the show. Afterward, they went backstage and met Tennessee Ernie Ford.

That March, when they all returned to Memphis, Scotty received a nice letter from Hal Kanter, addressed to his home at 1716 Tutwiler, which he and Bobbie shared with her three sisters and a brother-in-law. Wrote Kanter: "I want to take this opportunity to thank you for your cooperation during your period of employment, and also thank you for your valuable contribution to the project."

On his return, Elvis bought a present for his parents—and for himself. After their Audubon Drive neighbors circulated a petition complaining about Gladys Presley's habit of hanging her clothes out to dry on a line, the Presleys began looking for a more private place to live. In March, Elvis purchased the home of their dreams—Graceland—which remained Presley's home for the remainder of his life, and has become a shrine to his memory. The two-story mansion had a $100,000 price tag and was the most conspicuous symbol yet of Elvis's growing wealth. The *Press-Scimitar* sent a reporter out to interview them. Elvis told the reporter he was going to put a "hi-fi" in every room. "I want the darkest blue there is for my room—with a mirror that will cover one side of the room," he said.

"We will have a lot more privacy, and a lot more room to put some of the things we have accumulated over the last few years," said Gladys. Vernon impressed the reporter as being a little "skittish" about the purchase. "Moving is going to be a problem," Vernon grumbled. "Although a moving company has said they will move us free of charge. We just had the old place fixed up like we wanted it. Now we have to start all over again."

The trappings of success were piling up around Elvis, but there were indications he was feeling the pressure of being a star. One day, shortly after he had purchased Graceland, he went out on his motorcycle dressed as a cop: black leather jacket, vest, helmet, sunglasses. He stopped by Sun Studio, but Sam wasn't there; he was hardly ever there anymore. Jack Clement was in the studio. "Me and my ole buddy were back in the control room shooting craps and in walks this motorcycle guy who looked like a cop," says Clement. "It was Elvis. He scared us."

One day sometime later, Elvis was cruising on Parkway Avenue when he saw Betty McMahan, one of his girlfriends from the projects. He pulled her over to the side of the road. Betty didn't recognize him at first. When she saw it was Elvis she was surprised at how bad he looked. "His face looked pitiful," she told a reporter for *The Commercial Appeal*. "He had bumps even on his shoulders."

✻ ✻ ✻

By the time Scotty, Bill, and D. J. arrived in Hollywood with Elvis on April 13 to begin work on his new movie, *Jailhouse Rock*, their last single, "All Shook Up," had been No. 1 for eight weeks. In 1957 stars just didn't come any bigger than Elvis Presley. They checked into the upscale Beverly Wilshire, but Scotty, D.J., and Bill weren't comfortable there and moved to the Knickerbocker. It was written later that the backup men were moved out of the hotel on Parker's orders, but that's not the way it happened. "We were the ones who instigated it," says Scotty. "We didn't want to get tied in with the crowds. We wanted to get up and walk up and down the street and look in the windows."

**Mike Stoller, Elvis, and Jerry Leiber in a posed shot at MGM
Studios at the time of the filming of *Jailhouse Rock*
(Photo courtesy Leiber & Stoller)**

Scene from *Jailhouse Rock* (Courtesy of Scotty Moore)

By this point RCA Records felt it was slightly ahead of the curve—they had "Teddy Bear" in the can for upcoming release—and they knew they could count on *Jailhouse Rock* to spawn a hit or two. For the first time, they saw the benefits of merging Elvis's recording career with his movie career. Steve Sholes could do no wrong in the eyes of RCA. He was moved from Nashville and put in charge of the pop division in New York. Whatever his private thoughts about the direction Elvis's music was taking, his lack of aggressiveness demonstrated he didn't want to rock the boat.

Jerry Leiber and Mike Stoller, the songwriting team who had penned "Hound Dog," were hired to write songs for the *Jailhouse* sound track. They were given a script and pretty much told to write songs that would fit in certain scenes. As usual, they laid down the tracks at Radio Recorders. When the song "Jailhouse Rock" was explained to them, Scotty and D. J. talked about how they could generate a jailhouse sound.

"It would have been nice if we had a big sledge hammer and could have done a sound effect, but we didn't have a sledge hammer, so we did it musically, " says Scotty. "That intro—when I'm doing a half-step drag, D. J. is doing a beat on the drums to imply a rock pile—we tried to do that on all the songs."

The *Jailhouse Rock* sessions were the first at which Scotty noticed that Elvis's heart was no longer in the music. Elvis once spent five or six hours doing gospel songs with the Jordanaires as a means of escaping the work at hand. "Some of that movie stuff was impossible," says Scotty. "That's the reason he would play the piano and sing with the Jordanaires, to psyche himself up. Once he got started, he would do the best he could."

Once, when a studio executive complained Elvis was wasting time with the Jordanaires, Elvis walked out of the studio and didn't return until the next day. Whenever Elvis criticized a song, he was told how much money it would earn. He didn't want to let anyone down, so he did the songs.

Scotty, Bill, and D. J. were written into a number of the film's scenes, but they had to buy their own clothes because they were not provided with a wardrobe. Scotty bought two new sports coats for $58.50 from Lawrence Douglas Clothes on the corner of Santa Monica and Vine, and a pair of shoes for $15.95 from Regal Shoe Shop on Hollywood Boulevard.

When they filmed the swimming pool scene, Scotty was in the background, playing his guitar. Portions of the scene were filmed early in the day; other portions were done later in the day. As a result, when the movie was released, Scotty noticed that some of the long shots showed him wearing sunglasses, while others did not. That glitch had somehow slipped past the continuity person and the film editors.

Scotty was also on the set when Elvis did the famous dance sequence. "What impressed me was that the choreographer had watched footage of Elvis doing his live show," says Scotty. "He staged that whole routine around Elvis's natural moves. He had to follow a routine, but those were his own moves. That is what he did on the stage all the time when we were playing." Scotty laughs. "Elvis would probably still be out there working on that scene if they had asked him to do something they had made up."

✳ ✳ ✳

In early April they did two shows at the Sports Arena in Philadelphia. Before the first show, Elvis met with a small group of high school reporters. Dressed in black, but wearing "spotless" white shoes, he showed up for the interview with five bodyguards. One of the students asked him what he thought of his movie *Love Me Tender*. "It was pretty horrible," answered Elvis. "Acting's not something you learn overnight. I knew that picture was bad when it was completed. I am my own worst critic. But my next picture is different."

Another student asked him when he would be drafted. "Everyone thinks I've been drafted already, but I haven't," he said. "I've only passed the physical. But I'm not definitely going in."

From mid-April to late August Elvis stayed off the road, vegetating in Memphis. Mostly, he tinkered with his new toys at Graceland. Of course, that meant Scotty and the boys were knocked back down to their $100-a-week salary for the duration. If food stamps had been invented in 1957, Elvis's band would have qualified for benefits. Luckily for Scotty, Bobbie had a good job and was able to bring home a paycheck. At one point Scotty applied for unemployment, but that lasted only a week or so, After picking up the first check, he decided it was too big a hassle. "I decided I'd rather panhandle," he said.

Finally, Scotty, Bill, and D. J. got word Elvis had more work for them. In late August they drove to Spokane, where they were to begin a five-city tour of the Northwest, after which they would go to Los Angeles to do another recording session for RCA Records.

The first concert in Spokane was sheer madness, with over 12,500 screaming teenagers, mostly women, testing the resourcefulness of the one hundred police officers there to keep order. The next stop was Vancouver, British Columbia. It was one of the few foreign concerts Colonel Parker ever booked for Elvis—perhaps because Canadian border officials did not require passports and visas for entry from the United States. Parker could go to Canada without having his citizenship challenged.

When Scotty and the others walked out onto the stage with Elvis, they faced 26,500 screaming fans, their largest audience to date. The stage was constructed on the back of two flatbed trucks parked at the north end of the stadium. A fence was put up around the stage, and between the stage and the audience was nearly one hundred yards of football field. When the music began, the crowd surged past the police officers onto the field and sat down in front of the stage. "We must have looked like ants to them back where they were sitting," says Scotty. "All they wanted to do was to get closer. They didn't care whether they had seats or not."

Stadium officials stopped the show and told the crowd it would not continue until they got back off the field. D. J. remembers how defiant the crowd was. Stadium officials couldn't budge them. "They tried and they tried, and they wouldn't move, so we finally started the show," says D. J.

Frightened by the surging fans, Parker told Elvis to cut the show short. When Elvis abruptly left the stage and made a dash for his waiting car, Scotty and the others were left onstage to face the fans alone. Says D. J.: "The kids all ran up there and the platform kind of tilted to one side." By the time they got their instruments loaded into their car, they were surrounded by fans. "They shook the car a little bit, thinking he was in there with us," says D. J. "But finally they let us go. It took about two hours for us to get out. It usually took us about two hours to get out of all the buildings." The media later called it a riot, but it wasn't really, says Scotty: "The fans were just trying to get closer to the stage to see, that's all." If they wanted to see a real riot, he thought, they should spend some time in China.

After two additional shows in Washington state, they went to Hollywood in the first week in September for the scheduled recording session at Radio Recorders. Steve Sholes wanted to get some new singles, but he was mostly interested in trying to put together a Christmas album. *Jailhouse Rock*, the movie, was scheduled for release in a few weeks, along with the single, and he had a single in the can, "I Beg of You," that had been recorded last February.

Scotty and Bill were especially eager for this session. Elvis had been talking to them for months about doing an album of instrumentals on which Elvis would play piano. The project was his own idea. Financially, they were getting desperate. Every time Scotty or Bill put something together that would allow them to make extra money or receive items in exchange for endorsements, Colonel Parker shot it down.

Earlier in the year, while they were headed out of Hollywood back to Memphis in Elvis's bright yellow limo, they were flagged down on the street by a couple of men from a local Chrysler dealership. Says Scotty: "They introduced themselves, saying they were with the biggest Chrysler dealership in town. They asked us to go to a restaurant and have a cup of coffee. They told us, 'Look, we know Elvis is into Cadillacs, but we will give you boys a brand new Chrysler every year and all Elvis has to do is say, 'My band members drive Chryslers.'"

Scotty thought that was a great idea. Finally, someone had offered them something—and it wouldn't cost the Colonel a penny. "Of course, Parker said no way. He said he would never approve anything like that," says Scotty. They received the same type of endorsement offer from the appliance division of RCA. "That was fantastic," says Scotty "They were going to give us stoves, refrigerators, whatever. But Parker shot that down, too."

After they completed work on the singles and the Christmas album, they got ready to record the instrumentals. "We had even picked the name out for the group: the Continentals," says Scotty. "Elvis booked studio time for us. We even rehearsed some songs for the album. But before we got started, Parker found out about it and shut us down."

There was an awkward scene in the studio in which Elvis physically backed away from Scotty and Bill and disappeared behind the protective wall of his entourage. Bill was furious. He slammed his electric bass into its carrying case. Scotty was more disappointed than angry. He just couldn't bring himself to believe that Elvis would treat them that way.

Scotty was desperate. Just how desperate can be ascertained by a look at Scotty's tax records. Because Elvis had cut back on his touring schedule, Scotty's income from Elvis in 1957 had dropped to $6,656.65. His total income, before taxes, from Elvis for three and a half years amounted to only $23,041.72. He earned an additional $4,642.79 from the movies and the RCA sessions. Compared to the incredible wealth Elvis was amassing, that wasn't much to show for three and a half years' work. When they had started out, they were Elvis and the Blue Moon Boys, the musical equivalent of the Three Musketeers: all for one, and one for all. Now Scotty and Bill were struggling to make a living wage.

The album of instrumentals would have given them an opportunity to make royalties from their music. When it was scrapped, Scotty—perhaps for the first time—saw things as they really were. There was never going to be any sharing of the wealth, as Elvis had promised. Scotty was a salaried employee, nothing more. His salary of $200 a week, when he traveled with Elvis, was about the same salary Elvis paid the members of his entourage—the Memphis Mafia, as they later were called—except the members of his entourage also received free automobiles and expensive gifts. Elvis never purchased cars for Scotty or Bill.

❋ ❋ ❋

When Scotty and Bill got back to Memphis, they sat down with their wives for a heart to heart. They had to do something drastic. They couldn't continue the way they were going. Before leaving California, they had tried to talk to Elvis about their situation, but they couldn't get through to him. Finally, out of frustration, Scotty and Bill agreed—with the support of their wives—to write out letters of resignation. They called D. J. and asked him to write a letter as well, but he told them he was in a different situation. He had been hired as a salaried employee from the beginning. He didn't have any reason to expect more from Elvis.

In later years, D. J. was more supportive of their decision. "I don't blame them one bit," he says. "They should have left before that. It was Scotty and Bill and Elvis who started out. They had a legitimate reason to complain. I told them, 'If I'd have started like you guys, I'd be right with you.'"

Elvis was still in Hollywood when he received the special delivery letters on September 7. First, he was shocked, passing the letters around for everyone to see. Then he became angry and accused Scotty and Bill of being disloyal to him. Colonel Parker had Scotty and Bill right where he wanted them. He knew the best thing he could do to help things along was to stand aside and not get involved. Steve Sholes told Elvis not to worry, that he would find him better musicians than Scotty and Bill. By the time Elvis returned to Memphis on September 11, the local media were on the story.

"I don't believe Scotty and I could raise more than fifty bucks between us," Bill Black told *The Commercial Appeal.* The newspaper ran the story on the front page. "I'm still living day to day."

Scotty was equally blunt. "He promised us that the more he made the more we would make," he said. "But it hasn't worked out that way." Bill said he had started working in the service department of Ace Appliance Company to help make ends meet. He said he was "embarrassed" over the way things had turned out. "We'd be put up in a big hotel, and certain things were expected of us because we were with Elvis. Like picking up a check for coffee, and tipping and things like that. We'd go out to eat where we could get it cheaper . . . We're not jealous of anyone, but we found out other people were laughing at us. Even the guys selling souvenir books were making more money than we were."

Scotty received a phone call from Elvis when he returned to Memphis. Elvis asked him what it would take to make him happy. Scotty suggested a $50 raise and a flat payment of $10,000 so he could pay off the debts he had acquired while touring with him. Elvis told him he would have to think about it.

Scotty and Bill did some thinking of their own. From day one, they had subsisted on dreams and promises. They didn't want to quit Elvis. All they wanted was something to show for their efforts. They would stand by their resignations if they had to, but in their hearts, they just knew Elvis would come around. He would see what Parker was doing to him. Once he understood, he would reward them for their loyalty.

"It was like Elvis had been kidnapped and taken off into a sideshow of a circus," says Scotty. "The thing that got me, the thing that wasn't right about it, was the fact that Elvis didn't keep his word. If I had instigated the idea of Bill and I receiving royalties, and had tried to get royalties from him, that would be one thing. But I didn't. It was all his idea. I tried to make it as palatable as possible. There were other things he could have done to compensate us: the endorsements, the deals for new cars—especially the album of instrumentals. Those things would have made a difference."

After conferring with Parker and others for several days, Elvis responded to Scotty's request for a $50 raise. In an interview with Bill Burk of the *Press-Scimitar*, Elvis issued an "open letter" to Scotty and Bill: "Scotty, I hope you fellows have good luck. I will give you fellows good recommendations. If you had come to me, we would have worked things out. I would have always taken care of you. But you went to the papers and tried to make me look bad, instead of coming to me so we could work things out. All I can say to you is good luck."

Elvis told the reporter that it was a mystery to him why they hadn't come to him to talk over their problems. "We've had our problems before—even some arguments—but we always settled them," Elvis said. "Every time they ever came to me and asked for something, they got it, no matter what. Had they come to me, we would have worked it out and they would have got more money."

With his next performance scheduled for the Tupelo Fair on September 27, Elvis said he would start auditioning new guitar players immediately. "It may take a while," he said, "but it's not impossible to find replacements."

When Scotty and Bill—and their wives— read the newspaper story, they knew it was all over. Despite his statements to the press, Scotty still refused to blame Elvis for what happened. In Scotty's opinion, Parker was behind it all; Parker had not told Elvis about their many requests over the years. Says Scotty: "Elvis didn't know. He never understood. It was Parker's doing. I tried not to be around him any more than I had to. I had heard stuff about him from other people when he first appeared on the scene and I was leery of him. Frankly, he was just a con man. I could see what he did with Bob Neal. He whittled away at getting rid of him. He wanted to get rid of the band. He wanted to get rid of anyone who was pre-Parker."

On September 18, 1957, Vernon Presley sent Scotty a brief, one paragraph letter: "This is to advise that, pursuant to your notice of September 7, 1957, we are accepting your resignation from our employment effective September 21, 1957, and, accordingly, enclose herewith notice of separation and your final salary check in the amount of $86.25, representing payment in full for all services rendered for us by you prior to September 21."

September 18, 1957

Mr. W. S. Moore, III
1716 Tutwiler
Memphis, Tennessee

Dear Scotty:

This is to advise that, pursuant to your notice
of September 7, 1957, we are accepting your resignation
from our employment effective September 21, 1957, and,
accordingly, enclose herewith notice of separation and
your final salary check in the amount of $86.25, represent-
ing payment in full for all services rendered for us by
you prior to September 21, 1957.

Yours very truly,

Vernon Presley

Vernon's letter to Scotty, September 18, 1957
(Courtesy of Scotty Moore)

SCOTTY AND BILL CALL IT QUITS: "TRAGEDY" STRIKES

nce he was officially unemployed, Scotty wasted no time looking for work. He booked Bill and himself for a sixteen-day engagement at the Texas State Fair. As it turned out, it was the most lucrative booking of their career. They played four shows a day from October 5 through October 20, and received $1,600, plus all of their hotel bills were paid by fair officials. It was double what they made working for Elvis. With typical understatement, Scotty describes it as "not a bad deal."

As Scotty read the newspaper accounts of their resignation—and Elvis's comments to reporters about Bill and himself—he realized Elvis just didn't get it. It wasn't about recognition, as Elvis told reporters. Neither Scotty nor Bill cared about fame. They certainly didn't begrudge Elvis his success. "We just wanted some perks, so we could stick a few bucks in the bank," says Scotty. "It was a fantasy thing for us. Working for Elvis, at the pay he was giving us, was better than digging ditches, but we felt we deserved better than that. We just wanted more money. Later, people wrote that it was Bill who talked me into resigning. That wasn't the way it happened. Bill was always more vocal about it than I was, but we were both pretty adamant about it."

Scotty and Bill looked back over the past few years with more than a little self-loathing over their reluctance to stand up for themselves. When Elvis signed with RCA Records, they could have fought to keep using the name, Blue Moon Boys, but they didn't want to rock the boat. Unlike Scotty and Bill, the Jordanaires had insisted on keeping their name and identity. As a result, many people thought Scotty and Bill were members of the Jordanaires!

When Scotty and Bill looked at the situation they knew they had brought a lot of their troubles on themselves by not speaking up sooner. In many ways, Elvis was like a child. How could they blame him? They knew their problems all originated with management, with Parker, who had masterfully used their silence as a weapon against them.

"When Bill and I quit, I'm sure he just rolled over and ha-ha'ed," says Scotty. "We didn't want to be around him any more than we had to. I never called him Colonel unless it was a slip of the tongue—and that would piss him off. Hell, later on, I got an honorary title of my own from Governor Winfield Dunn, so he didn't outrank me. I understand Parker is in bad health now and still won't admit to things that people know he did. I think I would be trying to make a clean breast of it." [Tom Parker died in January 1997.]

As Scotty and Bill got ready for their two-week engagement at the Texas State Fair, Elvis prepared for a homecoming performance at the Mississippi-Alabama Dairy Show and Fair in Tupelo. It would be his first performance without Scotty and Bill. From all accounts, he took their resignation hard. He told people he felt betrayed and let down. It never occurred to him to blame Parker.

One day during this time, Elvis went by Sun Studios to see Sam and Marion. Unknown to Elvis, Marion and Sam had had a fight and she stomped out of the studio and joined the Air Force. His visit to the studio only served to confirm his increasing suspicion that the world was an unfriendly place. He couldn't understand why everyone was fighting with each other.

For the Tupelo show, Elvis hired two Nashville session players to replace Scotty and Bill: Hank Garland, another of Scotty's heroes and a great jazz guitarist, and Chuck Wiginton on bass. Chuck was close friends with both Scotty and D. J. When the Jordanaires arrived at the venue, they were shocked to learn that Scotty and Bill had quit. They hadn't heard a word about it. Says Neal Matthews: "I didn't know for two weeks that they had left." After the show, Elvis told D. J. it just wasn't the same without Scotty and Bill. Scotty just had his own way of doing those guitar parts. "Elvis was very upset, I assure you," says Jordanaire Gordon Stoker. "He loved both of those guys."

When Scotty and Bill returned from Texas they received a telephone call from Tom Diskin, Colonel Parker's assistant. Elvis had four concerts scheduled for San Francisco and Los Angeles for October 26 through October 29. Diskin told Scotty that if they rejoined the group, Elvis would

150

"WE COVER THE NATION"

P.O.
417
MADISON, TENN.

October 17, 1957

Mr. Scotty Moore
1716 Tutwiler
Memphis, Tennessee

Dear Scotty:

Enclosed are the contracts for the engagement October
26-27-28-29, 1957. Will you please sign one copy and
return it to me. The other copy you may keep for your
own records.

Note on transportation that I have included the phrase
that should you travel with DJ in Elvis's limosene there
will be no charge to you for this transportation. Should
you decide to travel by some other method that would be
of course at your own expense.

The present plans are for us to stay at the Mark Hopkins
hotel in San Francisco. That would be for Oct 26-27th.
On the Los Angeles dates we of course will be staying
at the Beverly Wilshire.

Please return the signed copies to me here at the
Sahara Hotel in Las Vegas via air mail - special delivery.

Best regards,

Sincerely,

Tom Diskin

Letter from Tom Diskin outlining the terms for Scotty's
performances with Elvis, October 17, 1957

pay them $1,000 each, or $250 per show. Scotty and Bill agreed to rejoin
the band on those terms, with the understanding that any future
bookings would be on a per-diem basis. "Just send us some contracts,"
says Scotty, getting some satisfaction from knowing how the phone call
must have made Parker cringe. Later, they learned the phone call had
been made at Elvis's insistence.

On October 17, the day after they returned from Texas, Diskin sent
the contracts. In his letter, Diskin asked Scotty to send the contracts

special delivery to the Sahara Hotel in Las Vegas. The letter, which was formal and to the point, said Scotty and Bill could travel from Memphis to California with D. J. in Elvis's limousine at no extra charge, but then added—with a characteristic Parker jab—"Should you decide to travel by some other method that would be of course at your own expense."

Scotty and Bill took the limo. The drive took a day and a half. They met Elvis at the San Francisco Civic Auditorium and he acted as if nothing had happened. "Nothing was said that I can remember," says Scotty. "We laughed and went on and did the show like we used to do. There weren't any hard feelings visible with anyone. We didn't go there with a chip on our shoulder. I don't think it was even brought up."

From San Francisco, they went across the bay to Oakland for a concert the second night, then it was on to Los Angeles, where they were booked for two nights at the Pan Pacific Auditorium. Elvis and his entourage checked into the Beverly Wilshire Hotel. Scotty and Bill checked into the Hollywood Knickerbocker Hotel, where they got rooms for seven dollars a night. According to one review of the first concert, the auditorium was "packed to the rafters" with 9,000 cheering, screaming fans who threatened to "break loose in a riot at every hip flip by Presley."

They closed the show with "Hound Dog," with Scotty doing his patented guitar riff and Elvis rolling on the floor of the stage with a plaster dog critics later concluded was the RCA Records trademark. It was like old times. Elvis was at his best when he let the child in him come out and play. Scotty and Bill were among the few people in Elvis's life who knew that child.

A few days after they returned to Memphis, Scotty and Bill received a contract from Diskin for two days of concerts in Hawaii. Elvis went by ship, traveling on the USS *Matsonia*, but Scotty, Bill, D. J., and the Jordanaires took a United Airlines flight. This time they would break tradition and stay in the same hotel with Elvis, who had reserved the entire fourteenth floor of the Hawaiian Village Hotel. Scotty's $12-a-night room was plusher than he usually got on the road.

The two concerts at the Honolulu Stadium attracted nearly 15,000 fans, bringing in more than $32,000 to the promoters. The second day they performed for 10,000 civilians and military personnel from Schofied Barracks Army Base near Pearl Harbor. Scotty was happy to be back onstage again with Elvis and company, but with Elvis facing the draft, questions about their future lingered.

✳ ✳ ✳

In December 19, 1957, Elvis received word from the draft board that his induction notice was ready. He was told he could drop by the draft board office, if he wished, and pick up the notice himself. That way there would be less likelihood the news would be leaked to the media. That sounded like a good idea to Elvis.

The following day, Elvis stopped by Sun Studio to show off his letter of greeting from Uncle Sam. Jack Clement was there when he walked in.

"Jack," said Elvis matter of factly. "I got drafted."

"We got to talking," says Jack, who had served with honor in the Marines. In music circles Jack was sort of famous because *Life* magazine published a photograph showing him as part of the Marine honor guard protecting Queen Elizabeth during one of her visits to America. "I got the distinct feeling he was happy about it. He said, 'Well, might as well have fun.' I think he probably did. He seemed kind of excited, like it was going to be an adventure."

No one knows for sure what was going through Elvis's mind at that time, but certainly all those stories about Shanghai wenches, floating bodies, and exploding rockets that Scotty had shared with him out on the road were not far from his thoughts. Scotty had survived military service; so had Jack. Elvis, too, would survive. At issue was whether his career would survive.

That month "Jailhouse Rock" was the No. 1 record on the charts, but closing in quickly was Jerry Lee Lewis's "Great Balls of Fire." With production scheduled to begin in January on Elvis's next movie, *King Creole*, Paramount Studio wrote the draft board and asked for a sixty-day deferment, citing the enormous preproduction costs they had invested in the movie. The draft board responded that it would consider such a request, but it would have to come from the inductee himself. Elvis promptly wrote the board a letter requesting a deferment, to which the board responded in the affirmative. Elvis was given until the end of March to finish the movie.

On January 10, 1958, Scotty and the band checked into the Hollywood Knickerbocker. As usual, they planned to work on the sound track at Radio Recorders before filming began. Elation over the reconciliation with Elvis was short-lived. The Memphis draft board had thrown a wrench into Scotty's long-term career goals. Would Elvis put him and the others on some sort of salary during the two years he would be gone? Would Elvis even have a career when he got out of the Army?

153

SCOTTY AND BILL CALL IT QUITS:
"TRAGEDY" STRIKES

Songwriters Jerry Leiber and Mike Stoller were again put in charge of the session. They turned out a respectable slate of four songs for the movie, including "King Creole," "Crawfish," and "Trouble," but their hearts were not in the project. Seasoned session players were brought in to give the sound track a Dixieland feel. Paramount had given up trying to get Elvis to record on the soundstage. Not only did Elvis not like the size of the soundstage, according to Scotty, he hated the engineering process they went through to get recordings.

"In a studio, you'd say, 'OK, let's do a take' and reach over and turn on the tape recorder and start singing," says Scotty. "But on the soundstage, they had to wait for all this stuff to get locked up. The engineer up in the control booth would tell the people down below, 'OK roll.' Everything had a number and a countdown and you had a guy on the soundstage and he had to do something. You're talking about two or three minutes before everything was locked up and ready to go."

When filming began, Scotty, Bill, and D. J. played the part of Elvis's movie band. This time they were given a few lines to deliver. When Elvis sang "King Creole," Scotty, Bill, and D. J. stood behind him on the stage. At one point during the song, Elvis pretended to play a guitar solo. He can be seen looking back over his shoulder at Scotty, a sly grin on his face. That grin wasn't in the script; it was a private joke between Elvis and Scotty. With his eyes, he was asking Scotty if he was doing his fingers correctly on the solo. When they shot the close-up of his hands, Scotty put on Elvis's shirt and played the solo for the camera.

At one point, Scotty was handed a banjo to play. It was a prop and didn't have real strings on it. Scotty had never played a banjo, but pretended to play it for the scene. The more he thought about it, the more he realized that everything Elvis was doing had a "pretend" air about it.

Before they headed back to Memphis, they did two recording sessions for RCA. Elvis was distracted and the sessions didn't go well. They did get two hits: "Hard Headed Woman," which went to No. 1 in July, and "Wear My Ring Around Your Neck," which peaked at No. 2 in April.

On March 24 Elvis reported to the induction center in Memphis and then boarded a train for his basic training. As he left for exile into the army, his biggest musical competitor, Jerry Lee Lewis, scored a Top 20 hit with "Breathless." Elvis must have wondered if the Killer was going to leave anything for him. What he could not possibly have guessed was that "Breathless" would be the last Top 20 pop hit Lewis would have, his career soon to be destroyed by his marriage to his teenage cousin.

The week before he left, Elvis answered all the questions about what would happen to his "boys" in his absence. They were simply let go. He called Scotty and Bill to say goodbye. Says Scotty: "His attitude was like, 'So long, see you when I get out.'" Before leaving, he bought his girlfriend, Anita Wood, a new car. Scotty couldn't believe it. It was like a dream—or a nightmare. Why would Elvis buy his girlfriend a car and not buy one for Bobbie? They had their differences, sure, but Elvis had turned him and Bill out to pasture like broken-down mules, without a penny.

"We were supposed to be the King's men," says Scotty. "In reality, we were the court jesters. People only laughed at us."

✻ ✻ ✻

After Elvis received his physical at Kennedy Veterans Hospital in Memphis, he was sent to Fort Chafee, Arkansas, then on to Fort Hood, Texas, where he was allowed to rent a home in nearby Killeen for his parents. Despite his statements that he just wanted to be treated like any other soldier, Elvis was given special treatment by the Army. He was allowed to have a sports car, which he drove to visit his parents. Gladys cooked for him, but she was clearly not in good health. They had been told Elvis would be stationed in Germany; Vernon and Gladys planned on relocating in Germany to be near their son, but Gladys had reservations about going overseas.

When Elvis completed basic training on May 31, he was given a furlough, which allowed him to return to Memphis for more than a week. On June 10 he went to Nashville, where at Steve Sholes's frantic pleadings, a recording session had been arranged. Scotty and Bill were not invited to the two-day session. They were replaced by Hank Garland on guitar and Bob Moore on bass. D. J. was invited, but not as the main drummer. A number of sides were recorded at the session, including "I Got Stung" and "A Fool Such as I," which Scotty and Bill might well have adopted as their theme songs.

When his furlough was up, Elvis returned to Fort Hood. In August, as his training was coming to an end, he put his parents on the train to Memphis. The day after they arrived, Gladys was admitted to the hospital. When the physician saw that it was serious, he telephoned Elvis, who was given a leave to fly to Memphis. Gladys had an advanced hepatitis infection, but she was conscious and conversed with her son, reassuring him that everything would be all right. While at the hospital, Elvis ran into his old girlfriend from the projects, Betty McMahan, who was employed at the hospital. "He had on his uniform," she says.

"He just grabbed me, hugged me just like he always did. Just a good friend."

After visiting his mother, Elvis went to Graceland, leaving his father in the hospital with Gladys. The next morning Elvis returned to the hospital and stayed several hours. Early the following morning, Elvis was called back to the hospital: Gladys was dead. When Elvis received the news, he was overcome with grief.

At the funeral, nearly 3,000 mourners filed past the casket. Four hundred people crammed into the chapel, which had seating for only 300. Outside, sixty-five police officers were on duty to control the crowd that had gathered to get a glimpse of the mourners and the celebrities who had arrived for the services. Noticeably absent from the services were Scotty and Bill.

Later, it was rumored that they had not attended because they could not afford suits. That explanation was only partially true. Scotty had a couple of relatively new jackets he had purchased to wear in his movie scenes, so he did have something to wear if he wanted to go. What he could not afford were groceries. His total income for the year amounted to only $2,322, all of which resulted from his work on *King Creole*. He had received no income from Elvis since the concert in Hawaii.

When Elvis had an opportunity to give him work again—but didn't— during the recording session in June, it stung. Had Elvis forgotten what it was like to live day to day? Scotty felt the pain Elvis experienced over Gladys's death. He knew what Elvis was going through because he knew how devoted he was to his mother. What Scotty couldn't bring himself to do was to share that pain in a public way. People could think what they wanted to think.

❋ ❋ ❋

Scotty and Bill went their separate ways, though they stayed in close contact and occasionally worked together on recording projects. With the newly formed Memphis label Hi Records just getting off the ground, Bill started spending time at the label's headquarters, a recording studio named Royal Recording. While doing session work with guitarist Reggie Young, he often expressed resentment about the treatment he had received from Elvis. He told Reggie that toward the end of their association with Elvis, he and Scotty were told not to talk to the star, except onstage.

For the first week after Elvis left, Scotty drew unemployment. Then he entered into a partnership with Ronald "Slim" Wallace, the truck driver with whom Jack Clement had built a garage studio named Fernwood.

"Slim had two or three microphones and a little mono tape recorder," says Scotty. "I took a few pieces of gear out and we started recording this and that."

One day, Thomas Wayne Perkins, Scotty's former paperboy at his old Belz Street address, asked him if he could stop by the house and audition for him. Perkins's brother, Luther, was the guitarist in the Johnny Cash band, so Scotty thought it was worth a listen. The youngster, still a senior in high school, was so nervous when he arrived at Scotty's house that he sat on Bobbie's glass-topped coffee table and broke it. When he sang, Scotty liked what he heard—broken glass and all.

Scotty worked with Perkins at Fernwood, but their first demos attracted no interest from the major labels. At one point, he and Wallace thought Mercury Records was interested in Perkins, but for some reason a deal never materialized.

Without Bobbie's job at Sears, they would have been destitute that summer. "I don't remember if Bill had a day job or not, but we were both scratching to stay afloat," says Scotty. His work at Fernwood wasn't bringing in much money, but it helped him to keep the faith. Sooner or later something would break in his favor—he was certain of that.

One day Scotty was walking along the street when he ran into Gerald Nelson, a disc jockey from Kentucky. They had met some time back at a concert. Gerald told Scotty that he and Fred Burch, a college student, had written a song titled "Tragedy." Fred had snatched the title from a course he was taking on Aristotelian tragedies.

Gerald said he had played the song for Chet Atkins, who had told him it sounded like a hit, but was not a song he could do anything with in Nashville because it wasn't country enough. Encouraged by Atkins's assessment of the song's potential, they had driven to Memphis, to the very cradle of rock 'n' roll. "We played it for Sam Phillips," says Gerald, "but he said he couldn't use it either." As Scotty stood on the sidewalk and listened, Gerald sang the song to him, playing the music on his ukulele. Scotty loved it. He told Gerald he knew just the guy to sing it: Thomas Wayne Perkins. Fred and Gerald felt so encouraged by Scotty's reaction, they moved to Memphis to begin new careers as songwriters.

Unhappy with the technical limitations of Fernwood's garage studio, Scotty looked for a better place to record the songs. In exchange for studio time at Hi Records' studio, Gerald sang background on one of their sessions. When they went in to record Thomas Wayne's session, they discovered the studio had installed new equipment; the studio was going to use them as guinea pigs to test the new machine. Thomas Wayne

Scotty Moore, extreme right above, who being a member of the Elvis Presley Band almost since its inception, found himself jobless when Presley entered the army, put his business talents to work and started Fernwood label at Memphis. The venture went over with its very first release—"Tragedy" by Thomas Wayne, the other man in the photo, who was backed by the Delons, the three girls above. "Tragedy" has climbed to dizzy heights in the charts, and today nobody believes that Moore will go back to a band job again, however lucrative the offer.

Scotty (far right) holds a copy of Thomas Wayne's (center) record "Tragedy" (Courtesy of Colin Escott)

brought three girls from his high school—his girlfriend and her two friends—to sing background. Scotty and Bill were the only musicians.

"It was the first time [the tape machine] was used," says Fred Burch, laughing. "They couldn't get it to work. Finally, someone kicked it and got it going. They cut the song three times and ended up using the first cut. There was no echo in the studio, so they took the tape to WMPS radio, where they had two Ampex machines."

Using the technique he learned from Sam for adding "slapback" to a record, Scotty recorded a simultaneous dub on a master tape at the radio station. This time, instead of offering it to a major label, they put the record out on Fernwood Records. The A side was an uptempo song written by Nelson-Burch titled "Saturday Date"; the B side was "Tragedy."

When "Saturday Date" was released in September, it had little impact on radio. But because Scotty believed in the record, he kept pushing it well into the spring of 1959. Finally, lightning struck. A disc jockey in Kentucky flipped the record and started playing the B side in heavy rotation. As a result, phone requests for "Tragedy" started flooding into the radio station. Before Scotty knew what had happened, he had a hit record.

With its understated instrumentation and lush background vocals, Thomas Wayne's macho-breathless baritone carried the song. "Tragedy" was one of those '50s-type ballads that never failed to get dancers hot and bothered. It was a Memphis thing: a song written by novices barely old enough to vote, sung by the producer's former paperboy, with background vocals provided by high school girls, recorded on bartered studio time. It was the stuff of which Memphis magic was made.

"It was like it happened overnight," Scotty says. "We didn't have a dime to promote it." As the orders started coming in, they hired a national promotion man, Steve Brodie of Buffalo, New York, to push the record. "He said, 'I can make this a big hit,' so we paid him a nickel a record."

Scotty and Wallace added a third partner, Memphis attorney Robert Buckalew. Their most immediate problem was getting large orders of records pressed. Working together, Buckalew and Brodie persuaded record pressing plants to give them sixty days credit, since they knew it would be at least that long before the money started trickling in. Once that happened, Brodie started working the song on radio, beginning with his hometown of Buffalo. As it climbed the charts there, he focused his attention on larger markets.

By March, "Tragedy" had risen to No. 8 on the national charts, making it a million-seller. Ironically, without trying to compete with Sun Records, Scotty had stolen its thunder. Before "Tragedy" hit, only three records recorded in Memphis had ever scored higher on the pop charts, and they were all Sun releases: Jerry Lee Lewis's "Great Balls of Fire" and "Whole Lot of Shakin' Going On," and Carl Perkins's "Blue Suede Shoes."

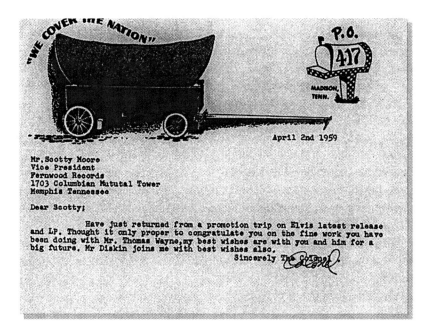

Letter from Tom Parker, April 2, 1959

Trying only to stay afloat, Scott had made history and a few bucks in the process. "We grossed about $600,000," says Scotty. "Of course, when the money started coming in and I sat down and started writing checks, it went [out] pretty fast. I remember writing one check for $150,000 to the pressing plants. Oh, that hurt."

After the record hit, Scotty sent a copy to Colonel Parker, who responded on April 2 with a letter. "Have just returned from a promotion trip on Elvis [sic] latest release and LP," he wrote. "Thought it only proper to congratulate you on the fine work you have been doing with Mr. Thomas Wayne. My best wishes are with you and him for a big future." He signed the letter "Colonel."

Scotty paid himself a salary from the record company with the agreement of the two other partners, but most of the money was funneled back into Fernwood Records. They rented an office downtown in the same building where their attorney (and new partner) was located. Later, they rented a building on North Main Street and installed a fully equipped studio. It was located next door to a delicatessen that specialized in corned beef. What Scotty remembers most about the studio is the plentiful supply of food. "I've never eaten so much corned beef in my life," he says.

That spring and summer, Scotty was on top of the world. He had a hit record and his own recording studio. It was another one of those rags-to-riches stories of which the music industry is so fond. In March he purchased a C-5 Classic Gibson guitar for $85 from Chicago Musical Instrument Company and a black El Dorado Cadillac with a red interior.

To promote Thomas Wayne's record, he organized a touring band made of himself, Bill, D. J. Fontana, and Reggie Young. Scotty was coming and going so fast, he sometimes lost his sense of direction. Reggie remembers one night when they returned to Memphis at three o'clock in the morning. "We pulled up in front of Scotty's house, stopping out in the middle of the street," says Reggie. "He just got out, left the car running, and went into the house and went to bed. Bill or someone slid over and took us home."

Scotty often booked Reggie for sessions at Fernwood. They got to be good friends and usually wound up the sessions by sitting on the curb drinking cheap wine. Reggie went on to become one of the premier session guitarists in the country, working in Memphis with literally hundreds of artists including Neil Diamond, Wilson Pickett, and Dionne Warwick, and then later in Nashville with Willie Nelson, Waylon Jennings, and Johnny Cash. But in those days he was just finding himself as a musician; the Blue Moon Boys were among his heroes.

"That whole deal of Scotty, Bill, and Elvis was unique," he says. "Scotty and Bill were as much a part of Elvis's music as he was. No one sounded like that. You always copy records you can play the parts to. Scotty's parts, they weren't real easy to play, but they were playable. They weren't something you couldn't figure out. I'm sure a lot of would-be guitar players sat down with Elvis's records and copied Scotty's licks. He was the first one to make people want to do that."

Fernwood followed up "Tragedy" with a number of Thomas Wayne recordings including "Scandalizing My Name," "Girl Next Door," "Just Beyond," and "Guilty of Love," some of which were written by Burch and Nelson. One Thomas Wayne release, "This Time," was penned by a newcomer to Memphis, a young Georgian named Chips Moman.[1] Unfortunately, none of Thomas Wayne's subsequent releases achieved the success of "Tragedy."[2]

In the aftermath of "Tragedy," Sharri Paullus, a songwriter whose physician husband had started a record label named Rave Records, took two instrumental ideas to Fernwood. For that project, Scotty asked Bill to play bass and saxophonist Ace Cannon to do the horn work. The finished product, with its gritty, hypnotic groove, is remarkably similar to records later recorded by the Bill Black Combo. The songs—"The Gambler" and "It's Not Fun Loving You"— were released on Rave Records.

As the year ended, Scotty reported his highest income to date— $13,547.64—but the money from Thomas Wayne's hit was quickly petering out at Fernwood.

✳ ✳ ✳

Elvis stayed on the charts in 1959 with songs recorded in Nashville before he left the country. He adjusted to the Army better than he, or anyone else, thought, but it was clear after he arrived at his station outside Friedberg, Germany, that he was going to receive special privileges. Originally, the Army said he would be assigned to the crew of a medium Patton tank. However, after he arrived in Germany in October 1958, it was announced that he would serve sixteen months as a scout Jeep driver. His father and grandmother arrived four days later and Elvis was given a pass to visit them at a luxurious spa several miles outside Friedberg.

---

[1] Moman went on to become one of the most successful record producers in Memphis. His 1969 sessions with Elvis Presley produced a numer of hits, including "Suspicious Minds" and "In the Ghetto."
[2] "Tragedy" was subsequently covered by a number of artists, including Bette Midler. Over the years, the publishing changed hands several times, eventually ending up with ex-Beatle Paul McCartney.

Elvis rented a two-story house for his father and grandmother, then was given permission to move in with them. The Army allowed him to commute to the base. If Scotty had any concerns about his friend's personal safety in the Army, they quickly dissipated when he read press accounts of Elvis's special treatment. It's sure not like it was in the old days, he thought. Hell, he's missing half the fun.

In November, Elvis's social life improved considerably when he was introduced to fourteen-year-old Priscilla Beaulieu at an Army party. Priscilla was the daughter of an Air Force captain stationed in Wiesbaden. He "dated" her several times, taking her to movies or for a drive in his BMW, but unknown to Priscilla, he also had an even younger German girl living in the house with his father and grandmother. He must have chuckled to himself over his involvement with the girls. Jerry Lee Lewis had married a girl only a year younger than Priscilla and he was being roasted by the press. When a reporter asked Elvis about Lewis's marriage, he said, "I'd rather not talk about his marriage, except that if he really loves her, I guess it's all right." Elvis was not as understanding of May-December romances when his father started dating a young married woman, Dee Stanley, only a year after his mother's death.[3] The same month he met Priscilla, he hired a South African fitness instructor to give him massages. He paid him $15,000, roughly the equivalent of the total salary he paid Scotty for the first three years they worked together.

Before his discharge from the Army in March 1960, it was announced that his next movie would be *G.I. Blues.* Colonel Parker was delighted to be getting him back in circulation. Elvis's income had dropped to only $2 million in 1958, Parker told Nashville reporters. On the day before he left Germany, the Army held a huge press conference for him at a gym in Bad Nauheim. He walked in the door, flanked by MPs and wearing red stripes and a gold braid. Standing near the door was Marion Keisker, by then a captain in the Women's Air Force.

"Hi, hon," said Marion.

Elvis was shocked when he saw her. "What do I do? Kiss you or salute you?"

Marion flung her arms around him.

The Army officer in charge was outraged. He accused Marion of staging the event. He ordered her to leave, but she refused, citing her position

[3] Vernon Presley married Dee Stanley on July 3, 1960, at the home of her brother. Elvis did not attend the ceremony.

as assistant manager of Armed Forces television. For Elvis, it couldn't have been a better sendoff.

✳ ✳ ✳

When Elvis returned to Memphis, he discovered the city's musical balance of power had altered considerably. Jerry Lee Lewis had fallen from grace and was in the midst of a nosedive into obscurity. Sun Records hadn't had a Top 20 hit on the pop charts since Johnny Cash's "Guess Things Happen That Way" in July 1958. The biggest hitmakers in the city were those two former members of the Blue Moon Boys: Scotty and Bill. Scotty had scored with his Top 10 hit with Thomas Wayne, and Bill had cracked the Top 20 with "Smokie (Parts 1 & 2)," recorded by the newly formed Bill Black Combo. Even as Elvis unpacked his bags at Graceland, Bill had another hit zooming up the charts, an instrumental titled "White Silver Sands." In April "White Silver Sands" was No. 13 on the charts and Elvis's "Stuck on You" was No. 11.

The Bill Black Combo evolved from the Hi Records session band that Bill had organized with Reggie Young. An executive from London Records, which had the distribution rights for Hi, was in the studio one day and heard them playing. He suggested they form a band. They didn't need much encouragement. "We were equal owners of the group," says Reggie. "We tried to figure who to name it after. It was either Bill or me. I had been working at the Louisiana Hayride with Johnny Horton, so I had some name recognition. But Bill had been with Elvis and knew more disc jockeys than I did." Thus the Bill Black Combo was born.

With Bill on bass, Reggie on guitar, Carl McAvoy on piano, Jerry Arnold on drums, and Martin Wills on sax, the Bill Black Combo popularized a whole new genre of groove-based instrumentals. "I tuned my guitar down a couple of steps, where it was real low, and I played rhythm with a pencil as a pick—that's how that shuffle kind of came about," says Reggie.

Bill Black was becoming the most famous bass player in America. A headline in the *Press-Scimitar* proclaimed, "Bill Black Getting the Top Breaks." The story, written by Robert Johnson to announce an upcoming appearance of the combo on the *Ed Sullivan Show*, said: "Things are breaking wide open for Bill Black, the Memphis musician who started out with Elvis, went with him all the way to the big time, then got lost for a time in the backwash."

As "Smokie (Parts 1 & 2)" peaked on the charts, Reggie received his draft notice. He left the group for two years, but when he returned he picked up where he had left off. Scotty and Bill remained friends, and

163

helped each other on projects whenever they could, but Scotty had his own thing going and never considered becoming a member of Bill's group. In his heart, Scotty still felt everything would work out with Elvis. He believed in Elvis, perhaps even more than Elvis believed in himself.

As expected, Elvis contacted Scotty and Bill when he returned to Memphis. He had a recording session scheduled in Nashville on March 21 and a television special with Frank Sinatra set for March 26 in Miami. Would they be able to hit the road again with him? Scotty said yes, but Bill declined, citing his responsibilities to the Bill Black Combo. Even without the success of the combo, it is doubtful Bill would have signed on with Elvis again. "Bill was upset because of the way they treated him" says his wife, Evelyn. "If it hadn't have been for him and Scotty and D. J., Elvis would never have been as popular as he was. He thought a lot of Elvis and he missed playing with him. He wasn't mad, it was more like he was disappointed. He would have liked to have stayed with Elvis until he died."

Scotty went out to Graceland to meet with Elvis. He hadn't seen him in nearly two years, but it was like old times. Elvis didn't say anything to Scotty about him not going to Gladys's funeral; Scotty didn't say anything to Elvis about being left high and dry. They talked about the upcoming recording session and the Sinatra show. Elvis told him RCA had offered to build him a studio at Graceland so that he could record whenever he felt like it. He asked Scotty if he would be interested in taking care of the studio for him. Scotty said that would be great, although they never talked about a salary.

Elvis complained about how ragged his Gibson J-200 looked. Scotty, who had obtained an endorsement deal from Gibson several years back, offered to send Elvis's guitar to the Chicago Musical Instrument Company to have it refinished and repaired, and to have his name inlaid on the finger board. After he left Graceland, Scotty asked O. K. Houck to ship Elvis's guitar to Chicago Instrument. In a separate letter to Chicago Instrument, Scotty wrote, "I would like for you to do some extra inlay work on the front, nothing too elaborate, something a little different possibly that he would like very much. I will leave the design of this to your discretion."

Elvis wanted the guitar to use at the session in Nashville, so Chicago Musical Instrument shipped it air express to Scotty in care of Chet Atkins at RCA in Nashville. The guitar arrived in time for the session. It looked great. Elvis was pleased with the work. Not until years later, when he began work on this book, did Scotty compare the serial number of the guitar he had shipped to Chicago with the serial number of the guitar that arrived in Nashville. At that time, he discovered the serial numbers did not match. Instead of repairing Elvis's old guitar, they had shipped a brand new guitar. Scotty was never able to find out what happened to the original guitar or get an explanation for the substitution.

March was a pivotal month for Scotty, not only in his relationship with Elvis, but in his relationship with Bobbie. Before Scotty left for the Nashville session, Bobbie got pregnant with their first—and only—child, Andrea, who was born on November 25, 1960.

After recording two ballads, "Stuck on You" and "Fame and Fortune," Elvis and the band boarded a train in Nashville and headed south to Miami. Scotty remembers seeing people lining the tracks along the way. The trip was supposed to be secret, but Parker, in an effort to get publicity, called every small town along the way. At some stops, Parker got Elvis to stand on the back platform, like he had seen presidents do, and wave to the cheering crowds.

When they reached Miami, they checked into the Hotel Fontainebleau. The television special was taped in the grand ballroom of the hotel and aired at a later date. Elvis was backed by the Nelson Riddle Orchestra, which was augmented with Scotty, D. J., and the Jordanaires.

In April there were more recording sessions in Nashville for an album, *Elvis Is Back*—two singles from these sessions, "It's Now or Never" and "Are You Lonesome Tonight," went to No. 1 later in the year—and additional sessions for the sound track for *G.I. Blues*. When filming began in May, Scotty and D. J. were hired as extras. "They had us wear these Barvarian outfits with short britches," says Scotty. "We had to get out there at five or six in the morning, when it was cool, and get leg makeup." Scotty laughs when he thinks about the leg makeup. "And you couldn't even see our legs in the movie."

By the start of summer, Scotty began to suspect that his earlier optimism might have been misplaced. No one was talking about going out on tour. The session work was nice—and it paid well—but it wasn't enough to support a family. His involvement in the movies was regressing. Elvis was back, but Scotty's income was plummeting. The money that had come in from "Tragedy" was gone now, spent on new ventures at Fernwood. More to the point, Elvis never again mentioned his offer of hiring Scotty to run a studio at Graceland. It was another promise that never materialized.

* * *

With Fernwood Records in dire straits—Scotty would sell his shares, or rather unload them, later in the year—he started looking around for a day job. Sam told him that in addition to the new studio he was building on Madison he was buying out a studio in Nashville. He needed someone to oversee both studios. Scotty hadn't had a regular job since his days as a hatter at the dry cleaners, but working for Sam seemed like a good idea. He would no longer be playing for thousands of screaming fans, but he would still be in the music business.

In June 1960 the *Sun-Liners,* a newsletter put out by Sun Records, announced the title of Johnny Cash's latest album, *So Doggone Lonesome,* along with a release from newcomer Bobbie Jean titled "You Burned the Bridges." Also in the newsletter was an announcement that Scotty Moore had joined the staff of Sam C. Phillips Enterprises as production manager. In that capacity, he would supervise all aspects of studio operation, including sessions, mastering, and new artist acquisition. "His will be a full-time job with Sun PI, et al., but he may get together with his old buddies, Elvis Presley and Bill Black, for a gig now and then," said the newsletter. "Persons wishing to utilize Sam C. Phillips Recording facilities for recording may reach Scotty in Memphis at JAckson 7-8233."

Scotty's photograph was prominently displayed in a *Press-Scimitar* feature that heralded the opening of the new studio at 639 Madison. Sam Phillips told the reporter, Edwin Howard, that he had invested $750,000 in the new facility in an effort to stay competitive. "Woodshed recordings have had it," Sam said. "You've got to have latitude today—all the electronic devices, built-in high and low frequency equalization and attenuation, echoes, and metering on everything."

The new studio, on a site formerly occupied by a Midas Muffler Shop, had all that and more. Howard asked if there was a possibility Elvis Presley might use the new facilities. "I don't know," said Sam. "Of course, RCA has its own studio in Nashville, and Elvis has been cutting there. But Ed Hinds of RCA's Nashville office is coming over for our opening. Something might develop eventually." Scotty knew there was fat chance of that: he knew Colonel Parker would never allow Elvis to record again in a studio owned by Sam Phillips.

The year 1960 was a watershed year for Scotty. At age twenty-nine, with a child on the way, he had come to terms with his life. For six years, he had been waiting for the economic situation with Elvis to change. Whenever he thought about it, it gave him a sinking feeling.

That's alright, Elvis, he thought, that's alright.

Shortly after he settled into his new routine at the studio, Scotty received a telephone call from someone from his past. Frankie Tucker had seen his photograph in the newspaper. She reminded him of their liaison in West Memphis in 1953. Then she dropped a bombshell: she had had his child six years ago, a little girl she had named Vicki. Would he like to see his daughter?

Vicki recalls her first meeting with her father with that type of fuzzy nostalgia usually reserved for a first Christmas or a first kiss. "I pretended I was asleep," she says. "He was rubbing my back and looking me over. He said [to my mother], 'Oh, she has my nose and she has your smile, your lips.'" For years after that initial introduction, Vicki made a mad dash for the television whenever she heard Elvis's name or voice. If it was an old show, she would see her father standing behind Elvis, always to his right; if it was new footage, she would wonder where her father was.

"If it wasn't him, I would be so disappointed," she says. "We saw each other only once a year—mostly because Mother's husband was jealous. He wouldn't allow Elvis albums in the house."

**Vicki Hein, her mother, Frankie, and Vicki's son, Nick
(Courtesy of Scotty Moore)**

CHAPTER

8

THE GUITAR THAT CHANGE
THE WORLD

hen Scotty started working at Sam Phillips's Recording Service, it had been two years since Sun Records had placed a record in the Top 20 in the pop charts.[1] The two major talents in Sam's stable were Jerry Lee Lewis and a newcomer named Charlie Rich, whose song "Lonely Weekends" had been a regional hit in 1959. Johnny Cash had moved on to greener pastures; Carl Perkins had dropped out of sight. The reigning Memphis hitmakers were Scotty Moore—with "Tragedy"— and Bill Black, with his "Smokie (Parts 1 & 2)." Elvis climbed back to the top of the charts in 1959 with "Stuck on You" and "It's Now or Never," but neither song was recorded in Memphis.

As head of production, Scotty presided over a state-of-the-art facility that the *Press-Scimitar* described as "plush" and "futuristic." It boasted a sundeck on the roof and an executive bar. Sam moved from his "no desk" office on Union Avenue to a penthouse office where he had a juke-box-like stereo hi-fi built into his desk. Seven gold records hung on the wall; none bore Elvis Presley's name. Although Sam didn't come right out and say so, the new studio represented a significant shift in his approach to the music industry. While his efforts previously had been focused on finding new talent for Sun Records, he now was more interested in selling studio time to other labels. Time was a less temperamental commodity in which to deal. As soon as he had the new studio up and running, he turned his attention to opening a studio in

[1]Johnny Cash's "Guess Things Happen That Way"/"Come in Stranger" peaked at No. 14 in July 1958.

downtown Nashville at the Cumberland Lodge Building. It was Scotty's job to oversee production at both facilities.

With Fernwood Records in disarray, Scotty brought Thomas Wayne over to Sam's studio, where he produced another Nelson-Burch ballad, "The Quiet Look," for Sam's new "Phillips" label. The record didn't hit, but Scotty continued to work with Thomas Wayne.

Scotty also engineered several sessions with Jerry Lee Lewis, one of which became a source of contention between the singer and the local musicians union. "I don't remember if they actually canceled his card or what, but he was in trouble with them and had been suspended," says Scotty. "He wasn't allowed to play until it was cleared up and Sam was desperate for a record. I did the tracks with another piano player, Larry Muhoberac, and got Jerry Lee to overdub his voice, so that way the union couldn't do anything."

Scotty wasn't antiunion; he was trying to help Sam out of a jam. In fact, it was during this period that Scotty became very active in the union, at one point serving on its board of directors. "In those days, the union was not affiliated with the AFL-CIO; it was strictly a fraternal-type organization," says Scotty. "They didn't want blacks or hillbillies in there. They couldn't keep you out, but they made it obvious they didn't want you. That pissed me off. I ran for the board of directors—and we got a new president in there. I told all the record companies, 'Someday you'll be glad if you just file the contracts and pay your taxes. If a guy wants to work for nothing, that's his business. Just make it legal.'"

Lewis's problems with the union were indicative of the turn his life had taken in general. Always temperamental, the roasting he took in the media for his marriage to his teenage cousin—and the subsequent nosedive his records took on the charts—made him even more unpredictable. One of the stories making the rounds at that time involved a tour he made with Chuck Berry. Lewis had been closing the show for several performances, so the story goes, when the promoter informed him it was Berry's turn to close. After an argument, Lewis finally agreed to go out first. At the end of a thirty-minute set, he whipped out a can of lighter fluid and soaked the piano and set it afire. "I'd like to see any son of a bitch top that," he reportedly said as he walked offstage.

In an effort to escape the notoriety—and perhaps cash in on the success Bill Black was having—Lewis recorded an instrumental in 1960 titled "In the Mood"/"I Get the Blues When it Rains." He released the song under the name "Hawk," but when the record, which was issued on Phillips Records, failed to fly, he dropped the moniker and went back to being plain old Jerry Lee. After several years of near misses on the

Scotty in Sam Phillips's studio, c. October 1960
(Courtesy of Colin Escott)

pop charts, he left Sun Records in 1963 and signed with Smash, a subsidiary of Mercury Records in Nashville. That move signaled more than a change of address, it represented a change in musical direction, nudging him from pop/rock to country.

Charlie Rich had been discovered by Scotty's A&R predecessor, Bill Justis, who himself had scored in November 1957 with a gritty Top 20 instrumental titled "Raunchy." Justis felt Rich was a superb pianist. He liked the demo tapes Rich brought him so much that he hired him as a session player in Sam's studio. One day, during lunch at Taylor's cafe with Rich and *Press-Scimitar* reporter Edwin Howard, Justis gave his new piano player some potent advice: "I keep telling you, Charlie: you're never gonna make it in the record business till you learn to play bad."

Sam released seven Rich singles on Phillips Records—including "Just a Little Sweet" and "School Days"—but the records never got beyond a regional audience. When Rich signed with RCA Records in 1963, Sam sent a telegram to the label stating that Rich still had an unfilled verbal contract with him. As a result of Sam's letter, RCA suspended Rich's contract and Rich sued Sam in chancery court charging him with breach of contract. The lawsuit was settled to Rich's advantage, but his rough new beginning with RCA produced only one minor hit, "Big Boss Man," and it wasn't until he moved on to Smash that he got a big hit with "Mohair Sam."

With the talent pool at Sun and Phillips becoming muddied by bad luck, lawsuits, and petty bickering, Scotty focused his attention on the operation of the studios. One day, while Sam was out of town, Scotty and engineer/consultant John Carroll started rewiring the control room of the Memphis studio. Sam was famous for being tight with his pennies. The best way to get something done, Scotty discovered, was just to go ahead and do it—especially if it involved the expenditure of money. When Sam returned to the studio and saw the mess—wires were strewn about the floor of the control room—he was moderately horrified, but when he saw the finished product a couple of weeks later, he was so pleased he asked them to rewire the studio in Nashville the same way.

What Carroll remembers most about those days were the long hours they put in. "I'd work all day at the television station and radio station and go down there and work all night at Sam's," says Carroll. "Scotty was doing pretty much the same thing, except he was doing it at the studio."

Each day, at one o'clock in the morning, Scotty and Carroll followed the same ritual. "Someone would go to the Krystals downtown and bring back a bushel basket of Krystal [hamburgers]," says Carroll. "It was nothing out of the ordinary for me to eat a dozen at a time."

According to Carroll, Scotty is one of the originators of the isolation technique of recording. "[Sam's] studio was fine as far as its acoustical properties were concerned, except you couldn't keep one instrument out of another instrument's microphone," says Carroll. "Scotty started using baffles. He'd partition areas for different instruments and that worked out real well. The general philosophy was to have a big open room and record it live like at a concert." Scotty got the idea of using baffles from the experiment that took place at the Hollywood soundstage when engineers constructed baffled rooms around them. That setup didn't work with Elvis, but it did work in Sam's studio once Scotty got the baffles properly placed.

Toward the end of 1960, Bill Black scored a monster hit with an instrument version of "Don't Be Cruel." Scotty talked to Sam about doing some instrumentals of his own. "Yeah, we'll do that," Sam told Scotty. But the weeks stretched out to months and it didn't happen.

That summer, Robbie Dawson, a young singer with a group called the Carousels, started doing backup work at the studio, backing Ace Cannon and others. Scotty started taking her out. "I remember one club where if you didn't have a tie they would loan you one," says Robbie. "Once I got to know [Scotty], I wanted to be around him. He's jolly, you might say. If you are a person he likes, he lets you know in a hurry." Sam told Robbie she sang like Kitty Wells, but her singing career never got off the ground. Her affair with Scotty in 1960 was brief (she also dated Elvis's cousin Bobby Smith around that time), but she was destined to reenter his life further down the road.

❊ ❊ ❊

In February 1961 Scotty joined Elvis for two performances at Ellis Auditorium in Memphis. Also in the band were D. J. Fontana, Floyd Crammer on piano, Boots Randolph on sax, and the Jordanaires. Conspicuously absent was Bill Black, who had continued to put distance between himself and the Presley organization. Bill was angry over the way he had been treated, and he occasionally expressed those feelings to family and friends, but mostly he kept his hurt feelings to himself.

The shows at Ellis Auditorium marked Elvis's first live performance since the Sinatra television special in March 1960. He had made three movies—and recorded three sound tracks—during the eleven months since that last performance. For the remainder of the decade, Colonel Parker would push him to complete three movies a year. The way Parker figured it, Elvis's price of $1 million per movie was more lucrative than doing a concert tour.

After the release of *G.I. Blues*, critics accused Elvis of abandoning

Hotel Fontainebleau

1. Heart Break Hotel — (E)
2. All Shook Up — (Bb)
3. Fool Such as I — (C)☆
4. I Got A Woman — (E)
5. Love me — (F)
6. Such a Night — (E)
7. Reconsider Baby — (E)
8. I Need Your Love Tonight — (G) Boogie
9. Thats All Right — (A)
10. Doing' The Best I Can — (G)
11. Don't Be Cruel — (D)
12. One Night — (E)
13. Are You Lonesome Tonight — (C)
14. Now or Never — (E)
15. Swing Down — (F)
16. Hound Dog — (C) (Get The Hell out)

Scotty's handwritten set list for the Ellis Auditorium shows, written on Hotel Fontainebleau stationary from their Miami stay in 1960 (Courtesy of Scotty Moore)

rock 'n' roll. Scotty found that amusing. He never thought they were playing rock 'n' roll. He considered it pop music. If his guitar solos were later used to define rock 'n' roll, that was fine as long as people realized it represented only one style with which he was experimenting. "I never liked the term 'rock 'n' roll' for Elvis and what we were doing," says Scotty. "Rock 'n' roll, to me, was strictly more black blues—Laverne Baker, artists of that era. That's what rock 'n' roll came out of. They used that term so much in their lyrics. What we did was more bop, more out of the old jazz-bop thing, with a country-blues feel to it. Like Bill Haley—I consider him more bop. He had a great jazz guitar player. That solo on 'Rock Around the Clock' will stand forever. The only thing I came close to with that type feel was the solo on 'King Creole.' Today, Michael Jackson is considered king of pop, but I don't consider anything he does pop. He's more rock 'n' roll. Is 'Don't Be Cruel' rock 'n' roll? No, it's pop. 'Heartbreak Hotel'? Go over the later things Elvis did. Are they rock 'n' roll? What he did is not even close to what the Rolling Stones do."

Certainly there was nothing rock 'n' roll about the concerts that day at Ellis Auditorium. Proceeds from the concerts and the $100-a-plate luncheon that preceded them were earmarked for local charities. It was the social event of the year. Tennessee governor Buford Ellington, who had issued a proclamation celebrating "Elvis Presley Day," was in attendance, along with Memphis mayor Henry Loeb. RCA used the occasion to honor Elvis for selling seventy-five million records. Scotty cringed whenever he heard numbers like that. He was lucky to eke out $10,000 a year.[2]

Amazingly, he was able to put all that out of his head when he was onstage. The music was the thing, the reason he endured everything. No matter how much time elapsed between performances, the onstage communication between Scotty and Elvis was always in sync. They possessed a unique—some would say psychic—ability to know where the other was going musically. At times, Scotty felt as though he were reading Elvis's thoughts; it was that intense. There were plenty of times—when Bobbie needed things or their daughter, Andrea, needed to go to the doctor, or when it was time to file his taxes—that Scotty wondered why he bothered to remain on call for Elvis, or why he played his guitar at all, but once they were onstage together and the music was flowing and the crowds were cheering, there was never any question about why he was doing it.

The two shows at Ellis Auditorium were typical Colonel Parker concoctions. They included an impressionist, a comedian, a tap dancer, and a team of acrobats. The music created by Elvis, Bill, and Scotty may have spawned a cultural revolution, but for Colonel Parker it was just business as usual. They played seventeen songs that day, beginning with "Heartbreak Hotel" and ending with "Hound Dog," the song they always ended with. It was their most requested song. "He'd start out, 'You ain't nothin' but a Hound Dog,' and they'd just go to pieces," says Scotty. "They'd always react the same way. There'd be a riot every time." Scotty wrote out the playlist for that day on a sheet of stationary he had saved from the Hotel Fontainebleau. There were sixteen songs on the list, along with the key for each song. After "Hound Dog" Scotty scribbled, "Get the hell out!"[3]

After the show, Elvis hosted an all-night party at Graceland. Scotty and Bobbie didn't go. They no longer felt comfortable in Elvis's private world. Elvis had flown Priscilla Beaulieu to Memphis from Germany for

---

[2]In 1960 Scotty Moore appeared on the Sinatra special with Elvis, played on his recording sessions, appeared in *G.I. Blues*, and went to work for Sam Phillips at his studio. His total income that year was $8,339.38, of which $1,582 came from Elvis Presley.
[3]See appendix.

Christmas, but she left after celebrating New Year's with him and was not there for the celebration that followed the shows at Ellis Auditorium. Elvis had asked her father if she could move to Memphis, but he told Elvis he didn't think that was a good idea. Priscilla made Parker nervous. Jerry Lee Lewis's career was destroyed almost overnight by his marriage to his teenage cousin; Parker urged Elvis to be discreet.

Actually, Elvis's attraction to Priscilla was not as much an aberration then as it seems today. In the 1950s, when Elvis came of age, it was not uncommon in the South for adult men to go out with fifteen- and sixteen-year-old girls. Scotty did it; Bill Black did it. Preachers of that era did not discourage such unions unless the men didn't do the "right thing" by marrying them if the girls became pregnant. It wasn't considered a perversion unless the girl was a relative.

In March Elvis flew to Honolulu to begin work on his next movie, *Blue Hawaii*. While there he performed in a benefit concert to raise money for a memorial to the USS *Arizona*, one of the battleships sunk in Pearl Harbor by the Japanese. Performing with him were Scotty, Floyd Cramer, Boots Randolph, the Jordanaires, and Minnie Pearl, who closed the first half of the show. Scotty had made several stops in Pearl Harbor while serving in the Navy, so the concert had a homecoming feel to it. "You feel this air of tranquility there," he says. "It's restful. It's in the air."

The Hawaiian concert was notable for two reasons: first, it was one of the longest sets Elvis had played in a while (forty-five minutes); second, it was the last public performance he would give for more than seven years. Wearing the gold jacket he had first worn in 1957, Elvis closed the show with a five-and-a-half-minute version of "Hound Dog."

It was the last time Scotty saw Hawaii.

✳ ✳ ✳

With Elvis all but invisible as a recording artist, Scotty settled into a new career as a studio manager and technician. The technology of recording had always fascinated him. He wasn't getting rich working for Sam, but it provided him with a steady income. By October 1963 he had obtained a new guitar under his endorsement deal with Gibson: a Gibson Super 400 (Sunburst model). He traded his old guitar—the blond Gibson S 400—to record producer Chips Moman for a set of vibes, a small classical guitar, and eighty dollars in cash. Scotty had been asking Sam for money to buy a set of vibes for the studio, but Sam said he didn't have the money. Scotty sacrificed his guitar.

Memphis was exploding with hit records. Carla Thomas had cracked the Top 20 in 1961 with "Gee Whiz," recorded across town at Satellite, the studio owned by Jim Stewart and Estelle Axton. They followed up that hit later in the year with "Last Night," an instrumental by a young group of studio musicians who recorded under the name of the Mar-Keys. "Last Night" peaked at No. 2. The following year, with the name of the studio changed to Stax, they scored with another monster instrumental, "Green Onions," recorded by Booker T. & the MGs.

Scotty told Sam that he really wanted to try his hand at doing instrumentals. Sam didn't say no; he didn't say yes. He kept putting Scotty off, promising to give it some thought. Scotty couldn't figure it out. The Memphis studio was often booked, but the studio in Nashville was generating more business. Scotty felt extremely frustrated. Memphis studios were gaining a reputation for churning out hit instrumentals: the Bill Black Combo; Booker T. & the MGs; the Mar-Keys. Why wouldn't Sam let him see what he could do? Maybe he could record a hit; maybe he couldn't. All he wanted was the chance to be competitive.

That fall, almost in desperation, Scotty asked Stan Kesler, who worked at the studio as an engineer—and several musicians—to come in on a Sunday morning when the studio was not booked. They had recorded three or four instrumental demos, when Sam Phillips showed up unexpectedly at the studio, interrupting the session. "I don't remember if he got angry, but it ended up I paid the studio myself, even though I was working there," says Scotty.

The tensions from the studio carried over into his marriage. Scotty and Bobbie did what couples often do in those circumstances: they bought a house, moving to Raleigh, a relatively new suburb in northeast Memphis, hoping a change in scenery would help. Scotty was miserable. He and Bobbie were fighting. Sam hadn't shown any interest in Scotty recording instrumentals. He was still being called in to play on Elvis's recording sessions for his albums and movie sound tracks, but that was not very satisfying financially or creatively. By that point, Scotty's only direct income from Elvis was a yearly bonus of $500.

To escape the frustrations he was experiencing with Bobbie and Sam, Scotty spent more time in the Nashville studio, where he met Billy Sherrill. The Alabaman was already working at the studio when Sam bought it; when it changed ownership he stayed on, working for Sam as an engineer. As a result, he and Scotty became close friends. They had a lot in common. Billy was six years younger, but they shared the same Southern heritage and they liked the same type of music. Billy hadn't worked for Sam long when he attracted the attention of executives at Epic Records in Nashville, who hired him as a producer. One of his first artists was newcomer Tammy Wynette. After leaving Memphis in 1956, she had moved to Birmingham, where she first got her foot in the door of the music industry as a songwriter.

During one of Scotty's trips to Nashville, Billy asked him why he hadn't done an album of instrumentals. Why indeed? When Billy suggested they do an album together for Epic Records, Scotty jumped at the chance. "I'd like to take the credit for having the idea," says Billy. "I think Scotty was too shy back then to want to be the star of his own album. I had always admired Scotty's style. I think he had the most unique style of any guitar player in the world. He did it before anyone else did it— those rock 'n' roll licks. I wanted to capitalize on the fact that he was the man who played the guitar that changed the world."

Billy Sherrill assembled an all-star cast for the session, which took place in late February or early March 1964. In addition to Scotty on lead guitar, he had D. J. Fontana and Buddy Harmon on drums, Boots Randolph on sax, Bill Purcell on piano, Jerry Kennedy on second guitar, Bob Moore on bass, and, of course, the Jordanaires.

"We gathered in a studio, and it was like, 'Well, what are we going to do?'" says Billy. "Someone said, 'Don't Be Cruel,' so we got Elvis's record out and listened to it and everyone did what they did on the record, except Scotty who would do what the voice did."

They went down the list:

Hound Dog	Milk Cow Blues
Loving You	Don't
Money Honey	Mystery Train
My Baby Left Me	Don't Be Cruel
Heartbreak Hotel	Love Me Tender
That's All Right, Mama	Mean Woman Blues

Billy wanted to title the album *The Guitar That Changed the World* and Scotty reluctantly went along with that, although privately he feared people would think he was boasting. Billy wanted to pay tribute to the man who had started it all. "I admire Scotty and I admire his contribution to music," says Billy. "He's in a class by himself. He is the rock 'n' roll player of the century. All those guys that came along, Jimi Hendrix, Eric Clapton, they can play faster, sharper, more compelling licks, but Scotty did it first. I'm sure there are better guitar players than Scotty that are around today. But they fed on his creativity. I don't know where he got his from—God, I guess."

The Guitar That Changed the World was one of Billy Sherrill's first projects as a producer, but he went on to become one of the most successful producers and songwriters in country music history. He had hits with Tammy Wynette, George Jones, Charlie Rich, Johnny Paycheck, Patti Page, and dozens of others. Today, when he looks back at the album he did with Scotty, he wishes more had been done to promote it. "The record company at the time didn't see the potential of the album and didn't work on it all that much," he says. "I think Scotty Moore made history. I was glad to be a part of that history."

Scotty was ecstatic over the album. For the first time in his career, he had a project that was his very own. For the first time, he had an album that would pay him royalties. When he got back to Memphis, he told Sam Phillips about the project. He thought Sam would be happy he had a deal with a major record label. Sam didn't say much when he told him; he sort of nodded and mumbled.

A few days later, Scotty received a hand-delivered letter from Sam dated March 17, 1964. "As you know I am real concerned about the events of the past week-end, and feel I must tell you that I feel a real trust has been handled with impropriety," Sam said in the letter. "I think under the circumstance [sic] all purposes, both for you and me, would be best served if you began to seek a new association." Sam was firing him because he recorded an album! Scotty couldn't believe it. Sam's letter continued: "I do not want you to feel that I do not appreciate your real and genuine dedication and concern for the companies you are associated with, but my faith has been severely taken to task, therefore, your continued affiliation with us will not be what I feel is a comfortable relationship. I do not, however, hold any malice in the matter and shall, and do, hold you in high regard. Also, your presence is welcome at all times and certainly until you make another connection that is satisfactory to you and your family. Further, please do not feel out of pride you have to leave immediately. This is not the case. As a matter of fact, you will be needed to help us avoid another 'immediate' departure. I shall be happy to recommend you, both as a person and as an employee, to whomever you approach for employment."

Scotty went home and told Bobbie.

"Aw, he does that all the time," Bobbie said.

"No, he means it this time," said Scotty. "He put it in writing."

Bobbie doesn't recall Scotty being particularly upset. "It was like, 'Well, I have to find another job,'" said Bobbie. "Sam had promised to do an instrumental album with him and he kept putting it off." Once Sam gave him his walking papers, Scotty started looking around for new opportunities. Stax Records was the hottest enterprise in Memphis, but it was pretty much a closed shop. Same thing with Hi Records, where

SAM PHiLLiPS RECORDING STUDIOS OF NASHVILLE & MEMPHIS, INC.

March 17, 1964

Mr. Scott Moore
639 Madison Avenue
Memphis, Tennessee

Dear Scotty:

As you know I am real concerned about the events of the past week-end, and feel I must tell you that I feel a real trust has been handled with impropriety.

I think under the circumstances all purposes, both for you and me, would be best served if you began to seek a new association.

I do not want you to feel that I do not appreciate your real and genuine dedication and concern for the companies you are associated with, but my faith has been severly taken to task, therefore, your continued affiliation with us will not be what I feel is a comfortable relationship.

I do not, however, hold any malice in the matter and shall, and do, hold you in high regard. Also, your presence is welcome at all times and certainly until you make another connection that is satisfactory to you and your family.

Further, please do not feel out of pride you have to leave immediately. This is not the case. As a matter of fact, you will be needed to help us avoid another "immediate" departure.

I shall be happy to recommend you, both as a person and as an employee, to whomever you approach for employment.

With kindest personal regard, I shall remain appreciatively for your association and hard work.

Appreciatively,

SAM PHILLIPS RECORDING SERVICE, INC.

Sam C. Phillips

Sam's termination letter to Scotty, March 17, 1964

THAT'S ALRIGHT, ELVIS

Willie Mitchell had been put in charge of production. Scotty had worked on some minor projects with Willie, but Hi Records was Bill's gig and the studio really didn't need a veteran guitarist/producer. Chips Moman was in the process of putting together his American Recording Studio, but it would be another year before he had it in full operation.

Scotty looked toward Nashville. He was motivated to begin a new life in a new city for more reasons than one. He and Bobbie had not been getting along. Not many marriages could have survived what they had experienced. The long separations, the road trips, all the glittery trappings of Scotty being "the man behind" America's reigning sex symbol dogged the relationship, but they probably weren't the most difficult to overcome. More damaging were the constant stream of work-related betrayals Scotty had experienced during their marriage. At age thirty-two, Scotty needed to try something different, and he needed to do it in new surroundings. He told Bobbie he was moving to Nashville.

"I think Scotty had been wanting to move to Nashville, and that was his opportunity," says Bobbie. "We weren't getting along too well at that time and that was when we separated. I didn't go to Nashville. We had just bought a house at Raleigh about six months before, so it didn't bother me too much, either. I thought, 'Well, now we can sell this house.' Sometimes you think something like that—a new house—will make you happy. But it doesn't."

Before leaving Memphis, Scotty sent Colonel Parker an acetate of *The Guitar That Changed the World*, along with a letter requesting an endorsement. "Recently I contracted with Epic Records, a division of Columbia to record instrumentally an album of Elvis' older hits," Scotty wrote. "With the understanding that if it met with any success the project would continue by volumes two, three, etc. I am enclosing herein, a copy of the first album and would deem it an honor if you would write the liner notes for Volume One. Of course, my first thought was liner notes by 'Elvis and The Colonel,' but realizing label policy knew this would probably be impossible. We have endeavored to present these selections with good taste and with a memorable flavor. Any thoughts you might have would be greatly appreciated. Here's hoping they will be pleasing to your ear."

Less than a week later, Scotty received a response from Tom Diskin, Parker's assistant. In a letter dated April 8 on Paramount Pictures letterhead, Diskin wrote: "Our hands are pretty well tied on what we can do on other labels, not only in the way of liner notes but there are restrictions that do not permit the use of Elvis' name in conjunction with another commercial record. We receive a great number of requests from the boys in the business and have to go along with the restrictions placed on us because of our association with RCA Victor. For that reason we have never done anything along the lines requested. We want to wish you good luck and hope that this LP is a big success, but mostly big royalties for you. KISSIN COUSINS is doing extremely well. We are still on the ROUSTABOUT picture. We are returning this acetate as we felt you may have use for it, and will be looking forward to the release of your album and I personally am going to buy one. You have to admit that is the best kind of endorsement."

It was yet another slap in the face. Scotty wasn't surprised, of course. He wasn't even offended. Actually, he never expected a response from Parker. Says Scotty: "If I had offered him $5,000 to write the liner notes, he might have done it. He never did anyone a favor that I knew of where he wasn't paid back tenfold somewhere down the line."

Buoyed by a contract for his first solo album—and dreams of royalties—he struck out for Nashville, leaving behind Bobbie and their three-year-old daughter, Andrea.

❉ ❉ ❉

When Scotty moved to Nashville in 1964, country music was in a state of flux, perpetuated to no small degree by the revolution in American music brought about by the music recorded a decade earlier by Elvis, Scotty, and Bill in Memphis. Country music didn't have a carved-in-stone direction in 1964. The biggest selling singles on the country charts were Roger Miller's "Dang Me" and Dottie West's "Here Comes My Baby." The hottest selling single on any chart was Roy Orbison's "Oh, Pretty Woman."

Former Memphis artists such as Orbison, Johnny Cash, Jerry Lee Lewis, and Charlie Rich were finding new success in Nashville, even as Elvis continued to record his albums and some of his sound tracks in the city, but country music's new wave—as represented by Willie Nelson, Tammy Wynette, Waylon Jennings, and others—was already in place, making Nashville both a pivotal and an exciting place to set up shop.

"I had made enough contacts in Nashville to start doing sessions, but I didn't want to do that," says Scotty. "My playing wasn't tuned in to the way they were doing sessions. Oh, I played on a few sessions. I really didn't care for that. You were restricted to three hours and had to do four songs and so on." Scotty was too much of a perfectionist to ever fit into the rigid studio system in place in Nashville—at least not as a player—and he knew that. The key to success in Memphis had revolved around unstructured sessions. That was the way he had learned it. He was too stubborn to learn new tricks.

Before Scotty left Memphis, Mort Thomasson, a recording engineer with Columbia Records, had talked to him about working for the record label as an engineer. He probably would have taken that job if he had not met studio owner Bill Conner. They discovered they shared a common goal. Conner wanted a bigger studio; Scotty wanted a studio, period. They found a studio that had gone on the market after its owners had filed for bankruptcy. It was in a good location, on Nineteenth Avenue, just off Music Row, so they pooled their resources and bought it. It had done business under the name Roi Studios. They renamed it Music City Recorders.

As Scotty's spirits soared over the purchase of the studio, they sank over the dismal showing his album, *The Guitar That Changed the World*, made on the charts and in record stores. It became clear to Scotty that the album was going to spawn neither hits nor royalties. Epic never pushed the album, reflecting a long-standing industry aversion to instrumentals. That was one way Memphis and Nashville were different. Memphis built an entire industry on instrumentals. Nashville avoided instrumentals whenever possible. That was one area where Scotty thought Nashville could learn a thing or two from its neighbor to the west. *The Guitar That Changed the World* never charted, dashing Scotty's hopes of receiving royalties for the music he helped create. The album didn't sell enough copies to pay production costs, and by 1996 $2,500 was still owed on the account.

Scotty brushed off that disappointment, as he had done so many others, and went about the business of building a new life. He and Bobbie weren't talking about divorce. Beyond getting a little breathing room, neither of them knew what they wanted from the other. All they knew for certain was that they didn't want to rush into anything.

However, a little more than a year after Scotty began his new life, tragedy struck his old friend Bill Black.

❋ ❋ ❋

For three successive years, the Bill Black Combo was named "Most Played" group in America by *Billboard* magazine and "No. 1 Combo" by *Cashbox*, a magazine published predominately for jukebox operators. By 1962 the group had four gold records—"Smokie (Parts 1 & 2)," "White Silver Sands," and "Josephine"—and a string of successful albums, including *Sexy Jazz, Solid & Raunchy*, and *Movin'*. It was reported in the *Press-Scimitar* that anything the combo released was given an automatic

Bill Black Combo, c. 1960. L to r: Bill Black, Carl McEvoy, Ace Cannon, Chips Moman, and Jerry Arnold (Courtesy of Colin Escott)

first pressing of 250,000. Bill reveled in the success, but the day-to-day business of looking after the group's interests, which increasingly involved television appearances and a worldwide touring schedule, became a chore. In 1962 he gave up leadership of the group to Bob Tucker, who already had replaced Reggie Young.[4]

For years, Bill had complained of headaches. His wife, Evelyn, thought it was from all the loud music and crowd noise, and the lack of sleep from being out on the road. In April 1965 he complained of pain across his temple and around his upper cheeks. Because he had not been out on the road recently, Evelyn talked him into going to the doctor.

[4]Reggie Young left the Bill Black Combo to become lead the guitarist for the house band at American Recording Studio. The band was popularly known as the 827 Thomas Street Band.

"I thought it was his sinuses, and he did, too," says Evelyn. "I took him to a doctor we had been going to. He took X-rays of his head and said he would get back in touch with us. About four or five hours later, he called and said he couldn't get a good picture. It was like fog. He wanted him to go downtown to the neurological floor at Baptist Hospital."

Evelyn took Bill to the hospital, but the admitting nurse mistakenly assigned him to the psychiatric floor. "He's not crazy," Evelyn told the nurse when she discovered the error. "I told her the doctor did not say psychiatric ward—he said neurological ward," says Evelyn. "She threw a fit and charged me $100 for the time we stayed there. I got the doctor's secretary to call her. I said I wasn't going to pay the $100."

Finally, Evelyn got Bill admitted on the right floor. After running some tests, the doctor took Evelyn aside and told her the news was not good. They had found a tumor on the left side of his brain. "We're going to have to open his head to see," the doctor said.

After the surgery, the doctor came out into the waiting room to talk to Evelyn. The prognosis was not good. He told her the tumor was about the size of a pecan. "I asked him if he got it all," says Evelyn. "He said they tried, but they had to take quite a bit of his brain to get what they got."

The doctor told her they would have to operate again. For that reason, they weren't going to sew him up. They were going to leave what he called a "floating incision." Before sending Bill home from the hospital, they would wrap his head in bandages. After he told Evelyn the bad news, the doctor broke down and wept. "What a waste for someone so talented," he said.

When Bill had recovered from the effects of the anesthesia, and was able to leave the hospital, Evelyn took him home to recuperate. The doctor told her not to discuss the surgery with him. If she needed to talk to others, he said, be sure to do it in another room where Bill wouldn't hear.

Evelyn was devastated by the news. Bill was only thirty-nine years old. They had three children—Nancy and Louis, both teenagers, and Leigh Ann, who was a little over a year old. Bill had been her lover, best friend, and soulmate since she was sixteen. She could not imagine life without him.

Over the next few weeks, Bill seemed to improve. Evelyn nursed him and took care of his bandages. She noticed that when the pressure built up inside his head, the bandages pumped up and down with each beat of his heart. But before long, his behavior became erratic, if only for short periods of time. One night he awakened and got out of bed while

Evelyn was asleep. He leaped down the eight steps from their bedroom to the ground floor—at that time they lived in a tri-level house—and ran out the back door into the driveway. Evelyn awakened when she heard him calling for his father. She ran outside and found Bill standing in his underwear.

"He was trying to find his daddy," she says. "But he had been dead for ten or twelve years." The doctors had told her not to argue with Bill, no matter what he said. With that in mind, she gently nudged him back toward the house.

"Bill, let's go back to bed," she said. "It's dark and your daddy's asleep. Let's not wake him up."

"Well, okay," Bill said, and went back into the house.

When Elvis heard that Bill was ill, he went by to visit with them. He took Evelyn aside. "He said he was sorry about Bill and that if anything happened he would not go to the funeral so it would not turn into a circus," says Evelyn. "He said he'd come back after everything was over with."

As soon as Scotty heard about Bill's surgery, he called D. J. They decided to meet in Memphis, with D. J. driving up from Shreveport and Scotty driving over from Nashville. "We met with Bill and had dinner with him," says Scotty. "He was his old jovial self and he looked great." They left thinking Bill had everything under control. However, according to Evelyn it was all an act for Scotty and D. J. Bill didn't want his friends to feel sorry for him. Even though neither she nor the doctors talked to Bill about the seriousness of his condition, she knew he was aware of everything.

One day, during one of his hospital stays, Bill greeted Evelyn with a question when she walked into the room. "Why you losing so much weight?" he asked.

"You know me," she answered. "I watch my weight."

Of course, there was a reason for her weight loss. "I was worried, that was what it was," she says. But her weight loss wasn't the only thing Bill had on his mind. That day's newspaper contained a story about actor Robert Taylor's death from a brain tumor. Bill showed the newspaper to Evelyn. The story described Taylor's symptoms and how the tumor had made him act.

"That sounds like me," Bill said.

By fall, Bill's condition worsened. The doctors had operated on him twice. They told Evelyn that if they operated a third time, it would leave Bill a vegetable. "They asked me what I wanted them to do," says Evelyn. "I asked the doctor if he would do it if it was his family. He said no."

Evelyn told them not to operate.

"The Blacks got upset with me," she says. "They said, 'We've always heard three is lucky.' I said, 'You may have heard everything, but hear this: I'm not going to let them cut on him anymore.'"

The last week of his life, Bill lapsed into a semicoma. He didn't say much toward the end. He smiled at Evelyn and squeezed her hand. On October 22, 1965, Evelyn and other family members were sitting in the hospital room with Bill when the nurse looked in on them. They had been there about eight hours that day. The nurse suggested they go get something to eat.

"I hate to leave him," Evelyn said.

"He'll be fine," the nurse said.

After eating, they returned to the room—but Bill was dead.

The funeral was held at Bellevue Baptist Church, with burial in Forest Hill Cemetery. Scotty and Bobbie went to the funeral with D. J. Fontana and his wife, Barbara. Scotty and D. J. were pallbearers. Afterward, they went out to Graceland to commiserate with Elvis. Everyone was stunned by Bill's unexpected death. No one knew quite what to say.

"Elvis was sitting out on his motorcycle when we arrived," says Bobbie. "The bodyguards were there. Priscilla came out the door and stood around with the bodyguards, but she didn't come over where we were and Elvis didn't introduce her to us. We didn't stay around too long." When Bobbie said goodbye to Elvis that day, it was for the last time. She would never see him again.

True to his word, Elvis went by to see Evelyn again after the funeral. This time, he took Priscilla with him. By then, Priscilla's father had relented and allowed her to move into Graceland with Elvis. "I told him how much I appreciated him coming by," says Evelyn. "I always thought a lot of Elvis. He didn't get messed up until after Scotty and Bill got away from him. He was just a young boy who loved music and loved to shake those hips and make the girls scream."

With Bill gone, Evelyn turned her attention to raising their young family. "It was a good marriage," she says. "He was gone a lot, but I took it in stride. I stayed with him through thick and thin. It's just a shame—someone dying that young."

9

"COMEBACK" SPECIAL:
A FAREWELL PERFORMANCE

Sometime after Bill Black's funeral, Scotty and Bobbie got back together. Death has a way of encouraging people to count their blessings. In 1966 Bobbie and Andrea moved to Nashville to live with Scotty. Andrea would turn six in time to start school that year. Bobbie was reluctant to give up a secure job with Sears, but she wanted Andrea to have a live-in father when she entered first grade.

By that time, Music City Recorders was up to speed. Scotty had settled into a routine as an engineer. Instead of playing music, he worked the dials that transferred the music to tape. To him, both aspects—performing and engineering—were equally challenging. As a musician, his job was to make his instrument complement the singer. As an engineer, his job was to transfer the singer's concept of the music to the reality of tape. Ideally, what the singer and producer heard in their heads would be what they heard on the playback in the control room.

In the beginning Scotty seldom did production work on his own. His main focus was on getting the studio established. However, he did continue to work with Thomas Wayne, who had moved to Nashville to help Scotty out in the studio. Eventually, Scotty expanded into production. He released several singles of Thomas Wayne, including "Don't Come Runnin'"/"Kiss Away," distributed on Racer Records, but none of the singles were hits—and Thomas Wayne's career continued to flounder.

Scotty, along with Rayburn Anthony, coproduced two singles by Jeris Ross, "Brand New Key" and "Old Fashioned Love Song," that made the country charts. When Elvis recorded albums or movie sound tracks in Nashville, Scotty usually was asked to attend the sessions. As a diversion from the day-to-day routine of operating a studio, the Elvis sessions were always welcome, but as a source of income they amounted to little more than pocket change.

By 1966 Elvis was churning out three movies a year, but he was making no public appearances and his recording career was almost nonexistent. Between October 1965 (the month of Bill Black's death) and October 1967, Elvis placed only one record in the Top 20, "I'm Yours"; he had not had a No. 1 record since March 1962.

Dominating the charts in the mid-to-late 1960s were British groups such as the Beatles and the Rolling Stones. From Memphis, a motley crew of young white and black teenagers under the direction of Jim Stewart, Chips Moman, and Willie Mitchell collectively made it the center of the American soul and pop universe with hits such as the Box Tops' "The Letter," Sam and Dave's "Soul Man," and Otis Redding's "(Sittin' on) the Dock of the Bay." Sam Phillips's studio got in one last hit with "Lil' Red Riding Hood," recorded by Sam the Sham & the Pharaohs and produced by Stan Kesler.

As the Memphis studios exploded with talent, Elvis sank further into the protective environment of Graceland. For the first time in his career, newspaper and magazine stories about Elvis focused on what he was *not* doing with his life. Had he given up on rock 'n' roll? An Associated Press article accused him of purposely hiding from the public. By the end of 1966, Elvis decided to marry Priscilla. She had been living at Graceland since 1961 and the rising tide of negative publicity made the relationship a potential threat to his career. Elvis proposed to Priscilla in December and they were married on May 1, 1967, at a private ceremony in Las Vegas.

Scotty had seen Priscilla from a distance on the day of Bill Black's funeral, but he had never met her. All he knew about her was what he had heard from mutual friends and what he had read in the newspapers. By then Elvis's love life wasn't a major concern for Scotty. Once again, his marriage to Bobbie was falling apart. The Nashville experiment wasn't working out the way they had hoped. In 1967 Bobbie took Andrea and moved back to Memphis, where she was able to get her old job back at Sears. The following year, after fifteen years of marriage, Bobbie and Scotty called it quits and filed for divorce. Bobbie worked for Sears until they closed their Crosstown branch and forced her into early retirement. She never remarried.

✻ ✻ ✻

By the spring of 1968, Scotty was again headed toward a serious relationship. Emily Hastings was a twenty-five-year-old hairdresser who was no stranger to the record business. Her sister, Charlene, was married to record producer Billy Sherrill, and Emily had dated Phil Everly and Johnny Rivers, two of the most successful entertainers in Nashville. Emily had run into Scotty at Sherrill's house over the years, but she never thought about him as a potential mate. He was a thirty-six-year-old studio owner, a quiet, behind-the-scenes player in the music scene; she was a striking, vivacious redhead in her prime, well known to the movers and shakers in Nashville. She liked the excitement that accompanied the music business and she liked the glitter and the fine things that usually went with it. Scotty was definitely not her type.

One day in early spring, during one of her chance encounters with Scotty, Emily told him she was having problems with her television. It was brand new, but she couldn't get it to work. Scotty offered to take a look at it. While there, Scotty asked her if she was involved in a serious relationship. She had been dating Freddy Bienstock, an executive with Hill and Range Songs, but it wasn't anything serious. Hill and Range was Elvis's publisher and in recent years Bienstock had taken on many of the responsibilities previously assumed by Steve Sholes. Bienstock wasn't one of Scotty's favorite people. He thought he used poor judgment in the songs he offered to Elvis. To Scotty's way of thinking, Bienstock and Parker were a matching pair of bookends: neither seemed to have Elvis's best interests at heart.

Emily agreed to go out with Scotty. She remembered him from Memphis, where, as a child, she had passed the dry cleaners and saw him standing in the doorway. "The first date we had, we went to a concert," she says. "We went to see a Spanish guitarist who was very famous. Scotty was absolutely in a trance. I didn't like it, because I didn't like that kind of guitar. Scotty kept looking at the guitarist's fingers. I've never seen anyone so excited. He talked about going backstage, but for some reason he didn't. I think it was because I didn't like it."

Emily was attracted to Scotty's lack of pretense. He was soft-spoken, polite, and never said anything bad about anyone. When she listened to *The Guitar That Changed the World*, the album produced by Billy Sherrill, she thought it was wonderful. But she thought it odd that she never saw him pick up a guitar. "He never mentioned Elvis," she says. "When we were dating, we would go places and musicians onstage would know him and they would introduce him and ask him up onstage. But that didn't impress me."

What did impress Emily was the way Scotty kept the conversation focused on her. The other men she had dated spent most of the time talking about themselves. Scotty didn't want to talk about himself. He was genuinely interested in what she thought about things. By May she had moved in with him. Scotty was living in Bellevue then, a fresh-air suburb on the western tip of Nashville.

Late one night the telephone rang. Scotty was at the studio and Emily was at home alone.

"Hello," she said.

"I'm trying to reach Scotty Moore," the caller said.

"Well, you've reached his home, but he's not here. Can I take a message? Who's calling, please?"

"Well, this is . . . ah, Elvis Presley."

"OK, fine. This is Elizabeth Taylor." Emily thought someone was playing a joke on her. The caller paused. Finally, Emily said, "Scotty is at a session. Why don't you call back later."

Later, when Scotty was home, the telephone rang again. The caller told Scotty that Elvis was trying to get in touch with him. When would be a convenient time for him to call back? Finally, Elvis called again. "I left the room," says Emily. "I always thought people were entitled to personal conversations."

Elvis told Scotty he had been asked to do a television special for NBC. The show would be taped, but he would be singing live in front of a studio audience. He hadn't done a live concert in seven years, since the 1961 benefit concert in Hawaii. Would Scotty be able to perform on stage with him? Scotty said yes, though not without some trepidation: he had not performed live since February 1961, when he had backed Elvis at Ellis Auditorium in Memphis.

Scotty hadn't seen Elvis since January, when they recorded "U.S. Male" for RCA. On that session Jerry Reed had played lead guitar and Scotty had played rhythm. By that time, Scotty had pretty much given up hope of ever again participating in a big way in Elvis's career. He was pleased to be invited to the sessions (pocket money was pocket money) and he didn't begrudge Elvis his success, but he never really expected ever again to share a stage with him.

When Emily came back into the room, Scotty told her about the conversation. They had planned on getting married in June, but since that was the month the television show would be taped they decided to postpone their marriage until August. Scotty asked Emily if she could get off work at the hairdressing salon to go with him to California.

"Scotty was excited about it," says Emily. "He was excited for Elvis because he knew it would be important for him. Elvis hadn't done a show before a live audience in a while. He was scared. We all were. I was scared for them."

Emily was in a whirlwind. She had only dated Scotty for three months, but he had proposed to her—and she had accepted—and now they were flying off to Los Angeles to do a television show with Elvis Presley. It was one hell of a romantic way to begin a marriage.

❈ ❈ ❈

By 1968 Elvis's films were no longer as popular as they once had been. NBC-TV approached Colonel Parker about doing a television special to be broadcast during the Christmas holidays. Parker agreed to let Elvis do the show, but made it clear he wanted it to follow the same format used by the movies. In addition, he said he thought the show should be built around Christmas songs. Steve Binder, hired by NBC to produce and direct the special, had other ideas. He wanted to do something with an edge: something a little more rock 'n' roll. Perhaps Elvis could talk to the audience and his musicians—initiate a dialogue with his fans.

Binder didn't mind sparring with Parker. Recently, he had produced and directed a television special starring Petula Clark. During the show, guest star Harry Belafonte had touched Petula on the arm, generating a firestorm of protest from viewers angered over what they perceived to be a violation of interracial etiquette. Binder hung tough with Parker, getting the Christmas playlist cut to one song, then, finally, to none. Then a battle arose over the band. NBC wanted to use its large orchestra. Binder had been talking to Elvis about his vision for the show. He knew Elvis wasn't happy about the direction his music had taken in recent years. For the show to capture the magic of the past, he knew he would have to take Elvis back to his roots.

Binder convinced NBC to allow him to add Scotty and D. J. Fontana. When Binder told Elvis he had NBC's approval, Elvis got so excited he called Scotty himself. But there was more to it than excitement. According to Elvis confidant Billy Smith, Elvis was scared to death about doing the show. In a way, Scotty and D. J. were Elvis's security blanket.

❈ ❈ ❈

The last week in June, Scotty and Emily flew to Los Angeles. Scotty would not check his guitar and amplifier into baggage; he carried both onto the plane. When they arrived at NBC's Burbank studios, they were held up in the hallway outside Elvis's dressing room. Once they got

**Scotty and Elvis: the "Comeback" special, 1968
(Photo © 1996 EPE, Inc.)**

inside, Elvis took Emily aside and explained the delay: Freddy Bienstock had been in the dressing room.

"I didn't know what to do," Elvis whispered to Emily. "I knew you went with Freddy."

"Now I know how you feel," she told him.

To avoid a scene, Elvis had Bienstalk unceremoniously ushered out a back door. "When I think about it, that was a nice thing for him to do," says Emily. "We would have walked in there and Freddy would have been sitting there. Elvis threw him out."

When Elvis saw Scotty, he fell into conversation with him immediately. There were no handshakes or phony greetings: they just started talking. To Emily, it was as if they resumed a conversation they had begun years before.

"Elvis looked great," says Scotty. "He was in good physical condition. Once we started talking, it was like old times, really. He was joking and talking about things we had done."

Emily sat next to Elvis, with Scotty at her side. D. J. sat across the room. The Jordanaires had been invited, but they were so heavily booked in Nashville they could not get away. Elvis's entourage filled the room, watching his every move. Says Emily: "Elvis picked up a guitar. I noticed he had on one of those wide things around his wrists. I said, 'What are those?'"

195

"Well, I do karate, and they are from that," he said.

"Well, they are stupid," said Emily. "They look like something from a concentration camp."

The room grew quiet. You could have heard a pin drop. Everyone looked at Emily. Finally, out of self-defense, she said, "Well, they do!"

"Hmmm," said Elvis.

"Elvis kept playing and he talked a while, but I could tell he was angry," says Emily. "Scotty didn't care one way or another. He just laughed. After that, they always put me next to Elvis. They were waiting for the next thing. I didn't know any better. Whether it was Elvis or the President, it didn't matter to me. I wasn't impressed. I had heard Elvis's music and certainly liked it, but I had never been a person who was starstruck. What he did for a living was to perform; what he was as a person was separate. I respected him for his creativity, but I wasn't going to get down and kiss his feet."

They talked about the show and the songs they could do. Then the subject of dinner arose. "We talked about going out to eat, but you can't do that with Elvis," says Emily. "You have to bring it in or go to his house. As we were getting ready to leave for his house, someone—I think it was

Lamar [Fike]—kept saying, 'We can't go yet, the car is not ready.' Elvis got flustered. He said, 'What do you mean we aren't ready yet?' Lamar kept saying, 'The car is not around yet.' I kept thinking, what is the big deal? Finally, one of the guys leaned over and said to me, 'We can't reach Priscilla.' I thought, what does that mean, you can't reach Priscilla? By then, it must have been right at twelve midnight or maybe one. In the limo, they kept calling the house, calling the house. When we arrived, Elvis told me Debbie Reynolds lived next door and he pointed out the house. The first thing he did when we walked in was to ask where Priscilla was. Everyone looked at each other."

"She'll be here," someone said. "I guess she's on her way."

"Uh-huh," said Elvis.

Everyone in Elvis's entourage was solicitous of him, but he was clearly irritated. They sat in a large circular room and tried to carry on a conversation. It was difficult to talk because everyone was so ill at ease. Elvis kept asking for Priscilla.

"Finally, someone came in and said dinner was ready," says Emily. "Just as we were being seated, in walks Priscilla. I was seated next to Elvis. There was an empty chair on the other side of Elvis. Priscilla came in and sat down. There was no conversation between them. No hello, goodbye, go to hell, where have you been? There was just this cold stare with heaping hunks of horrendous hate."

Midway through dinner, Elvis turned to Priscilla. "Where were you?" he said.

"Dance lessons," she said.

"It's two and three o'clock in the morning and you were at dance lessons?"

"Yes, that's where I was."

After dinner, Elvis showed Scotty, Emily, and D. J. around the house. They went into a sunken den that had a large fireplace with a mantel. Emily noticed a beautiful carved stone chariot on the mantel and commented on it. She was just making small talk.

"I know absolutely nothing about it," said Elvis.

"It's beautiful. I don't think I've ever seen anything like it."

"I'm sorry I can't give it to you because I don't own it. We're just renting this house."

"I wasn't asking for it," said Emily, slightly offended. "I was just admiring it."

Later, Emily asked Scotty about the incident.

"Elvis felt if you said you liked something, he was supposed to give it to you," Scotty said.

At first, that bothered Emily. Then, the more she thought about it, the more it embarrassed her to think that Elvis thought she was asking for a gift. When they returned to the living room, Emily asked Elvis for directions to the restroom. He told her he had no idea where it was located.

"Well, could you ask someone?" Emily said.

"Sure," Elvis said. From the look on his face, Emily could tell that he was embarrassed.

"When he found out, he got up and took me around to where we had been before and he pointed to the door," said Emily. "He said, 'It's in there.' I went into the bathroom and it was mirrored and I just knew there were cameras behind those mirrors. I had heard the stories. I said to myself, 'No, I'm not going to go.' I held it. When I got back with Priscilla again, we went back to the bedroom. I told her I had rather go to the one back there. She said that was fine. She was very nice—a tiny, petite woman, very small. I picked up that there were problems in the marriage.

"One of the bodyguards told me she was going with Mike Stone, who was the karate instructor. At the age I was, I didn't understand. I guess he told me so that I would tell Scotty. Everybody was nervous and you could see that something was wrong. The same guy told me that was the reason we had to delay leaving the studio. 'Normally, when we start home,' he told me, 'we can reach her at Mike's house and she goes home.' It was like, well, you're with Scotty, so we can tell you this.

"Priscilla had wonderful things to say about Scotty. She said Elvis talked about Scotty a lot and he represented an important part of Elvis's life and he had helped Elvis through some tough times and had never belittled him. She was so pretty, even with all that makeup on. She was like a little china doll. I must have weighed 120 pounds at the time. I would have made three of her. She was so much smaller than I was. It was like she had a child's body, but she was very, very pretty and very nice."

When Emily and Priscilla returned to the living room, Elvis started talking about their daughter, Lisa Marie. She had been born on February 1 at Baptist Memorial Hospital in Memphis, which would have made her five months old at the time. Elvis asked the nurse to wake her and bring her out to the living room.

Not surprisingly, Lisa Marie was unhappy about being awakened in the middle of the night. She cried when the nurse brought her out into the living room. Elvis bragged about Lisa Marie, obviously the proud father, but he made no effort to hold her. After a few minutes, the screaming baby was taken back to bed. It was an awkward moment for Elvis. He had asked for the baby without being really sure what to do with her.

Elvis, Scotty, and D. J. went into another room to talk in private. Emily and Priscilla went into the bedroom. "She showed me her closets," says Emily. "She had a makeup counter that must have been six feet long. I had never seen so much makeup."

Scotty thought it was unusual that Elvis wanted to talk to them in private. He usually felt free to talk in front of his bodyguards. When they were alone, Elvis asked if they would be interested in doing a European tour with him. Scotty and D. J. both said they would love to do it.

"He had talked about it when he got out of the Army, but he hadn't mentioned it again since then," says Scotty. "He turned to me and asked if I still had the studio in Nashville. I said, yeah, and if we are going to do the European tour let me know ahead of time so I can get someone to fill in for me. He asked me what would be the chances of us going into the studio and just locking the doors for a couple of weeks to see what we could come up with. I told him sure, to just let me know when. He didn't say what was on his mind. I know he was tired of the movie songs. He might have wanted to go back to where we were in the early years. Knowing his mindset at that point in time, it gave me renewed hope. He just wanted to try something without somebody saying, 'That song fits this scene in the movie.'"

Elvis talked about his favorite 78 records from his teenage years, about how he had just about worn them out on the phonograph. He asked Scotty if his studio had the capability to transfer the records to tape. Sure, Scotty said. Elvis asked if he would mind doing that for him. He said he would get the records together when he returned to Graceland.

After they talked for a while, Elvis took them all out to the garage to see his cars. As they stood there admiring his fleet, Priscilla walked up behind Elvis and—in an obvious gesture of conciliation—lovingly put her arms around his waist. Elvis coldly pulled her arms away. "I thought, oh, oh, trouble in paradise," says Emily. "There was real anger there."

By that time, it was approaching dawn. With a wake-up call at 5:30 A.M., Scotty and Emily returned to the hotel to freshen up before reporting to the NBC studios at Burbank.

✳ ✳ ✳

On Thursday, June 27, they started taping at seven o'clock in Studio Four. They began with the amusement pier segment, then moved on to the "Little Egypt Club" and the discotheque segments. Elvis did well on the vocals, nailing them on first takes, but he sometimes floundered on the dance steps. Once he was supposed to break a bottle over an extra's head, but it wouldn't break. Elvis cracked up and everyone laughed. During one of the dance segments, a female dancer was supposed to slide her arms down his leg, but she was a little off target and ran her hand along his crouch. Elvis broke out into laughter. "I really like this," he said.

Except for a constant stream of women coming into the dressing room to see Elvis, Emily was the only woman allowed backstage. "At first there weren't any women in the room with him, but then he got used to me being around, and I started to see one woman after another," says Emily. "I didn't object to that, but they were kissing all over each other with other people in the room. It was more the women doing it than Elvis. I was the only other woman in the dressing room. Maybe that was the girls' way of letting me know they were with Elvis. Later, when I saw Priscilla again, I felt uneasy. I felt like I had betrayed her because I knew something she didn't know. I felt sorry for her, but I didn't know what to do. Scotty's reaction was that it was none of my business. He said, 'What you see is what I lived and this is why I don't want to be part of it anymore.' Then I began to understand."

When Elvis laughed, everyone laughed. If something funny happened—and he did not laugh—no one else in the room laughed. Says Emily: "Elvis said things to people I would not have liked if I had been one of them. Things like talking down to them, being sarcastic, treating them with total disrespect. He never did that with Scotty. He never said to Scotty, 'Go get me this or that.' He treated Scotty entirely different than the way he treated the others."

At one point, Emily said she wished she had a Coca-Cola.

One of the bodyguards looked at her in horror. "Elvis drinks Pepsi," he said.

"I can't help what Elvis drinks," said Emily. "I drink Coca-Cola. That's what I want."

Suddenly, the room sank into a stone cold silence.

"You," said Elvis, motioning to one of the bodyguards. "Go get her a Coke."

The bodyguard hurried down the hall to get the Coke.

"There was a line he wouldn't cross with Scotty, and that was obvious," says Emily. "He would watch Scotty, and before he said something to Scotty he would think about it, whereas with someone else he would mouth off. He always had something to say about someone who left the room and I always felt like he never did that with Scotty. I think Scotty knew everything there was to know about Elvis, but he never brought up his faults. They had this mutual respect for each other and there was a line neither one of them would cross."

✳ ✳ ✳

One of the best ideas Steve Binder had was to place Elvis on a small stage in the round. With him on the stage were Scotty, D. J., Charlie Hodge, and Alan Fortas. Off-camera was an electric bass player. Although Hodge was an accomplished rhythm guitarist who had been with Elvis since he got out of the army, he was there primarily to offer moral support, along with Fortas, a member in good standing of the "Memphis Mafia." Fortas, the nephew of former Supreme Court Justice Abe Fortas, who resigned from the High Court in 1969 under scandalous circumstances, sat on the stage with his back to the camera and never attempted to play a musical instrument. A Memphis high school football hero, Fortas had joined Elvis's entourage in 1958 and served primarily as a bodyguard, although for a time he managed Elvis's Circle G Ranch located south of Memphis.

Before going onstage, Elvis, Scotty, and D. J. rehearsed in the dressing room, picking, jamming, singing, cutting up—it was like the old days. Binder told them to play anything they wanted to play when they got before the audience. By the time they hit the stage at six o'clock that evening, they were ready for anything. Elvis wore a black leather outfit that had been chosen especially for him by a costume designer who mistakenly thought Elvis was famous for wearing black leather. The outfit was uncomfortable, but Elvis liked the way he looked in it.

"I was really surprised at how good looking Elvis was," says Emily. "His photographs did not do him justice. He was absolutely gorgeous. There isn't another human being who looked like Elvis. He had charisma and he was destined to be who he was. I thought, what a magnificent looking man, just gorgeous. But he wasn't a man I would have personally been attracted to. I admired him more than anything else."

The nearer they came to show time, the more anxious Elvis became. "He kept saying, 'I'm nervous. I won't be able to do this. What if they don't like me?'" says Emily.

"Scotty, don't let me come in too soon," said Elvis.

"Don't worry about it," said Scotty.

When they walked out on stage, their guitars were already in place. Scotty had his Gibson 400 Sunburst and Elvis had his Gibson J200, a natural-grain flattop model that Scotty had obtained for him from the manufacturer. They began the show with some of their early material: "That's All Right, Mama" and "Are You Lonesome Tonight." At one point, Scotty suggested a song title. Elvis looked shocked. "That's the first words you've said onstage in fourteen years," he said, smiling.

It was the best Elvis had sounded in years. The music was lean, sparse, just like it had been that first week in Sun Studio fourteen years ago. During the first couple of songs, Elvis kept glancing at Scotty, who was sitting to his left. Scotty's brightly colored guitar shone in the camera lights. It was bigger than Elvis's guitar, it was better looking, and it sounded better than his guitar. Elvis decided he just had to have it.

"Scotty was playing lead for a while and all of a sudden Elvis wanted to play lead," says D. J. Fontana. "So he goes over and grabs Scotty's guitar." D. J. was horrified. He knew how meticulous Scotty was about his guitar. "I thought, 'What are we going to do here.' Scotty wasn't very happy about that. Elvis was a flogger and I knew he was afraid he'd scar up the guitar. It worked out, but oh boy, he doesn't like anyone to touch that guitar."

Elvis played Scotty's guitar for the remainder of the show. It is the guitar with which he was most often photographed in promotion photos for the show; it is the guitar on the cover of the videocassette. At one point, Elvis said, "I think I'm gonna put a strap on this and stand up." He looked over at Scotty. "Got a strap?" he asked.

Scotty didn't have a strap.

Elvis stood, balancing the guitar on his thigh as the strummed and sang, "One Night with You." If Scotty was fuming on the inside, he never showed it. He kept going, never missing a beat, playing Elvis's guitar with the same determination and skill he had done with his own. Elvis was the star, so he wanted the biggest, flashiest guitar—but there was more to it than that. Elvis, above anyone else, knew how Scotty was about his guitars. By taking his guitar from him onstage, Elvis was subjecting Scotty to a test of their friendship. They both knew what the gesture meant.

They did two hourlong shows in the round that night. Critics later were unanimous in their praise of the performance. People who had not been around in the early years to hear Elvis, Scotty, and D. J. together were amazed at the stark power of the music. When the show aired on December 3, 1968, it was the highest rated program of the week. Writing

Scotty and Emily on their wedding day
(Courtesy of Emily Sanders)

in the *New York Times*, Jon Landau said: "There is something magical about watching a man who has lost himself, find his way home." From that point on, the show was referred to as Elvis's "Comeback" special.

* * *

On the plane back to Nashville, Scotty and Emily sat in silence, more tired than anything else. They didn't talk about the show. They didn't talk about Elvis. They viewed the trip as sort of a midsummer outing. For Emily, it was also a lesson in Elvis Presley economics. "The trip ended up costing us money," says Emily.

Despite her young age, she was savvy to the ways of the music business. Emily could tell that Scotty had a lot on his mind. The "Comeback" special was more than just a seminal event for Elvis, it was a potential turning point for Scotty. A part of him wanted to be excited about the European tour Elvis discussed with him and the talk of a behind-closed-doors recording session at his studio in Nashville. Another part of him was afraid to be excited about it. At thirty-six, he didn't want to be disappointed again.

On August 28, 1968, less than a month after they returned from Los Angeles, Scotty and Emily were married. In many ways, Emily was Scotty's exact opposite. She was outgoing, vivacious, a risk-taker who encouraged him to push the envelope. Scotty fell hard for Emily. In the throes of middle age, he was mesmerized by her vitality and her youthful optimism. For the first time in his life, he awakened each morning as excited about the woman lying next to him as he was about his music. It wasn't so much that Emily made him feel younger, it was that she made him feel alive.

Scotty and Emily bought a small, A-frame house on one of the highest hilltops in Nashville. It was a gingerbread house, warm and rustic, a romantic enclave for two people starting out on an adventure. Scotty pushed himself at the studio, working fourteen- and sixteen-hour days. He wanted to give Emily everything she wanted (and deserved). With his income from the studio hovering around the $12,000-a-year mark, he knew that would be difficult. For that reason, he looked with growing anticipation toward touring with Elvis. It was just the financial infusion he needed.

Scotty waited for word from Elvis.

Sometime that fall he received a small briefcase from Elvis. It was filled with 78-rpm records, many of them showing obvious wear. "When I saw them, I remembered them from when I first went to his house," says Scotty. "He played them on one of those wind-up record players."

Scotty with Elvis's favorite 78s (Photos by James Dickerson)

Scotty examined the record collection. Included were Ray Charles's "I Got a Woman"/"Come Back," Roy Hamilton's "Hurt"/"Star of Love," Fats Domino's "Ain't That a Shame"/"La-La," and Carl Perkins's "Matchbox"/"Your True Love." "I made two copies," says Scotty. "I sent one copy to him and filed the other one in the studio. I didn't want to ship the 78s because they were already in such bad shape, so I kept them, planning to hand them back to Elvis personally at our next meeting—but I never saw him again."

When the television special aired, Scotty received a letter from Jim Beedle, a disc jockey at WXCL in Peoria, Illinois. "I watched the 1956 gang totally wipe out NBC a couple of weeks ago, and the nostalgia was great," he wrote. "I have always been a fan of the great Elvis, and it was so good to see him back in action again. I really think what I dug about his records at the beginning was that knocked out lead man, and then found out it was you. I play the Epic LP *The Guitar That Changed the World* quite often on my shows, and it never fails, someone will call and wonder who that was." Beedle ended his letter by thanking Scotty "for bringing back 1956—the original happening."

Scotty waited for word from Elvis. The year was drawing to a close. The few times he tried to contact Elvis directly, his calls were shunted aside, lost in the underling shuffle. He wasn't surprised. He figured it was Parker's doing.

When he finally heard something, it wasn't the news he expected. Word came that Elvis was going to record a new album in Memphis. It would be produced by Chips Moman at American Recording Studios. It would be the first time Elvis had recorded in a Memphis studio since the early days at Sun. Scotty thought that maybe the new album would be used as a send-off vehicle for the European tour. At last, something was happening. Scotty waited for a call to report to the studio. That call never came.

Unknown to Scotty, Chips Moman refused to record with anyone except his house band. Moman had a string of more than one hundred hits using the same band, and he wasn't about to change his way of doing things, not even for Elvis Presley. As a tribute to Scotty, Moman took his blond Gibson to the studio and gave it to Reggie Young to play on the session. "That's what I thought of Scotty," says Moman. "His music changed my life. If I had it all to do over again, he would have been invited to that session."

Early on, Moman had a run-in with Parker over publishing rights to the songs Moman brought to the session. Parker called him aside and told him the publishing would have to be assigned to Elvis. Moman bristled at that suggestion. "I'll tell you what," he told Parker, "if you feel that way we'll just wrap this session up right now and consider these songs very expensive demos."

Parker backed down and the session continued.

The Memphis session gave Elvis his first No. 1 hit since 1962, "Suspicious Minds." Critics said it was Elvis's best work since the early days at Sun. Scotty was used to disappointments, but Emily was not. It was one thing to be let down by Elvis—he was used to that—but it was something else to feel that he was letting down Emily.

Scotty took the exclusion as a personal affront. What he did not know at the time was that it was not Elvis's or Parker's decision to exclude him from the session. It was not even Moman's decision, since using musicians other than his own house band was never a consideration for him. Moman could no more have used other musicians than Scotty could have upended his sock drawer. The 827 Thomas Street Band was at the core of his belief system.

Unknown to Scotty, Moman was one of Scotty's biggest supporters. "One of the things I missed with Elvis was his old band," says Moman. "I always liked Scotty and Bill and D. J. Fontana. I thought they were really unique. In my opinion, up until the 827 Thomas Street Band cut him, no one took an interest in his music after Scotty and Bill were gone. It was just a job for him. You could hear it on his records. Everything was rushed. I always thought it was sad that Scotty and Bill didn't stay their whole career with Elvis. They were unique together."

If the January 1969 Memphis recording session was a disappointment, news that same month that Elvis was planning a Las Vegas engagement was an even bigger blow. Scotty was told flat out there would be no European tour. Scotty met with D. J. and the Jordanaires to discuss the Las Vegas job. For them to all drop everything they were doing in Nashville to go there for two weeks would amount to a significant loss of income.

"We got together and did an estimate," says Scotty. "I don't remember the figure, but we told them we would have to have 'x' amount to make it worthwhile. They hit the ceiling, I'm sure. If we had known they were going on the road, it might have changed the picture. We might have sacrificed on the chance the other things would happen, but no one told us anything about going out on the road afterward."

Says Gordon Stoker of the Jordanaires: "We would have had to get out of thirty-four scheduled sessions. It wasn't financially feasible for us to do it." When Parker refused to pay them what they would have lost by giving up their work in Nashville, Scotty, D. J., and the Jordanaires said they would have to decline the offer. Parker responded by hiring James Burton, a respected session guitarist in Los Angles, to put together a band for the engagement. Reportedly, Burton was paid $5,000 a week as the band leader.

"The Vegas thing was the crowning blow," says Scotty.

Scotty washed his hands of the entire affair.

Then he put his guitar in its case and didn't perform live again for twenty-four years.

The Jordanaires with Scotty, center, at his home, 1996
(Photo by James Dickerson)

10

BEHIND CLOSED DOORS
WITH RINGO, TRACY, AND
A CAST OF THOUSANDS

"I live way the fuck out in Crib Death, Tennessee—my nearest neighbor is three-quarters of a mile away," says blues singer Tracy Nelson, describing the location of her farm west of Nashville, where she's lived for more than twenty-five years. There are many ways to get to that farm, but the road that led her there began in 1969 at Music City Recorders.

That year, Tracy and her band, Mother Earth, were out promoting their self-titled debut album. When the tour ended, they looked up from the road haze to get their bearings—and found themselves in Nashville. Their record label wanted a new album from them, so they decided to record it there. They rented a farm outside town and, working with producer Pete Drake, recorded a complete album at a studio named Bradley's Barn.

One day Drake took Tracy by Music City Recorders to meet Scotty.

"Of course, I knew who he was," says Tracy. "I was mystified by this Scotty Moore." She asked him about his guitar. He said, "Oh, I never play anymore."

It had only been a few months since he had retired his guitar, but—like the Wild West gunfighters who hung up their guns—the gesture had represented a serious commitment to abstention. Once he made up his mind to put his career as a performer behind him, Scotty devoted the same meticulous attention to detail when he started setting up a studio. Working with a Memphis carpenter, he rebuilt the interior of the studio, designing it with sound quality in mind.

"I kept thinking about wood," he says. "Why is there wood in a Stradivarius violin and in guitars?" He asked the carpenter about different types of wood. The carpenter suggested balsa, but that didn't sound right to Scotty. The carpenter then suggested cypress, a coniferous evergreen that thrives in the lowlands of Louisiana and Mississippi.

"We started checking around and found we couldn't get it in Nashville," says Scotty. "It would cost an arm and a leg to have it shipped in, so the carpenter went back to Memphis and checked with a couple of places and found a place where he could get the raw stuff right out of a mill. He brought back some samples. When I saw them, I knew that was it."

The cypress was cut into one-by-twelve planks and installed untreated on the studio walls. The raw, rough appearance of the cypress looked great and absorbed sound. It was perfect. Well, almost perfect. A couple of weeks later, when the soft, absorbent wood dried, it shrank, leaving half-inch cracks between the planks.

"I thought, 'Well, I'll be damned,'" says Scotty. "I went and got me a fruit tree sprayer and filled it up with water. Every few weeks, I wet the suckers down. It worked—and it also helped recycle the air in there. It took out the cigarette smell and made it seem fresh."

Scotty had no problem keeping the studio booked. To keep up with demand—and to support his new wife—Scotty worked as an engineer, pulling twelve- and fourteen-hour days. One of his regular clients for over five years was the Air Force, which used the studio to record its syndicated radio program, *Country Music Time*. The program was produced quarterly by the Air Force recruiting branch and distributed to radio stations across the nation. It was hosted by Technical Sergeant Perry Bullard and featured a wide selection of recording artists, including Ferlin Husky, Jimmy Dickens, Stonewall Jackson, and Charlie McCoy. The program was taped in the studio and transferred to vinyl discs and mailed out in six-disc sets to radio stations. In between the banter and the music were commercials designed to lure new recruits into the service.

❊ ❊ ❊

After their meeting with Scotty, Tracy and Drake decided to book Music City Recorders for another session with Mother Earth. Unlike the sessions with the Air Force, which were staid and well-heeled, the sessions with Tracy were wild and woolly.

At age twenty-two, fresh from the hippie and rock scene in Los Angeles—where Tracy was labeled the "new" Janis Joplin by the music

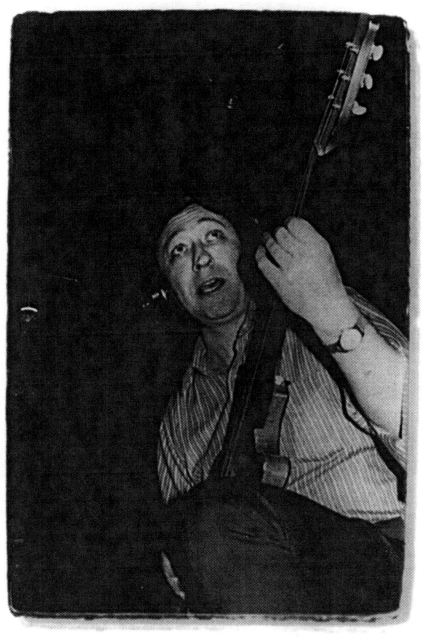

Scotty playing 6-string bass in his studio, c. late 1960s
(Courtesy of Emily Sanders)

BEHIND CLOSED DOORS WITH RINGO, TRACY,
AND A CAST OF THOUSANDS

Scotty with Tracy Nelson in the studio
(Courtesy of Scotty Moore)

press, a comparison Tracy despised ("I'm a better singer than she could have ever been")—she reveled in shocking the Nashville musicians who gathered around her in the studio. She talked like a man, cussed a blue streak, and used her simmering sexuality to her advantage. Occasionally, she showed up at the studio flashing a stash of marijuana.

Pete Drake's wife, Rose, laughs when she thinks about it today. "We had never heard women use four-letter words like that," she says. "When Tracy got around those country guys, she was so polite. Then, when she found out it embarrassed them, she just would not hush. She loved it. Scotty blushed, everyone did. Hippies hadn't really hit Nashville yet. They had the hippie look here but not the hippie ways. Pete took her into the front office and told her women didn't talk like that—and that just set her off. Some days she'd come in and say, 'Well, I'll be good tonight,' or she'd say, 'You guys have had it tonight.' They were afraid to bring people into the studio because they didn't know what Tracy was going to do next."

Scotty might have blushed, but he loved every minute of it. "We just hit it off from the beginning," he says with a wink. "If I hadn't been married to Emily, Tracy and I might have gotten together."

With Scotty as engineer, Mother Earth recorded a second album at Music City Recorders. When the album—*Make a Joyous Noise*—was released, it contained two discs: a "city" one and a "country" one. Playing on the country one, which was recorded at Music City Recorders, were D. J. Fontana on drums, Larry Butler on piano, Boz Scaggs on rhythm guitar, and the Jordanaires. A couple of times, Scotty brought out his guitar to play a couple of licks.

"We were just flabbergasted to have him on the session," Tracy says. "What was amazing was to sit around with Scotty every day. I'd think, 'Jesus, look at this. I'm shooting the shit with Scotty Moore.' If you got to be holed up in a room with someone, Scotty's the type of person you would want to do it with. He's very witty and has an appreciation of irony.

"I was curious about why he put his guitar away and on occasion I would ask him about it. He would say, without saying it, that he didn't want to talk about it. He felt really burned by how things went. He just decided the music business sucked and he didn't want to be in the middle of something like that. The studio was sort of a haven for him."

* * *

Ringo Starr and Scotty Moore had something in common. One had recently gone through a professional divorce; the other was in the process of getting one. By June 1970, when Ringo arrived in Nashville, the Beatles had announced their breakup. No one was surprised. Any fool could see there was trouble in Beatleland.

When "Let It Be" topped the charts in April, the No. 3 trailer on the charts was John Lennon's "Instant Karma (We All Shine On)." Ringo had already released a solo album, *Sentimental Journey*, a collection of standards produced by George Martin. Although there would be more chart toppers from the Beatles—"The Long and Winding Road" went to No. 1 on June 13, the week before Ringo arrived in Nashville—the Beatles clearly were pursuing separate careers.

Pete Drake met Ringo in England, where he had gone to do session work. George Harrison had introduced them. Pete was the premier pedal-steel guitarist in America. A native of Atlanta, Georgia, he moved to

Nashville in 1959, where his innovative guitar work made him a legend among studio musicians. Although his work pushed numerous singles to the top of the country charts—including Roy Drusky's "I Don't Believe You Love Me Any More" and George Hamilton IV's "Before This Day Ends"—it was not until he released a solo single, "Forever," that the public discovered his talents. By the time he met Ringo, he had recorded with Bob Dylan, Joan Baez, and Elvis Presley. For George Harrison, who had been experimenting with slide guitar, Pete was the real thing, someone he himself wanted to recruit for an album.

"Come on over to Nashville, and we'll do an album," Pete told Ringo.

"Well, OK," Ringo said.

When Pete returned to Nashville, he booked time at Music City Recorders for the latter part of June and asked Scotty if he would engineer the session. With Scotty's help, he put together twelve of the city's finest session players, including D. J. Fontana on drums, Jerry Reed on guitar, Charlie Daniels on acoustic guitar, Charlie McCoy on harp and electric bass, Jerry Kennedy on dobro and electric guitar, Buddy Harmon on percussion, Shorty Lavender and Jim Buchanan on fiddle—and, of course, the Jordanaires. All of the players were well known to Scotty. He especially liked Jerry Reed, with whom he had worked on sessions with Elvis. Jerry was the only man besides himself and Chips Moman who had ever stood up to Colonel Parker. That in itself was enough to endear him to Scotty.

The first thing Ringo did when he arrived in Nashville was to go to Ernest Tubb's Record Shop to get a stack of genuine country albums, then he went to Sears Roebuck to buy toys to ship back to his children in England. Pete registered Ringo at two hotels. At the hotel where he did not stay, he was registered under his own name. It was an attempt to sidetrack the fans and reporters who had gotten word of the session. Ringo actually stayed on the fourth floor of the downtown Ramada Inn. The hotel no longer exists, but at the time it was popular with celebrities who came to town to record on Music Row.

When Ringo arrived at the studio the next day, he was greeted outside the door by an off-duty policeman with a clipboard. Pete had hired him to keep out the curious and to provide protection for the ex-Beatle. Standing next to the cop was Emily Moore.

"Name, please," said the cop.

"Ringo Starr."

The cop ran his finger down the list on the clipboard.

"Ringo, Ringo, Ringo," he mumbled. Then he looked the "funny" Beatle squarely in the face. "Don't see it. You can't come in."

Thomas Wayne Perkins adjusts the microphone for Ringo
during the *Beaucoup of Blues* sessions. Ben Keith is at Ringo's left
(Courtesy of Scotty Moore)

Emily was dumbfounded. "That's Ringo Starr," she said. "He's the
reason you're here."

"Oh, yeah," the cop muttered. "Ringo Starr—you can go in."

What little ego Ringo still possessed—the press was already
wondering aloud what poor Ringo would do without the other Beatles—
was deflated as he entered the studio to face a roomful of Southern boys,
most of whom bore a healthy skepticism of Ringo's ability to do justice
to country music. Emily went in behind Ringo and told Scotty about the
incident. Scotty fell out laughing, but didn't tell the others. He kept it to
himself.

"Ringo was real quiet, but he was like one of the guys—a super nice
guy, real laid-back," recalls Rose Drake. "With Scotty being real quiet
and Ringo being real quiet, there didn't seem to a whole lot of extra conversation in the studio."

For D. J. Fontana, it was the first session he had ever played on in
which the singer was a drummer. Ringo played on a couple of songs, but
he was there to sing, not to play drums. "I have to give Ringo credit,"
says D. J. "Had it not been for him, that band would have fallen apart.
He was such a stickler for tempo. The guys would say Ringo wasn't a
drummer. I'd say, 'The hell he isn't!'"

The sessions lasted three days, going from about six o'clock in the evening to one o'clock in the morning. The studio was always packed. To satisfy public demand for information, Pete and Scotty allowed reporters from the *Nashville Tennessean* and the *Nashville Banner* into the studio for brief glimpses of the session. Incredibly, the reporters got Ringo mixed up with songwriter Sorrells Pickard, who wrote four of the twelve songs used on the album. When Ringo read the newspaper stories the next day, describing him as a heavyset, goateed man in a red shirt, he couldn't believe it. "They didn't even know who Ringo was," says Rose. "They kept describing Sorrells. Every move he made, the newspaper got it totally confused with Ringo."

After reading the newspaper story, Ringo protested to everyone around him: "But I didn't do that. I didn't do that!"

To everyone's surprise, Ringo blended in exceptionally well with the other musicians. If every once in a while they had a little fun with him, it wasn't because they didn't like him. Southern boys only fun around with people they like, or people they think they might be about to like. Sometimes Scotty or Pete would conclude a playback of a vocal with a comment that maybe it needed a little more echo.

Laughing good-naturedly, Ringo would respond, "Yeah, I guess we do."

One time they kept moving him away from the microphone until he was all the way out of the studio and down the hall and almost out the back door.

"Just a little bit further," they told him each time he moved.

"But you can't hear me," Ringo protested.

"We know, we know," they said, laughing.

Ringo took it all in stride.

"He worked like a real trooper," says Scotty. "They were using head arrangements that they made up on the spot. He only had the three days to learn the songs. He would start singing, and all the pickers would put it together."

"Whatever we wanted to do was fine with him," says D. J. "Sure, he struggled with the vocals, but I thought he did a good job. He's not a bad singer at all. He has that little English accent—yeah, I'd buy that album, sure would."

The day after they wound up the session they all piled into Pete's bus and went to Tracy Nelson's farm to take photographs for the album cover. Nashville photographer Marshall Fallwell, who was friends with both Scotty and Pete, was hired to take the pictures. He had been allowed into the studio for the entire session and did an admirable job of documenting the madness.

Ringo Starr, front row, fourth from left, with the band from the Nashville
sessions, photographed at Tracy Nelson's farm. D. J. Fontana sits on
Ringo's left (Photo by Marshall Fallwell Jr., courtesy of Rose Drake)

As surprised as anyone was Tracy Nelson. "We were sitting around
the house one day and Pete or Rose—I forget which one—called and
said, 'We're on our way out with Ringo Starr to take some pictures.' They
didn't want to give us any warning so no one would know where he was.
When they pulled up, I, of course, was trying to throw together some
lunch. Ringo was a vegetarian and all I had in the house was bacon."

Tracy, who had never met Ringo, was impressed by his shyness. "He
was very sweet," she says. "We had these horses and cows, and they
would come right up to the house. They wanted to take pictures of him
with a horse and it scared the hell out of him. I had to coax him to put
his hand out to give the horse sugar, but he ended up making friends
with the colt."

Before leaving Nashville, Ringo gave Pete one of his silk shirts. Pete had kidded him throughout the session about his wild clothes, which, in the land of rhinestone shirts and oversized cowboy hats, took more than a little gall on Pete's part. Ringo may not have had a deep appreciation of Southern humor, but he knew a good heart when he saw one. The shirt was an acknowledgment of that. The album was titled *Beaucoup of Blues* (after the lead cut) and was released by Apple Records. Pete did the project without anything in writing from Apple. People told him he was a fool to work that way, but he had faith it would work out.

"I think the world will be shocked when his record comes out," Pete told a Nashville writer. "[Ringo] worked his tail off. This should be the thing that puts Nashville music on Top 40 stations." Also expressing confidence in the album was Tommy Hill, the manager of Window Music Publishers, which held the American publishing rights to the songs. "I believe this is one of the best things to ever happen to Nashville," Hill said.

When the first single, "Beaucoup of Blues," was released in October, *Cashbox* selected it as one of its "Picks of the Week." Said the review: "This is a fine country single that because of Ringo's name and the pop overtones of the song itself should be going well on the pop side in short order." The song also was praised by *Billboard* and *Record World*. Unfortunately, the single never made it out of the 80s on the charts, but it did open the door for other hit singles by Ringo. Today the album, which was rereleased in 1995 by Capitol Records, is regarded as a landmark work by the ex-Beatle.

For his part, Scotty chalked up another "first," becoming the only person to work for the two most influential independent labels in record history: Sun Records and Apple Records.

✳ ✳ ✳

Speeding down the entrance ramp to Interstate 240 in Memphis, Thomas Wayne Perkins crossed four lanes of traffic, picked up speed, then shot across the median into incoming traffic, slamming into a car driven by Vance Simelton of Little Rock.

Seven hours later, Thomas Wayne was dead.

Police determined his death to be an accident, although there were indications he had floored his accelerator as he came off the ramp. They couldn't prove what he was thinking when his car went out of control— only that it did go out of control—so they wrote it up as an accident. Vance Simelton was in the wrong place at the wrong time.

Thomas Wayne was buried on August 17, 1971, at Madison Heights

Baptist Church in Hendersonville, Tennessee. Those who attended the funeral couldn't help but think how tragic it all was—and how ironic that his only success bore the name "Tragedy."

For more than a decade, Thomas Wayne had struggled to re-create the success of that 1959 hit. Scotty recorded countless sessions with him, released singles on his Belle Meade label, which he had begun shortly after moving to Nashville, and promoted him at every opportunity. Nothing worked. The public had decided Thomas Wayne's place in history was as a one-hit wonder. In the end, the best Scotty could do for Thomas Wayne was to offer him work in Music City Recorders. Scotty understood what Wayne did not understand: hit records are a flirtation from the public, not a promise of a long-term relationship.

Scotty wasn't surprised when he heard about Thomas Wayne's death. His behavior had grown more and more erratic over the years. "Every once in a while he would tend to get high and flip out on me," says Scotty, who attributed some of Wayne's problems to an ongoing and long-running dispute with his ex-wife, Charlene. In fact, he had gone to Memphis on the weekend of his death to resolve a conflict with Charlene over their daughter, Maria Elena.

Hugh Hickerson was also among those not surprised at Thomas Wayne's death. Hugh was an audio technician who often worked at Scotty's studio. After Thomas Wayne left Music City Recorders, he worked for Pro-Sound Productions, and then for a recording studio named NAR, where he was employed at the time of his death; Hugh continued to have contact with him on a professional level. They became friends, according to Hickerson, but were not what you would call "drinking buddies." Shortly before he died, Thomas Wayne made a startling confession to Hickerson. He confided that he had once parked his car across both lanes of the interstate one night—and turned off his lights. He did it at a blind curve that would have made it impossible for traffic coming at a high rate of speed to stop. Fortunately, the highway patrol arrived on the scene before an accident occurred. They found him sitting in the car, waiting for whatever was going to happen.

"He said he was arrested and they were going to send him for psychological evaluation, but he got an attorney who got him out of it," he says. "We talked about it. The impression I had was that he was doing it in order to achieve a violent end to his life."

The last time Hickerson saw Thomas Wayne was at the NAR facility on Division Street. He went to the studio late one night to repair some equipment. He didn't see Thomas Wayne when he walked in, but since he knew his way around the studio, he went to the back room where the equipment was located. Later, when he finished working, he walked back out into the studio. Someone was at the piano, but he couldn't tell who it was. As he walked closer, he saw that it was Wayne. From the look on his face—and the weird sounds he was making—he thought he might be in trouble.

"Is anything wrong?" asked Hickerson. He walked around the piano, taken aback by what he saw.

Thomas Wayne was having sex with a woman on the piano bench. Neither Wayne nor the woman was fully undressed, but they displayed no embarrassment at being interrupted.

"Excuse me," Hickerson said, and left. He never saw Thomas Wayne alive again.

"I sensed that he was very distraught with his life," says Hickerson. "Thomas Wayne wanted to regain that part of his life that he had lost. He was a nice guy, but he was one of those guys that, if you were around him, you could sense that he was suffering. There was some pain he was feeling. If he had not avoided that psychological evaluation, that might have enabled him to see it through. His death was such a tragedy, not only for himself but for the other man involved in the accident."

✻ ✻ ✻

Two of the three people with whom Scotty was most closely identified professionally—Bill Black and Thomas Wayne—were now gone, felled under tragic circumstances. At least Elvis was still going strong. Not going strong was Scotty's marriage. The harder he worked to provide for Emily, the longer the hours he put in at the studio, the more they seemed to argue about him never being at home. The more neglected Emily felt, the harder Scotty worked to make her happy. The faster that circle spun, the more Scotty drank to dull the pain. Then the drinking itself became an issue.

By late 1971 Robbie Dawson had come back into his life. She had married a military man and moved to Japan. When she began having problems with her husband, she returned to the States and called Scotty, initiating an affair that lasted well into 1972. One result of the affair was a daughter, Tasha, born on July 19, 1973. After the affair ended, Robbie moved to Mississippi, where she lives today. "I never asked Scotty for anything," says Robbie. "Just him knowing he has a daughter is enough for me. I loved him from day one—and, to the day I die, I will love him."

Emily never knew about Scotty's affair with Robbie. It was the drinking that got to her. One night, Scotty came home from the studio, maneuvered around the three sharp turns that made the drive up to his

Robbie Dawson with Scotty's daughter Tasha, c. 1980
(Courtesy of Scotty Moore)

mountaintop home an interesting exercise in motor-vehicle dexterity, only to be greeted by an empty house and a locked door.

When he couldn't find his keys, he smashed in the door with a sledge-hammer and went upstairs and went to sleep. "I knew then that the relationship was out of hand, and that's when I walked," says Emily. "Drinking kills a relationship, and I didn't want it to get any worse than it was."

Emily moved out of the house and filed for divorce. It was granted on November 22, 1972. "Scotty is not a person I ever thought I would marry, but I really fell in love with him," she says. "I will always love Scotty; we will always be close. I never doubted that Scotty loved me. I'm sure a lot of what happened was the pressure of him trying to do things for me. He pushed himself to the limit in a lot of ways."

In 1973, within months of the divorce, Scotty sold Music City Recorders and started working as a freelance engineer: have ear, will travel. Mostly he worked out of Monument Studios. He worked nights and slept days. Mort Thomasson, one of Monument's owners, preferred to work days, so that arrangement worked out well for everyone. Scotty had his own key, and he came and went as he pleased.

Gail Pollock was working for Monument when she met Scotty. He impressed her as a nice man, but she knew nothing about his background. He never talked about his past. One day Gail was in her office talking to a man who had dropped by to book studio time. Scotty came in to book some time for himself. Gail introduced the two men. They exchanged pleasantries and Scotty left.

"Is that the real Scotty Moore?" the man asked.

"Well, that's his name," Gail answered.

"You mean, the Scotty Moore, the one who played with Elvis?"

Gail had no idea what he was talking about. "No," she said. "He's an engineer."

Thomasson, who was sitting there when the conversation took place, laughed when the man left. "Scotty will dance at your next two or three weddings," he said.

"Why?" she asked, still not getting it.

"For not telling that guy he played with Elvis."

"Did he, really?"

"Hell, yes," Thomasson said.

Gail was speechless. "I didn't even know Scotty played guitar," she says. "I saw him several times a week—probably just about every day—and it never came up. He never mentioned it and no one else did either. I asked him about it, and he said, 'Yes, I'm guilty.' That was all that was said."

✻ ✻ ✻

Fiercely independent, Scotty's mother, Mattie Moore, lived alone on the farm for twelve years after the death of his father, Scott. As a teenager, she had promised to spend all her days with Scott—and she kept her word. She never remarried. She never built a new life to replace the one she had lived with Scott. Of course, living alone on a farm in Crockett County was not like living alone in a city. She had neighbors who cared about her. Help was only a phone call away.

By February 1975 her health was failing and she was admitted to a Jackson hospital for surgery. She wanted to go home to recuperate, but there was no one there to take care of her, so she was persuaded to enter a nursing home where she could receive twenty-four-hour-a-day care. Mary Ann Coscarelli, a dark-haired, dark-eyed schoolteacher who had met Scotty shortly after his divorce from Emily, volunteered to go to Jackson to look in on Mattie. She and Scotty dated off and on, and she lived with him briefly, but their relationship was volatile, punctuated by frequent arguments—which Scotty attributed to her hot-blooded Italian ancestry—but she thought the world of Scotty and was happy to do anything she could to help him.

Mattie was grateful for the visits. "She and I got on quite well," says

Mary Ann. "She was a very feisty lady, a very strong lady. I was concerned about her, as I would be for any human being going through that type of problem. I went to serve as a liaison, to keep the family members informed as to her condition."

Mary Ann's visits didn't extend past February. Mattie didn't recuperate well after her surgery, and, at age eighty-three, she passed away before the month was out, only days away from the anniversary of Scott's death. Mary Ann and Scotty went to the funeral together. Afterward, they gathered at Mattie's house with the rest of the family to reminisce about old times.

For Scotty, it was a hurtful time, because it reminded him of the isolation he felt growing up on the farm. He had learned that it was possible to feel loved by one's family and isolated from them at the same time. It presented an emotional dichotomy that would trouble him for the remainder of his life. What Scotty felt in his heart and what he was able to express were not always identical.

After his mother's death, Scotty threw himself into his work at Monument. He had lost both parents, his musical alter-ego (Bill Black), the symbol of his musical independence (Thomas Wayne)—and he had endured three divorces, the last of which had left him emotionally drained. Studio work is a notoriously effective salve for bruised spirits. The rooms are usually dim, almost dark, purposefully built to provide a womblike environment. Because music has a life of its own, it is easy to get lost in the mechanics of transferring it to tape; the process offers a unique opportunity to control and manipulate emotions with a flick of a switch or a turn of a dial.

Scotty thrived in that environment. If anything, he worked too hard. He engineered demo sessions for would-be singers and songwriters, as well as regular sessions for established artists. ("Just about every country singer in town came through at one time or another," says Scotty.) Sometimes he engineered sessions just for the hell of it, or just to help someone he felt had talent. Harpist Cindy Reynolds falls into the latter category. "[Scotty] made a tape of me with D. J. Fontana on drums and Bill Humble on bass," she told a reporter for the *Nashville Tennessean*. "[He] played it for producers in town just to get work for me—for no other reason." Others Scotty worked with during that time were saxophonist Norm Ray and harmonica player Terry McMillan.

Gail Pollock recalls Scotty working so hard he looked "like a turtle" because of back and neck strain he received hunched over the soundboard. "It was set up so he had to look to his side," she says. "He would sit for hours with his head turned to the right. He started walking stiffly

223

**Gail Pollock, arranger Don Tweed, and Scotty in the studio
(Courtesy of Scotty Moore)**

and couldn't unbend his neck. You could feel a knot on his shoulder. He
had to go to a chiropractor."

It was during this time that he renewed his friendship with Carl
Perkins. For the past decade, Perkins had toured with the Johnny Cash
band. He was a regular on Cash's network television show that ran from
1969 to 1971, and often was spotlighted with solos. The exposure
brought him a contract with Columbia Records that led to several albums, including *On Top* in 1969 and *Boppin' the Blues* in 1970. But by
the mid-1970s, Carl's career was once again in a down cycle.

Scotty had always liked Carl and respected his work, so in 1975 when
Carl asked him to play on "EP Express," a song he was recording for

Mercury Records, Scotty took his guitar out of storage and did the session with him. The lyrics of "EP Express," which was written by Carl, consisted of song titles from Elvis's recordings.

Despite their shared musical ancestry at Sun Records, it was the first time Scotty and Carl had ever recorded together. "I enjoyed his music," says Scotty. "He was a good ole country boy like I thought I was. We considered ourselves friends."

❄ ❄ ❄

One day Scotty bumped into another Sun Records alumnus—Jerry Lee Lewis—at a disc jockey convention. They met in Mercury Records' hospitality suite. They sat around talking, having a few drinks, going over old times. Of course, Scotty and Jerry didn't have any *good* old times. One thing led to another, and the subject of Scotty's guitar playing came up. Jerry told him he wasn't good enough to play guitar in his band.

D. J. Fontana, who was there with his wife, Barbara, remembers what happened next. "Chairs were going every which way, and Scotty and Jerry were rolling out in the floor," he says. "I thought, 'Damn, what are they doing?' Scotty was just beating the fire out of him, really. They were fighting to kill each other."

The sight of two forty-something-year-old men slugging it out in public is not a pretty sight in the best of circumstances. In this case, D. J. was friends with both men, so it wasn't something he wanted to witness. He hurriedly got Barbara to her feet and led her to the door.

"I didn't want to get in the middle," D. J. says. "I knew Scotty could take Jerry. I don't think they have ever really gotten along. They like each other, I think, but they just have different attitudes. When I saw them out there wrestling, I thought, 'Shit, I'm going home.'"

As the months went by, Scotty seemed to withdraw more into himself. He rented office space in the building at 1609 McGavock that housed Monument's warehouse. And with his mind made up about never performing again, he settled in for the long haul. Working as an engineer was about as far away from the music business as you could go and still stay in it. It was where Scotty wanted to be.

❄ ❄ ❄

On August 16, 1977, Scotty was at the studio when he received a telephone call from Emily. He was surprised to hear from her.

"Have you heard about it?" she asked. "About Elvis—he's dead. It's on the news."

What Scotty thought and felt that day is a blur to him today. Elvis's death came as a total surprise, a lightning bolt out of the blue—at least the timing of it struck him that way. At a deeper level, that psychic part of him that always knew what Elvis was thinking before he even thought it was not surprised that his old friend had met a premature death.

"I always said he would never grow old gracefully," says Scotty. "I don't think he could handle it. Maybe in the back of his mind that was part of it—that he had a death wish. We'll never know. I look at pictures of him taken the last year and I can see the drugs. When he started putting on weight, he looked like he could be on anything. He looked loose—like he was coming unglued, falling apart."

When Emily hung up the telephone after talking to Scotty, she felt sorry for him. Just because they were divorced did not mean she did not feel his pain. "I never saw Scotty cry, but that was the only time I ever heard his voice break and I knew it was great turmoil for him," she says. "He was truly crushed. That was a part of his life—and a friend for life, someone he cared about. There was real sadness in his voice."

The Memphis Police Department homicide squad initially reported Elvis's cause of death as either heart failure or an accidental overdose of drugs. Before the day was over, spokesmen for the police department denied that a drug overdose was a suspected cause of death. In the years following his death, countless theories evolved about his final days.

Scotty has no special insight into Elvis's death. They had not spoken since the "Comeback" special televised in 1968. When he thinks of Elvis, he thinks of the man he knew in the early years, when he was young and vibrant and ready to set the world on fire. He never met the bloated, awkward Elvis he saw in photographs in later years: that Elvis was a stranger to him.

With Elvis's death, Scotty lost more than a friend. He lost the hope that their "misunderstanding" would ever be resolved. That wasn't something Scotty thought about all the time, but it was something that was always in the back of his mind—the possibility that at any given moment the telephone could ring and it would be Elvis and everything would be like it was in the old days. The telephone would never ring, he knew that now. The waiting was over.

Three days before Elvis died, Memphis songwriter Sharri Paullus, whose physican husband had once treated Gladys, called Vernon to tell him that she had written two songs for Elvis. One of the songs, "Heartbreak Avenue," was perfect for him, she said. Vernon told her to send the demos over to Graceland. "I can't promise he'll do them, but he will listen," he told her.

When Elvis came in that night, he listened to the songs. Vernon called Sharri back the next day. He told her Elvis loved "Heartbreak Avenue."

"He said he could do the same thing with it that he did with 'Heartbreak Hotel,'" he said. "We'll send over a car for you tomorrow."

The next day, as she waited for the car to arrive, Sharri turned on the radio. That's how she learned that Elvis was dead. There would be no car for her that day, or any other day. "I couldn't believe it," she said. "That's what you call getting close."

On August 18, 1977, Elvis's funeral was held at Graceland, then followed by a ceremony and burial at Forest Hill Cemetery.[1] Pallbearers included Joe Esposito, Lamar Fike, George Klein, Charlie Hodge, Billy Smith, Jerry Schilling, and his personal physician, Dr. George Nicholopoulos. Producer Felton Jarvis was scheduled to be a pallbearer, but he was unable to attend. Scotty did not attend the funeral. He stayed in Nashville.

Minutes after he heard about the death, Colonel Parker booked a flight to Memphis for the purpose of meeting with Vernon over merchandising rights to Elvis's name. The King might be dead, but that was no reason for the kingdom to suffer. Elvis was worth as much dead as he was alive, maybe more. At the funeral, Parker wore a bright blue shirt, opened at the collar, and a baseball cap. If he had any feelings for the man he called "son," he kept them to himself.

227

[1] On October 2, 1977, Elvis's body was removed from Forest Hill Cemetery, along with that of his mother, and both were reburied side by side at Graceland. The relocation was spurred by a bizarre incident earlier in the year when three men wearing dark jumpsuits were arrested and charged with trespassing on cemetery property.

11

UP FROM THE ROCK,
ONTO THE ROAD

C arol Burnett and Dolly Parton could not have been more different. Dolly was bubbly, effervescent, charmingly democratic in her approach to those with whom she worked. By contrast, Carol was intense and standoffish, someone who avoided eye contact and conversation.

Carol and Dolly were in Nashville to tape a television special at Opryland, "Carol and Dolly Together Again for the First Time." Before they taped the show, they gathered at Monument to record the music. Scotty was the engineer. When they moved over to Opryland for the actual taping, he went there, too—pulling duty on the soundboard as a freelance engineer.

At the studio, Carol sat with her husband and daughter on one side of the control room. They talked among themselves, but avoided conversation with the staff. It was almost as if they had pulled their wagons into a circle as a means of self-protection. Carol didn't feel entirely comfortable in Nashville—and her discomfort showed. Of course, Dolly felt right at home in the studio. Over the years, Scotty had engineered a number of her demo sessions—back before she became famous, when she was Dolly Parton, the wannabe—so he was used to her gregarious, down-home ways. Unlike Carol, Dolly has the same engaging personality offstage as she does onstage.

When Dolly walked into the studio, she was wearing an oversized sweater that hung down to her knees. The massive sleeves were wadded up to her elbows. The baggy sweater belonged to her husband, Carl, a large man who would have filled it out nicely. As she entered the control room where Scotty was seated, she whirled about in a modelesque manner with her arms extended.

"Scotty, I knew you wanted to see me in a sweater," she said, laughing.

From the mid-'70s to the early '80s, Scotty engineered a number of television shows, often working with Hugh Hickerson at Opryland Productions. "I don't think a lot of people knew about Scotty's background," says Hickerson, who is today head of engineering at the facility. "A lot of the artists he worked with probably didn't know. I don't think Ann-Margret or Carol Burnett knew. I think a lot of the country artists would have known." The anonymity suited Scotty. Talking about Elvis—or guitar picking—wasn't high on his list of things to do.

Ann-Margret's show, which was taped at the Opry House in February 1977, was titled "Ann-Margret . . . Rhinestone Cowgirl." Her guests were Bob Hope, Perry Como, and Minnie Pearl. With Hope and Minnie Pearl on the set, Scotty and the others were pretty much kept in stitches. Told they would have to run through a number one more time, Hope grinned and said, "Want to take it from where we got off the plane?"

Producer Gary Smith told reporters for the *Tennessean* that they were doing the show in Nashville because they thought a country flavor would result in higher ratings. Leaving Los Angeles to do the show, he said, had cost them about $75,000 extra, but he thought the added expense would be worth it in the long run. Smith was impressed with the facilities.

What he didn't know was that, technically, it was still a work in progress. For several years, Scotty and Hickerson had struggled with the Opry House management to make changes to improve the acoustics and technical capabilities of the facility. Scotty says that when he first started working there, Mort Thomasson "saved [his] butt" by coming up with a solution to a technical problem.

"They had an orchestra pit—well, it wasn't actually a pit; it was built flush with the floor that came down from the audience—and we were having problems with the bottom end of the strings," says Scotty. "On the way home one night, I stopped by Monument. It was seven or eight o'clock and Mort was still there. We started chitchatting and I explained the problem to him. He had never been out there, so he asked me to explain how it was set up."

Scotty explained how the orchestra pit was about two feet below floor level and had open space between it and the basement floor. "That's the problem," Mort told him. "It's like a big bass drum." Armed with that perception, Scotty went back to the theater and dropped in 80-cycle cutoffs on the strings and boosted it to a level where the strings could be heard.

"I didn't know it at the time," Scotty says, "but Mort had firsthand knowledge of that problem from when he worked at Columbia, where their Studio A was built on coils. The whole floor had coils under it. It was the same thing I was dealing with at the Opry House."

Scotty enjoyed working with Ann-Margret, but apparently she was unaware of his long association with Elvis. Of course, Scotty knew about her longtime romance with Elvis, but he saw no reason to bring it up. When Scotty recorded the orchestra in the studio at Monument, Ann-Margret came by to do scratch vocals. She would sing the actual vocals live when the show was taped, but the music would be prerecorded.

Gail Pollock was in the studio when Ann-Margret did her vocals. "She is such a beautiful creature," she says. "At that point, country music was not big like it is now. She was of a larger magnitude star than what we normally dealt with. She was so perfect it hurt your eyes to look at her— but she's not that great a singer."

Scotty did so many television shows during that time, often sharing engineering duties with his friend Conrad Jones; they have since all blurred in his memory. He did three remote shows called "Nashville on the Road," and a series of thirteen hourlong programs called "Music Hall America," which featured a cast of kids who sang and danced in a park.

One show he did with Conrad was the Joey Heatherton special. Working with them in the control room was Conrad's cousin, Terry. During a rehearsal, Heatherton wandered about in the audience, singing on a riser. She kept yelling up at the control room for more feedback because she couldn't hear herself. "Terry pushed the talk back that went into the auditorium and said, 'Hell, the commodes are white capping up here now it's so loud,'" says Scotty.

Jones says Scotty was such a perfectionist he was a "fanatic" about little things. "He would not accept the fact that we were using [light-weight] 10 KC telephone lines," he says. "We would have to tweak and twist every knob there trying to get a little more high and low end, which the telephone lines just lost. Gosh, he would hound Hugh Hickerson and myself into oblivion. He had been a session musician. He really had trouble accepting [the limitations of our technology]."

Whenever musicians from Scotty's past showed up to do a television show, he made it a point not to leave the control room to talk to them. "I don't know how many Johnny Cash shows we did with Carl Perkins, Jerry Lee Lewis—people who would have loved to talk to him— but unless it was sound related, he stayed in the control room. He was not Scotty Moore, the picker. For years, we tried to get him [to perform again], but he would just look at you and grin and say, 'Elvis is dead.'"

One of the things Conrad remembers best is the way he and Scotty watched the clock. As the second hand moved toward the clock-out time, they would look at each other and grin. In Scotty's briefcase, which he carried with him wherever he went, was a bottle of Johnny Walker (Red). The instant the big hand hit the mark, the briefcase snapped open.

❈ ❈ ❈

It was while he was working as a freelance engineer that Scotty became a businessman. In 1976, when Monument decided not to renew its lease for the building it was using as a warehouse, Scotty was approached by the building's owner about purchasing it. The owner said he would make him a good deal on the building. Tommy Hill, an employee of Gusto records, told Scotty where some equipment could be picked up at auction for a good price. He said that if Scotty wanted to bid on the equipment and open a tape-duplication business, he would put up money as a partner.

Scotty bought the building and the equipment, then opened a business under the name Independent Producers Corporation (IPC). The business made copies of tapes in large quantities for studio owners, songwriters, and musicians who needed cassettes to distribute—or sell—to potential clients and customers. Scotty hired a woman to operate the plant, and he allowed his nephew Jerry to oversee the accounts payable and receivable. Scotty supervised the overall operation of the business, but continued to work as a freelance engineer.

Soon after he started the tape-duplication business, Scotty's daughter Andrea came to Nashville to live with him. She enrolled in classes at Nashville Tech and worked part-time at the tape plant for about six months. When she became homesick, she went back to Memphis to live with her mother. The following year, when she was nineteen, she returned to Nashville to live with Scotty.

For the past eight years, Andrea had only visited Scotty once a year, usually at Thanksgiving, so living with him required some adjustment on her part. "It was kinda tough," she said. "I've always been real picky and didn't date too much. The first thing he told me was that I needed to be on the pill. That way he didn't have to worry."

Although reestablishing parent-child bonds with Scotty proved more difficult than she imagined, Andrea enjoyed working at the tape plant. "He's a good boss," she says. "My mother always said he paid people well. He treats his employees like family." Her best memory of those years, she says, was "just sitting around drinking" with her father. "Once I got to be an adult, I think he could relate to me better."

❋ ❋ ❋

For Scotty, the '80s offered an opportunity to put his past behind him. He became Scotty Moore, the engineer, the businessman; many people he worked with had no idea he even played a musical instrument. Scotty Moore, the guitar legend, ceased to exist.

In 1982, IPC, of which Scotty was president, bought a print shop, which they named Villa Printing. Located on Edgehill and Villa Place, it specialized in small-order jobs. As the demand for cassettes increased at the tape plant, so did the difficulty in obtaining cassette inserts from local printers. Owning his own print shop would enable him to do faster—and better—work at the tape plant. Within a couple of years, the name of the print shop was changed to IPC Graphics and it was relocated downtown. At that point, both businesses were incorporated into the same company.

By 1980, Gail Pollock, who had been helping Scotty part-time at the tape plant—"I was like unpaid help whenever they needed it because Scotty and I were friends"—learned that he wanted to hire someone to handle the graphics and do the layouts on the eight-track labels. "I said, 'Scotty, why don't you just hire me?'" she says. As a result, Gail left Monument to work full-time for Scotty. People joked that she was to Scotty what Della was to Perry Mason: his right hand, his shoulder to cry on, his business advisor.

Occasionally, an enterprising writer tracked down Scotty and asked for an interview, but with a few exceptions, he begged off, saying he really didn't have anything to say. Elvis was dead.

Just because he gave up performing, however, did not mean he lost interest in guitars. In March 1987 Allan Cartee, with whom he had worked on previous occasions, called and told him he was leaving town and wanted to sell his guitar. He had a Gibson Super 400. Would Scotty be interested in buying it?

"I told him I wasn't playing any longer," says Scotty. "But he brought it by to show me. He had bought it for a session and it only had been played one time."

Scotty bought the guitar for $1,500. He saw it as an investment, if nothing else. The guitar sold for about $5,000 new.[1] He didn't know if he would ever play it in public, but as an investment, he thought he couldn't

---

[1] In 1992 Scotty asked Gibson the price of a Super 400. They said they only made them on special order and cost $12,500.

go wrong. He added the guitar to his collection, which still included the original Ray Butts amplifier he had bought in 1955. Scotty, the collectible, became Scotty, the collector.

❊ ❊ ❊

One day Chet Atkins called up and asked if he could bring someone over to meet Scotty. Guitarist Mark Knopfler was in town doing an album with Chet and had asked if he could meet him. As the three of them sat in the back office of the tape plant and talked, Chet noticed that Scotty had an old RCA 77DX microphone on his desk. It was practically an antique.

"Does it work?" Chet asked.

"I'm sure it did, until someone cut the cable off," said Scotty.

Scotty was using the microphone as a paperweight. When Chet showed an interest in it, he gave it to him as a gift. The gesture had unexpected results. Some time later, Chet showed up at the office carrying a guitar case. When Gail told him Scotty wasn't there, he opened the case on the counter to show her what was inside. It was a Chet Atkins Gibson "Country Gentleman" guitar.

"It was a real dark mahogany instrument," says Gail. "It was gorgeous—it was one he had used himself." Chet left the guitar for Scotty as a gift.

❊ ❊ ❊

In September 1989 Scotty ran into Carl Perkins at a Music Row party honoring Carl for a No. 1 song he had cowritten for the Judds. Scotty and Carl stood out on the porch for more than an hour talking. "We never did do an album together," Carl said.

"Hell, I haven't played in years," said Scotty. "I wouldn't know what to do with a guitar."

"It's just like falling off a bicycle—you never forget how," Carl said, laughing.

Scotty said he would think about it.

It was shortly after that meeting that Carl was diagnosed with throat cancer. Scotty kept in touch with him. Carl told him he didn't think he would ever again be able to sing. The radiation treatment had destroyed his saliva glands, making it impossible for him to do vocals.

Scotty told him they would do the album as soon as he whipped the cancer.

Carl said he didn't know if he wanted to whip it.

In 1989 ABC-TV accepted a proposal from Priscilla Presley and Jerry

Schilling for a weekly series to be titled *Elvis*. The thirty-minute program would focus on Elvis's early years with Scotty and Bill. The idea was to show the teenage Elvis, as he was in the beginning of his career, not the slick, seasoned performer he became in later years.

Jerry, who had met Elvis while playing football in Memphis, ended up working for the entertainer. He was on Elvis's staff from 1964 to 1976, and subsequently became a manager for the Beach Boys and the Sweet Inspirations. After Elvis's death, Priscilla hired him to be the creative affairs director of the Presley estate.

Priscilla and Jerry, along with a third investor, produced the television series themselves. Actor Michael St. Gerard, then twenty-five, was chosen to play Elvis, Jesse Dabney was picked to play Scotty, and Blake Gibbons to play Bill Black. Chosen to be the singing voice of the young Elvis was country singer Ronnie McDowell.

Immediately after Elvis's death in 1977, Ronnie cowrote a song about the entertainer titled "The King Is Gone." Partly as a result of the success of that song, Dick Clark Productions asked him to do sound-track vocals for a 1979 television movie about Elvis. Ronnie scored several hit singles on the country charts in the late '70s and '80s, including "Wandering Eyes," "Older Women," "Unchained Melody," and "Watchin' Girls Go By." When time came for Priscilla and Jerry to chose a vocalist for their series, Priscilla requested Ronnie. His voice was so close to Elvis's, she said, she sometimes could not tell them apart.

Jerry Schilling had met Scotty several times over the years, but by the time he became a salaried employee, Scotty's contacts with Elvis were limited to occasional recording sessions. As a result, Jerry didn't have a strong personal relationship with Scotty. When he asked Scotty to be a consultant for the TV series, he wasn't sure what to expect. He had heard the stories about Scotty shunning the spotlight. To his surprise, Scotty said yes.

"Knowing Elvis the way I did, I knew the support system he needed," says Jerry. "Scotty was like the rock in the foundation that Elvis depended on. That is why Scotty was his manager in the beginning. Scotty was low-key, strong, honest, certainly a talented musician—and he gave Elvis a lot of strength. They were out there on the road and there wasn't anyone else. Scotty was the rock, sort of like Peter was the rock of the church. Knowing Elvis and Scotty the way I do, I can see why Elvis depended on him."

To his surprise, Scotty enjoyed being a consultant for the show. He especially liked the actor who played him in the series. When it aired in February 1990 most critics were unanimous in their praise of its

235

authenticity. Robert Oermann, music critic for the *Nashville Tennessean*, wrote: "By any measure, *Elvis* is extraordinary television . . . when you're dealing with the most famous entertainer in world history, the truth is more fascinating than any fiction could ever be." To hammer home the point, Oermann's article bore a headline that said NEW PRIME-TIME PRESLEY SERIES EXHIBITS ASTONISHING AUTHENTICITY. Unfortunately, television viewers were not as receptive of the series and it was not renewed for a second season.

✻ ✻ ✻

By 1991 Scotty had grown accustomed to being a "former" guitarist. It had a comfortable feel to it, like a pair of old shoes. Over the years, countless requests for information, artifacts, guitar-playing tips, and personal appearances arrived at his tape duplication business. Gail answered the letters for him and screened calls for him, but he turned down all requests for personal appearances.

One day Jerry Schilling received a telephone call from someone in the Rolling Stones organization. They wanted to know if he knew how to get in touch with Scotty. If so, would he mind asking him if he would meet the Rolling Stones? They were in the middle of their Steel Wheels tour and would be happy to fly Scotty to one of their concerts.

"I called him, and he was at the tape factory," says Jerry, who told him about the request from the Stones. "He said, 'That might be a kick.'"

Jerry relayed the message to the Stones, with the admonition that he was certain Scotty would not want to perform. A few days later, the Stones business manager called Jerry back.

"Did you talk to Scotty?" Jerry asked.

"Sure did," said the business manager.

"What'd he say?"

"He said, 'Why don't you call me back in a week.'"

Obviously flustered by his conversation with Scotty, he asked Jerry what he should do next.

"Call him back in a week," said Jerry.

To everyone's surprise—including his own—Scotty agreed to go to St. Louis to meet the Stones. It was an all-expense-paid trip. They had offered to take care of everything. When he boarded the plane in Nashville, he carried only an overnight case—no guitar case. He was serious about not performing.

Scotty arrived at the St. Louis airport early in the afternoon and took an airport van to the hotel. "I didn't try to contact any of them—I figured they would get me up on the game plan," says Scotty. "Later on that afternoon, someone called me and told me what time we would leave the hotel for the stadium."

That evening they all piled into a caravan of vans. To Scotty's surprise, Emmylou Harris also had been invited to the concert. He was a big fan of hers, but had never met her. "That was a double dip for me," says Scotty.

After attending a press party at the stadium, Scotty went backstage to watch the show. "I stood on the right side facing the audience," says Scotty. "Johnny Johnson, Chuck Berry's piano player, was there. Chuck wrote 'Johnny B. Goode' about him. He went out and played a number with them. They did a hell of a show. I was not a big fan, but after they did that show, I became a fan. I timed them. They did two hours and forty minutes nonstop."

After the concert, they returned to the hotel, where they had dinner in a private room that had been closed off for them. "Then we went up to Keith's room—and him and me got plastered," says Scotty. "He had several guitars there. He wanted to learn the lick to 'Mystery Train,' so we played until four-thirty or five o'clock that morning. I got up the next morning, and, with two hours' sleep, flew back to Nashville hurtin'."

For Keith Richards, the encounter with Scotty was a dream come true. "For a few brief hours, it was like sitting at the feet of the master . . . digging the cat himself," he says. "Scotty—what a gent!"

When Scotty arrived in Nashville after his visit with the Stones, he called Jerry Schilling and told him about the trip. To Scotty's surprise, he had become an instant celebrity among his own employees, all of whom seemed shocked that their Scotty Moore had palled around with the Rolling Stones. Says Jerry: "He said, 'Jerry, you know the only thing is that when I came back about thirty people here at the factory wanted one of those T-shirts. I don't want them to give me any, but if you could get me a good deal on them I would like to buy them for everyone here.'"

"We were so surprised he went," says Gail Pollock. "For years, we had been trying to get Scotty to crawl out from beneath the rock."

❈ ❈ ❈

By 1992 Scotty felt like he had been hit by a rock—a big one, at that. The printing shop wasn't getting enough orders to stay afloat. "The economy took a nosedive that year," says Scotty. "The big companies were already running three shifts a day. They cut prices and ran them on their third shifts just to keep their employees."

In a effort to keep the printing shop afloat, Scotty sold the tape plant in February to Gail Pollock. She changed its name to "We Make Tapes."

**Carl Perkins, left, with Scotty at Sun Studio in Memphis, c. 1992
(Courtesy of Scotty Moore)**

Unfortunately, that transaction was not enough to save the printing business. With each passing day, it plummeted ever deeper into debt. To
make matters worse, the tape plant was one of its biggest clients. "What
we did print-wise was nowhere enough to keep the print shop running,"
says Gail. "[It] didn't do well because it didn't have enough work from
just us to keep it going."

Early in 1992, while Scotty was agonizing over his failing business
interests, he received a phone call from Carl Perkins.

"When do you want to do the album" Carl asked.

Scotty was speechless. He had talked to Carl several weeks earlier at
Christmas. Since then Carl had learned the cancer had gone into remis-
sion. He was ready to sing again.

"Carl, I haven't picked up a guitar in twenty-four years," Scotty said.

Scotty had grave doubts about his ability to pick up where he had
left off, but he was not about to let an old friend down, especially one
that had licked cancer.

In March, Scotty and Gail Pollock drove to Carl's home in Jackson to talk to him about recording again. They met in his studio, which was at the rear of the house next to the swimming pool. Carl suggested they do the album in Memphis at the old Sun Studio, which had been reopened in recent years for recording sessions.

"Scotty was sitting there, thinking 'I can't play a guitar—no way,'" recalls Gail. "Carl was singing and practically doing a show for us right there. Scotty kept thinking, 'I can't do this.'" But Carl was convincing. They agreed to book time in April at Sun Studio.

As they stood in Carl's carport before leaving, Scotty suggested Carl write a song about Sam Phillips for the session. "Remember how he kept pushing you?" Scotty said.

Carl grinned. "Damn, Sam," he said.

The next day after church Carl called Scotty. He read him the lyrics to the song he had written overnight. He had titled it "Damn Sam."

Carl had worked in Sun Studio several times since the '50s, so he was more familiar with it than Scotty, who had not been inside the studio in nearly thirty years. When he saw it, he was surprised at how little it had changed.

"It was the same ole room with acoustic tile on the wall and ceiling," says Scotty. "Of course, it didn't have the same equipment. It needed a little paint and cleaning up."

239

In addition to Scotty and Carl, the lineup for the session included Carl's sons, Stan and Greg, D. J. Fontana, Paul Burlison, James Lott, Donnie Baer, Johnny Black, Willie Rainsford, Joe Schenk, and Marcus Van Storey.

"It was so neat to watch those old guys," says Gail. "Marcus told me he was supposed to be in the hospital that week. I said, what for? He said, 'Oh, they wanted to check my heart, but I wouldn't miss this for the world.'"

They did three sessions at Sun, with each lasting about five hours. Among the songs they recorded were "Blue Suede Shoes," "Mystery Train," and "Damn Sam." Since Carl was still recuperating, he couldn't sing for long periods at a time.

"He was very, very skinny—and his shoulder was hurting real bad," says Gail. "I had some stuff I used to rub on Scotty's shoulder sometimes, so I went and got it and rubbed his shoulders with it. He was not well, but he did a great job on the session."

When Scotty returned to Nashville and listened to the tapes, he wasn't happy with the quality of the recording. "I thought we had enough material, but some of the tapes were garbled and weren't usable," he says. "So I hired a remote audio truck and took it to Carl's house. His wife graciously let us move some furniture out of the den to get the drums in there and we recorded half a dozen songs there in his den. Tracy Nelson came down and did two songs with us."

Scotty titled the album *706 ReUnion: A Sentimental Journey*. He released it on Belle Meade Records label and sold it by mail order. A glowing review by Michael Price in the Fort Worth *Star-Telegram* said the Moore-Perkins alliance had "yielded the richest roots-rock album since Fort Worth's Ray Sharpe delivered his 'Texas Boogie Blues' collection in 1980 . . . Moore's playing—though he has claimed to be rusty from inactivity—packs as much brisk authority as it did those nearly forty years ago, and Perkins's voice soars."

In May 1992, a few weeks after he returned from Memphis, Scotty filed for bankruptcy. The printing shop stopped production in June and vacated its offices in August. Scotty was both embarrassed and angered by the bankruptcy: embarrassed because he didn't like to feel he had let other people down; angry, because bankruptcy "makes you feel like a criminal or something."

The bankruptcy forced Scotty, at age sixty-one, into an early retirement. He no longer had a studio or a tape plant or a printing shop. He did have a guitar or two. Two weeks after the session in Memphis with Carl, Scotty received word that Marcus Van Storey had died of a heart attack.

Gail, who recalled her conversation with Marcus, felt he "died a happy man" because of his participation in the session. She wondered if it would have made any difference if he had gone to the hospital instead of playing in the session.

✻ ✻ ✻

While Scotty was deciding what to do next—whether to look for an engineering job or consider performing again on a regular basis—he accepted a booking with Carl Perkins at Ellis Auditorium in Memphis. The concert, scheduled for August, was part of the "Good Rockin' Tonight" show, a festivity of the annual "Elvis Week" celebration. By 1992 Graceland had become Memphis's leading tourist attraction. The previous year, 670,000 people had passed through the front gates, with the number increasing each year.

Also appearing on the "Good Rockin' Tonight" show were the Sun Rhythm Section—minus Paul Burlison, whose wife, Rose, was ill—guitarist James Burton, D. J. Fontana, Ronnie McDowell, and the Jordanaires. Scotty was nervous about performing again. His last performance had been the

1968 "Comeback" special—twenty-four years ago. Anyone would have been nervous under those circumstances.

Ronnie McDowell had met Scotty, but had never talked to him at length. Between sets at the auditorium they got to know each other. When Scotty told him he was "scared to death" about performing again after so many years, Ronnie reassured him, then suggested he go out on the road with him and his band as a means of getting his chops back in shape. Scotty said he'd think about it. "To me, Scotty and Bill were as much a part of it as Elvis," says Ronnie.

Gail watched the show from the rear of the auditorium. "It was one of those, 'You have to be there' performances—it was electric," she says. "It was a great show. But it was very difficult on Carl. The doctors told him he could do twenty minutes—and he did an hour and twenty minutes. He could hardly talk afterward."

Scotty was hooked.

A week after the Memphis performance, Scotty went to England with the Jordanaires for performances at more than a dozen venues. Carl was booked as the headliner, but had to cancel at his doctor's insistence and was unable to make the trip.

"I'll never forget the first show," says Ray Walker of the Jordanaires. "Scotty was uptight. He looked a little pale—and he had this quizzical look in his eye, almost like he wasn't going to walk on stage. But when he did, those people came unglued. They recognized him, and when he hit that guitar lick, it happened again. They absolutely came unglued."

"I couldn't believe it," says Scotty. "We'd do those shows and people my age and older would come through the lines, their hands absolutely shaking, with tears rolling down their faces—and the majority of them would have their little grandkids with them carrying Elvis records to get signed."

The following year, Scotty and D.J. went to Jackson, to appear on a telethon with—and for—Carl Perkins. When it came to public performances, there weren't many people who could get Scotty to say yes. Carl was among the few who could.

Unknown to Scotty, his old friend James Lewis was watching the telethon at his home a short distance away in Crockett County. As a joke, he called in a $100 pledge if the telethon sponsors would get Scotty to sing. "Of course, I had never heard him sing a note in his life," says James, laughing.

Scotty didn't sing that day—and he didn't find out about the pledge until three years later.

When Lee Rocker, the former bassist with the Stray Cats, first started playing rockabilly in the late '70s, disco audiences looked at him like he was crazy. Didn't he know Elvis was dead? Over the next several years, the Stray Cats—with singer/guitarist Brian Setzer and drummer Slim Jim Phantom—almost single-handedly introduced a new generation to the music created at Sun Studio.

After the Stray Cats split up in 1993, Rocker joined with guitarist Mike Eldred and formed a new group named Big Blue. They went to Memphis to record their debut, self-titled album. Long before they booked the session, Eldred wrote Scotty a letter, telling him how much he had been influenced by his playing. He never expected to hear from him. To his utter surprise, Scotty answered his letter.

The end result was that Scotty agreed to sit in on their Memphis session.

"I said, 'Scotty, you want me to send a limo [to Nashville] to pick you up?'" says Rocker. "He said, 'No, I've got a car.' I asked him if there was anything we could do. He said, 'No, not really. I'll just put my guitar in the car and drive over to Memphis.'"

Rocker was amazed once they began the session. For years, the Stray Cats had emulated the early work Scotty had done at Sun—and not just the picking. They moved microphones around, trying them at different distances, they experimented with analog delays on the tape. They did everything they could think of to get that sound.

When Scotty walked into the studio, Rocker thought, finally, he would discover the secret. To his surprise, there was no hoodoo magic involved. "Scotty came in and put a microphone in front of his amp— and that was it," he says, laughing. "I realized we had wasted a lot of time trying to get that sound. It's his sound."

Scotty played on two of the album cuts: Jimmy Reed's "Shame, Shame, Shame" and "Little Buster," a song written by Rocker and Eldred. "I didn't want to go back and cut Elvis stuff," says Rocker. "I think he enjoyed playing on something that was new."

In 1994 Gary Tallent, Bruce Springsteen's former bassist, asked Scotty if he would play on a session he was producing with Sonny Burgess. "The funny thing about it was that I was trying to direct him to play like he played thirty years ago," says Tallent. "He would look at me, like 'that's thirty years ago.' In some ways it's like he's starting fresh again."

Tallent was amazed that he remembered Scotty's old licks better than Scotty himself remembered them. "We have studied what he did more than he has—and I guess that's true for anyone in this [business]. Basically what he does is instinctive. He doesn't rely on a bag of tricks. He just plays and figures it out as he goes along. Rock 'n' roll is improvised music—and that's how he goes about it. It took that situation for me to realize—of course, that's rock 'n' roll."

✳ ✳ ✳

For most of the summer of '94, the media was swamped with stories of a massive Elvis tribute that was going to be held at the Pyramid arena in Memphis. The event would be offered to the public on pay-per-view television and Mercury Records would subsequently release an album of material recorded live at the concert. The list of performers signed up for the concert was impressive: Tony Bennett, Melissa Etheridge, Chris Isaak, Michael Bolton, Carl Perkins, Bryan Adams, Aaron Neville, Dwight Yoakam, Tanya Tucker, and Travis Tritt. It would be the biggest Elvis tribute ever.

In late September, two weeks before the event was scheduled to take place, Scotty received a call from one of the producers. Would he be interested in putting together a band and performing at the concert? Scotty was taken aback. The concert was only two weeks away.

"D. J. and I were already booked with Ronnie [McDowell] in Indiana on that same date with the Jordanaires, so I told him we couldn't do it," Scotty says. "I said I wasn't going to cancel on them and I didn't think any of the others would either."

The producers called back and said they would be willing to add Ronnie to the program. That would be fine, Scotty told them, except for the fact that they were booked at the other venue. "Finally, they said they would buy out the show for us—whatever the promoter thought he would lose by rescheduling the show, they would pay it," says Scotty.

With everyone agreed to those terms, Ronnie's date in Indiana was rescheduled. As Scotty got ready to go to Memphis with D. J., the Jordanaires, Ronnie, and the members of his band, faxes started arriving from the producers on a daily basis. Unfortunately, they would not be able to use Ronnie's band. However, Scotty persuaded them to use two members of the band: Kevin Wood, the guitarist, and Steve Sheppard, the keyboard player.

They arrived in Memphis the day before the concert. When they went to rehearsal, they discovered that most of the other performers had not yet shown up. To help the producers, Ronnie offered to fill in for them.

Before the rehearsal began, Don Was, the musical director, committed two major gaffes. First, when the Jordanaires were mentioned, he

L to r: Thom Bresh, Carl Perkins, Scotty, and Ronnie McDowell, c. 1994
(Courtesy of Scotty Moore)

said, "Oh, are they still alive?" Second, he told Scotty what key he would be playing his songs in. Scotty set Was straight on the Jordanaires in quick order, then told him he would do Elvis's songs in the same key he had always done them.

"Scotty actually saved the show," says Ray Walker of the Jordanaires. Gordon Stoker agrees: "If it hadn't have been for Scotty, [the show] would have been in serious trouble."

A few hours before showtime, what had thus far been merely unpleasant, suddenly became a nightmare for Scotty. "I had been going through this hassle with them—it was horrible—then we broke to go back to the hotel to get dressed and eat," says Scotty. "It was then that one of those honchos came around and said they were running low on time. Ronnie would have to do his song on the pay-per-view preshow teaser. If there was still time during the main show, he could do his number then.

"I thought I had covered every crack, but someone outsmarted me. We had rehearsed with all those other guys and we would have looked like assholes if we hadn't played. I called Ronnie's manager, Joe, and he did the worst thing a manager could do—he told Ronnie, who just slipped out of the hotel and went back to Nashville. He was that hurt."

Scotty felt horrible about what happened to Ronnie—"They had a right to cut acts, but it was the way they did it"—but he and the others went ahead and did the show. They backed Chris Isaak on "Blue Moon," Michael Bolton on "Jailhouse Rock," Carl Perkins on "Blue Suede Shoes," and Bryan Adams on "Hound Dog."

As Scotty reveled in the excitement of the packed arena, halfway across the country his old Navy buddy Frank Parise watched on television.

✳ ✳ ✳

On July 4, 1995, Scotty, D. J., and Carl Perkins performed at the third annual "American Roots" concert at the Washington Monument. The event was organized by the National Park Service and the National Council for the Traditional Arts. It rained that day, and what Scotty remembers most about the concert was how hard the stage hands had to work to keep the equipment dry. "In the wings stood Moore, looking as stoic as ever, cradling the kind of Gibson guitar that helped launch countless rock careers," wrote Mike Joyce for the *Washington Post*. "When he and Fontana joined Perkins onstage, it was strictly 'go cat go.'" The reporter wrote that Scotty was still laying down "sparkling solos."

At sixty-three, Scotty still had the fire and the burning desire to perform. It's not the sort of fire that grows cold with age. Throughout 1995 and 1996, Scotty toured with Ronnie McDowell. Typically, Ronnie does his regular show, performing the country hits he racked up over the years, then concludes with a forty-five-minute tribute to Elvis, which features Scotty, D. J., and the Jordanaires. "The people react great to him," says Ronnie. "We were in Laurel, Mississippi, doing a little show at a fair. The young girls just screamed everytime I mentioned their names. Scotty leaned over to me and said, 'Man, this is just like 1955.'"

"We'll do autographs, and people will make comments like, 'You don't realize how many memories you brought back,'" says Scotty.

Ray Walker of the Jordanaires still gets a kick out of watching Scotty onstage. One of the things Scotty is famous for—at least among fellow musicians—is his reluctance to deviate from the playlist. "Sometimes Ronnie will say, 'This isn't on the list' [and go into a song he hasn't told Scotty about]," says Ray, laughing. "Scotty just laughs and says, 'There you go.'"

Ronnie knows it drives Scotty crazy when he improvises. "He hates the way I do my show because I don't stick to a format," says Ronnie. "Everything I do is off the cuff, and my band is used to that. Scotty would like for me to stick to a format.

Scotty Moore, c. 1994 (Photo by James Dickerson)

"I say, 'You mean to tell me Elvis stuck to a list?'

"He says, 'We never veered off of it—what we wrote down is what we did.'"

But Scotty knows it's all in fun. And the fun doesn't stop on stage. Musicians are notorious practical jokers. One night, after engaging in a serious conversation with Johnnie Walker (Red), says Ronnie, Scotty dropped off to sleep on the bus. While he was asleep, slumped over in one of the plush chairs, the boys in the band decorated him with fruit— a banana in his pocket, grapes in his lap and in his hand. When he awoke and rubbed his face, he was a mess.

Scotty didn't get angry. That's life on the road.

"Outside of us, Ronnie was the first person outside Scotty's [immediate circle] that had a personal appreciation of him," says Ray Walker. "Scotty could see that he was safe with him. That was really a good marriage for Scotty."

Spliced between continuing performances with Ronnie, Scotty spent much of 1996 working on a compilation CD and a film documentary to celebrate the contributions Scotty, D. J., and Bill Black made to American music. In addition to a Woodstock session with Keith Richards, Levon Helm, and The Band, Scotty and D. J. recorded songs with the BoDeans, the Mavericks, Cheap Trick, Tracy Nelson, Steve Earle, and others.

"D. J. and I hadn't actually heard of [the BoDeans], but when we met them we found out they had grown up on Elvis music," says Scotty. "Turned out, they were real easy to work with."

Following the session with Cheap Trick, Bun Carlos, the drummer, asked D. J. and Scotty to sign his snare drums. Later, as Scotty happened to be walking past, Carlos asked D. J. to sign his sticks. Overhearing the request, Scotty never missed a beat. "You must have a wood-burning stove," he interjected.

Of course, 1996 wasn't all work and no play. Early in the year, Scotty received an invitation to guitarist Les Paul's eighty-first birthday celebration. Scotty had not been to New York City since the mid-1970s, but Paul was an early hero of his. He broke with tradition in this instance and boarded a plane, party-bound for Iridium, a jazz club on West 63rd Street.

"Les didn't know until an hour into his set that Scotty was there," says Dan Griffin, who accompanied Scotty to the party. "Les got a guitar and put it in Scotty's hands and dragged him onstage before he could say no. They were thrilled to sit there and play with him. They played some jazz songs I didn't know, and some standards."

For Scotty, who first heard Paul on "How High the Moon," the thrill was mutual. "If it hadn't been for Les Paul, us guitar players might be playing harpsichords," he says. "He invented the electric guitar. Every guitar player there is should bow down at his feet."

❊ ❊ ❊

Scotty began his professional life out on the road—and now, in the twilight of his career, he's back on the road again. Approaching age sixty-six, he has emerged from his bout with bankruptcy and accepted the fact that he will probably have to perform for the rest of his life to put food on the table. There's no bitterness in him about the way things turned out. He believes in Elvis as much today as he did in 1954. It is scandalous that his total take from fourteen years with Elvis amounted to only $30,123.72, but never will you hear him blame Elvis for that, not even on his darkest days.

"To me, and it's a sad thing to say, but without Scotty, Elvis wouldn't have been as big," says Keith Richards. "It was Scotty and Bill Black's rapport—and Scotty's ability to understand the space he was working in. Elvis got big so quick, he overshadowed the band. Parker, the beloved Colonel, being the man he is, saw no percentage in the band. It is really scandalous what Parker did to Elvis. I'm sure the Colonel told him [Scotty and Bill] were being paid a fortune. Knowing this business—and knowing the Colonel—I would put money on it."

"Scotty truly respected Elvis for his abilities and he cared about him as a human being," says Emily Sanders. "He never said an unkind word about Elvis. If there was something that troubled Scotty, it was something that saddened him because Elvis didn't come through on something—but he never cursed him."

"Why would I?" says Scotty. "He was like a brother to me."

Today, Scott lives in a rural area northwest of Nashville in a two-story house that sits off the road in a clump of tall trees. He has a large kitchen that is heated by a wood-burning stove. It is the room he spends the most time in. He has converted the actual living room into a studio. A second room, located just off the living room, was converted into a sound booth. He has a small soundboard and an assortment of equipment he uses to edit both sound and videotape.

One night in 1996, as work on this book was concluding, Scotty called me following a storm that left eight inches of snow around his house. He said his electricity had gone out, but his telephone worked just fine. Scotty was home alone, as usual. Unfazed by the darkness—and below freezing temperatures—he assured me that he was doing just

Scotty at home, c. 1996 (Photo by James Dickerson)

fine. On his wood cookstove simmered a can of beans, which he planned to wash down with his favorite scotch. Once he finished the beans, he said, he would use a candle to make his way up the dark stairway to his bedroom. The world would look different after a good night's sleep. It always had.

Scotty Moore (right) is a guitarist, recording engineer,
and record producer, who lives near Nashville,
Tennessee. James Dickerson (left) is the author of *Goin'
Back to Memphis* (Schirmer Books, 1996), among other
books, and is a Nashville-based freelance journalist.

I'M STILL HERE

It's been eight years since I finished work on this book, and all I can say is that after heart and brain surgery, I'm glad to still be here. More about the surgeries later, but first I want to bring you up to date on what I've been doing for the past few years.

One of the first things that I did after *That's Alright, Elvis* was published was to hit the road in the fall of 1997 with my co-author to promote the book. We began our book tour with a train ride to New York City, a re-creation of the ride that Elvis, Bill, and I made on our first trip to New York. Only this time around, there were two major differences: The first was that since I lived in Nashville, and Memphis no longer had direct train service to New York, we had to go all the way to Birmingham, Alabama, to board the train—and the second was that nearly fifty years after my first trip, train service had gotten worse. I thought the modern trains, especially the Pullman cars, would really be knockouts, but the old ones were much better.

On the first leg of our trip, from Birmingham to Atlanta, a TNN camera crew accompanied us on the train, taping everything we did. That wasn't too bad. The interviewer had two qualities I find irresistible in reporters—blondeness and perkiness. We said good-bye to the camera crew in Atlanta, and stayed there a day or two doing interviews and a book signing that attracted an Elvis impersonator or two. I can live with that, just barely, but when they try to talk like Elvis I want to run out the back door.

Scotty Moore on the train to New York to promote *That's Alright, Elvis.* (Photo by James L. Dickerson.)

From Atlanta, we went to Washington, D.C., where we did more interviews and book signings, and then on to Philadelphia for more of the same. The best part about Washington was a black cab driver from Alabama who talked about how much he missed soul food. I felt fine, but I kept breaking out in a cold sweat whenever I had to walk more than a few steps at a time. James kept asking me if I felt all right, and I told him I did, which was the truth, except for maybe feeling more tired than usual.

We had signings planned for New York, but they had to be canceled because the publisher ran out of books. The best part of the trip was playing a concert in Central Park with Ike Turner, Joe Louis Walker, and Matt "Guitar" Murphy. The fans were disappointed that I didn't have books to sign, but they were very enthusiastic about the concert. After the show, we were all standing around backstage, talking and posing for pictures, with me on one end, when Ike said, "Scotty, you've got to stand in the middle—you're the fly in the buttermilk with this one." That cracked me up. It was hard to believe that it had been nearly half a century since Ike and I had started out in Memphis.

We ended the tour back in Birmingham, but had to cancel a scheduled book signing there because the store was unable to get books.

Gail Pollock picked us up at the train station and drove us back to Nashville. We had dinner along the way and Gail said that she was shocked that we sat at the same table. "I figured you two wouldn't be speaking after that trip," she laughed. I guess she thinks I don't travel too well. She should know. She's been my faithful traveling companion for almost twenty years.

Scotty, seated, with D.J. Fontana and Bill Black Combo, from left, Mike Leech, Reggie Young, Ace Cannon, Jerry 'Satch' Arnold, Bobby Woods, and Bobby Emmons at the reception for their Grammy nomination. (Photo courtesy of Rusty Russell.)

Not long after the book tour ended, I learned that a song from *All the King's Men* was nominated for a Grammy. "Goin' Back to Memphis" (we borrowed the title from James' book of the same name) was an instrumental recorded by the Bill Black Combo. D.J. Fontana and I wanted to pay tribute to Bill Black on the album, so we asked Reggie Young, who had been one of the founding members of the Bill Black Combo, to re-organize a group to do the recording. He brought in five other Memphis music veterans: Mike Leech, Ace Cannon, Jerry "Satch" Arnold, Bobby Woods, and Bobby Emmons.

We didn't win the Grammy, but it was an honor to be nominated.

* * *

POSTSCRIPT

The year after the release of the book and the CD, it seemed like I was always on the go, whether to promote the book and CD, or simply to perform. I continued to perform a lot with my friend Ronnie McDowell, but he got a booking in October 1998 in Paducah, Kentucky, that I initially turned down. Later, I had second thoughts about not going and decided to drive up there with Gail and surprise him.

I arrived at the venue early and set up my amplifier on the stage. Then I left, knowing that Ronnie wouldn't see my amplifier until he walked out on stage. Once Ronnie and the band arrived, I returned to the venue and went backstage without anyone in the band seeing me. Gail took a seat in the audience to watch the show. It was while I was alone backstage that I started sweating all of a sudden. It was sort of like what happened on the trip to New York. I thought it was because they hadn't turned on the air conditioning. I took off my coat, but that didn't help. Then I took off my tie. I was burning up like I had a high fever, but I felt fine otherwise.

Scotty with Bonnie Raitt. (Photo courtesy of Scotty Moore.)

Finally, I got Steve Shepard's attention on stage. He is the keyboardist and he was positioned so that he could see backstage. He saw that I was in trouble and he got Gail's attention in the audience. When she came backstage, I told her that something was wrong. When we returned to Nashville, I was so weak that I couldn't walk up the stairs. Two weeks later, I underwent a triple-bypass heart operation that was followed with bouts of anemia, kidney failure, and the loss of hearing in my left ear.

All that sounds pretty grim, but less than five months after having that heart surgery, I flew to Europe and did thirteen shows. That was when I joined up with Pete Pritchard, a bass player that had played with me on my first English tour in 1992. He's been a good friend ever since. He helped me put together a band that has stuck with me for several return engagements in the United Kingdom, France, Belgium, the Netherlands, Finland, Norway, Denmark, Sweden, Switzerland, and Germany.

Jimmy Russell is the drummer. He's tasteful and he doesn't pound the bass drum all night long. Liam Grundy plays keyboards and David Briggs plays second guitar. Paul Ansel does the vocals. When they're not playing with me, they play with other bands. The fact that they have other gigs makes me appreciate them even more when they drop what they're doing so that they can tour with me.

I love to go to Europe because there I am looked on more as an influence to their guitar heroes than as Elvis' lead guitarist. I have a great time there seeing fans not only my age, but younger fans that seem to get younger with each trip. At one show at the Mean Fiddler in London, there was a young man about twenty who stood right in front of the stage and sang every word to every song. When it was time for me to take my solo, he pointed to me, and when it was time for D.J. to do sometime special on the drums, the young man pointed at just the right moment. I laughed all through the show.

Scotty on 2001 tour in Norway with, left to right, Vidae Thomt, Steve Shepherd, Ella Shepherd, Peter Pritchard. (Photo courtesy of Scotty Moore.)

While I'm talking about new friends, I should tell you about Jacques Vroom. At the tail end of the book tour in 1998, I went to Arlington, Texas, in a Winnebago to sign books and do as many radio interviews as possible. It was a miserable ride. The only time I could get any sleep was when the vehicle was parked. At any rate, Jacques showed up at one of the signings and introduced himself. At that time, he put out a rock 'n' roll memorabilia catalog and he asked me about items that he could obtain for his collection. You couldn't say enough nice things about him, really. We hit it off right away and he's traveled with me on many occasions, often using his airline connections to get my tickets upgraded to first class.

I was doing some shows with ex-Stray Cat Lee Rocker, when his former bandmate Brian Setzer called him and asked if it were true that I was playing with him. Lee told him that I was, and he invited him and former Stray Cat Slim Jim Phantom to the show. Veteran drummer Earl Palmer also showed up, so when the time came to do "Mystery Train," Lee invited them all up on the stage to play along with us. That was a great night. It was the first time that all three Stray Cats had played together since 1992.

Scotty with Lee Rocker in Memphis. (Photo courtesy of Scotty Moore.)

On another night with Lee, we went to San Francisco to do a show. My good friend Tracy Nelson was there, as was Jacques, who had flown there with me. Before we went on stage, we gathered in one of the tiny backstage dressing rooms. Tracy made herself comfortable on the couch, stretching out the full length of her body, and Jacques sat in one of the chairs. They were watching me put powder on my hands, something I always to do to keep them from getting wet and sticky when I play guitar, when Jacques asked, "By the way, Scotty, what are you using the power for?" I smiled, and said, without missing a beat, "To powder the crack of my ass." Tracy laughed so hard that she rolled off the couch onto the floor.

Scotty with Keith Richards, D.J., and Ron Wood. (Photo by Paul Natkin.)

* * *

In March 2000, I was inducted into the Rock 'n' Roll Hall of Fame in the sideman category. I had mixed feelings about that. I was happy to be recognized for my contributions to music, but saddened that they felt they had to rewrite history to do it. When Elvis, Bill, and I made those first recordings, it wasn't as Elvis Presley and his sidemen. We were a band, just like the Beatles were a band. We were called either "Elvis, Scotty, and Bill" or the "Blue Moon Boys."

POSTSCRIPT

For the Rock 'n' Roll Hall of Fame to ignore that is tantamount to giving the Beatles an award inscribed, "To John and Paul, but not to their sidemen, Ringo and George." I'm not upset about it, just frustrated that people would use an award to rewrite history. Giving me an award under those conditions was a slap in the face to Bill Black and D.J. Fontana. How can you ignore Bill and D.J. and still honor rock 'n' roll? The Hall of Fame is just a big political thing. If you know anyone that wants to buy a trophy from the Hall of Shame, I've got one that's for sale.

The best part about going to New York for the ceremonies was that it provided me with an opportunity to make a record with Paul McCartney. Two days after the ceremony at the Waldorf-Astoria, D.J. and I went to Sear Sound studio to re-record "That's Alright," with Paul replacing Bill on bass and Elvis on vocals. D.J. was happy to go to New York for the session, but he didn't go to the Hall of Fame ceremony because he was too pissed off. I don't blame him.

Scotty in a New York studio with, left to right, D.J., Karen Fontana, Paul McCartney, and Gail Pollock. (Photo courtesy of Scotty Moore.)

The session was the brainchild of Atlantic Records head Ahmet Ertegun. The idea, as he explained it, was to do a television documentary and a CD, with D.J. and I doing a series of sessions with guest artists. It didn't turn out exactly that way. D.J. and I did the session with Paul, and we did a few sessions at Abbey Road Studio in London, but not all of them were used on the CD or on the television special.

I expected Paul to come into the studio with an entourage, but he arrived with a man he had gone to school with as a youngster. Paul was a nice, everyday good guy. It felt like we had known each other forever. The studio was filled with people carrying clipboards and pens, but none of them had any business being there. They didn't fool me, and I'm sure they didn't fool Paul, either.

"All the people with clipboards didn't bother Paul in the least," said Gail, who had accompanied me to the session. "He's a vegetarian, so they had all the snacks laid out, vegetarian-style, and he was going around doing his dips, totally unbothered."

Paul told D.J. and I that he was a fan of our early work, and we told him that we were big Beatles fans—and we are. What I didn't tell him was that when the Beatles were at their peak, from the mid-sixties to the early seventies, I was working as a studio engineer in Nashville and I didn't have much time to listen to the radio. I got turned on to the Beatles' music because of all the people that came into the studio to record sound-alike songs. And, of course, I later engineered Ringo's Nashville album.

When time came to start the session, Paul said that he would have brought Bill's bass to the session, but he was concerned about trans- porting it in an unpressurized cabin. I laughed and told him the story about when we were traveling with the equipment strapped to the roof, and hit another car, sending the bass skidding out onto the road. As we inspected the damage to the cars, we heard Bill in the distance testing the bass . . . thumpty thump, thumpty thump. Paul got a good laugh out of that, as did Elvis and I at the time. I'm pretty sure that tough old bass would have survived the flight.

Finally, we got down to business. We recorded "That's Alright" live, with Paul singing and playing bass. The only overdubs we made were when the song was played back so that Paul could add "slap back" to the recording by sitting down and slapping his hands against his legs in time with the music.

Afterward we went into the control room to listen to what we had done. After two playbacks, Paul asked, "Well, Scotty, do you have anything else you want to do here?"

I laughed. "I've done more here today than I did the first time."

Paul laughed, and said, "Well, as soon as we get the orchestra and the girl singers, we'll be through." It was a joke, of course, because when we first recorded "That's Alright," Elvis was years away from adding orchestras and girl singers to his records. After the session, when they posed for photographs, Paul saw Gail and Karen Fontana enter the room, and he said, "Here come the girl singers!"

Later, Paul told *Pulse* magazine: "I love the early Elvis stuff, and it was such an honor to work with those guys. I mean, Scotty, to me, some of those early solos were just mind-blowing. Where some of them came from, I don't think he knows. You talk to some of those guys—'Well, I was just goofin' around, Paul.' They're so self-effacing."

* * *

Scotty at his home studio. (Photo by James L. Dickerson.)

One of the things in recent years that has given me a lot of enjoyment is my home studio. I added a room onto my house and built a stone wall out from the base of the addition. Now I can not only do my own recording projects without leaving the comfort of home, I can engineer and produce other projects.

I did an album with Ronnie McDowell at my home that I am particularly proud of, and I'm proud of my part in Alvin Lee's album, *Alvin Lee in Tennessee.* D.J. played drums, Pete Pritchard played bass, and I played on a couple of tracks, in addition to making production suggestions. Stan Dacus engineered the album, which was interesting since both Alvin and I had connections with him that went back to the 1970s. At my suggestion, an old friend of mine, Willie Rainsford, played keyboards. Later, Alvin told BlueSpeak.com: "[Scotty] was the original raw sound . . . A lot of his runs are based on jazz notes but played with rock 'n' roll energy. He transcends all styles and every solo he plays is a singable tune in its own right. If anyone has ever done more for the guitar than Scotty Moore, I don't know who it is."

Scotty with Ronnie McDowell at Horseshoe Casino in Tunica, Mississippi. (Photo courtesy of Scotty Moore.)

* * *

In November 2003, I was driving my tractor, mowing the grass out behind my house, when my right leg started hurting. I didn't think too much about it. Aches and pains seem to go along with operating a tractor, mainly because you're using muscles that you normally wouldn't use. The next day I was sore and stiff when I awoke, so I went to an osteopath. He injected my hand with the medication that he usually used to take out the stiffness, but he didn't seem concerned about the leg pain.

POSTSCRIPT

A couple of weeks later, Gail brought me a stack of photographs to autograph. When I tried to write out the dedications, I got the letters all wrong. I would think one thing and my hand would write something else. I had a hard time making the letters. We had to throw away a lot of photographs because I ruined them. It was then that Gail noticed that I was clinching my hand and holding it close against my chest. She encouraged me to go to a doctor and get a checkup, but I didn't see any reason to do that. Other than the problems with my hand and leg, I felt fine. Besides, two ailments out of a possible thousand that could affect a man my age, didn't seem so bad.

"I thought he might have had a stroke," says Gail. "For two weeks, he wouldn't go to the doctor. On December 2, three days before a party that Gibson Guitars put together to celebrate his birthday and his 50-year association with them, he went into town to sign papers for the production company that was going to film the party—and he couldn't sign his check! It was darnedest scrawl you've ever seen. I was fussin' with him all the way home, giving him hell about not seeing a doctor."

Late that afternoon, I received a call from Ira Padnas, a New Orleans anesthesiologist who organizes a music festival each year, the Ponderosa Stomp, to feature the old timers of rock 'n' roll, jazz, and rhythm and blues. He had come to Nashville for my party and had called Gail to get directions. I felt comfortable talking to him because I knew him and trusted his judgment. I gave him my symptoms and he told me that it sounded like a bleeding problem, not a stroke. He told me to go to a hospital right away. I didn't, mainly because of the party. I didn't want to ruin it for everyone. I postponed making a decision until the next day, hoping that the problem would go away. When I awoke the next morning, the problem was worse, so I called Gail and asked her to take me to the hospital.

When we pulled up at the hospital, the valet attendants were nowhere to be found, so Gail let me out of the car and left to find a parking place. While she was gone, I went to the admitting office and checked myself into the hospital. My primary doctor, Bryce Dixon, was there and sent me up to intensive care, where they gave me a CATscan. Later, they told me that I had a two-inch thick hematoma on my brain.

They said they needed to operate on me immediately, but they couldn't because of the anticoagulation medication I was on. Instead, they gave me packed platelets all day to build up my blood. Two days later, they took me into surgery and operated on my brain. The next several weeks are still a blur to me.

After the surgery, the surgeon, Dr. Harold Smith, told Gail that he was amazed that I had been able to walk into the hospital. "He shouldn't have been able to walk with something that size inside his head," explained the doctor. "Luckily, there was no damage to the brain waves. For the past two or three weeks, his brain was jammed against the other side of his skull and when we took out the hemotoma, the pressure that had been there was suddenly released and caused his brain to flop back against the other side. Essentially, we rattled his brain."

I was in the hospital for thirty-three days, but I don't have any memory of the first three weeks. My memory begins in the hospital room, after they moved me from intensive care, and basically all I remember about my stay is how bad the food was.

When I was released from the hospital on January 8, they told me not to drive my car since my motor skills were not up to par. They seemed to know what they were talking about, so I didn't drive my car; but they didn't say anything about not driving my lawn mower. The grass was so high in my backyard that I didn't see any harm in taking a spin on the mower. Everything was fine until I drove too close to a ditch that ran alongside the house. The mower toppled over into the ditch, with me on it. I wasn't hurt, but it did put a scare into me.

I called Gail and told her I had a problem.

"What kind of problem?"

"You'll see when you get here."

When she saw the mower, Gail was amazed that I wasn't hurt. We got the tractor out of the barn and wrapped a rope around the tractor and the mower and pulled the mower back up out of the ditch. It wasn't a big deal. I just got too close to the edge. It's an occupational hazard for guitarists.

Every morning, when I wake up, all my bones crack. It didn't do that before the surgery. I don't know whether things will ever get back like they were before the surgery. I don't know why I was chosen to survive Elvis and Bill. I did everything they did. I spent all that time on the road, eating bad food, getting no sleep, just enjoying what we were doing. Why I made it this far and they didn't, I'll never understand.

* * *

POSTSCRIPT

When Johnny Cash died, it was another chink out of the wall. I knew Johnny when we were all just starting out. We weren't close, but we followed each other's careers. I don't think we miss Johnny as much as we thought we would because he was ready to go at that point in his life. It was his wife, June, who kept him going. When she died, he apparently didn't see any reason to continue without her. I hope they remember him from the old days..."I Walk the Line," and that sort of thing.

One friend that Johnny and I had in common is Marty Stuart, who played in Johnny's band for a while and married one of his daughters. I got to know Marty when Johnny went to the facilities at Opryland Productions to record his television specials. Marty spent so much time with me in the control room, asking questions about the machinery, that the director had to look for him when he was needed on stage.

I never realized I had an impact on Marty until the week of my brain surgery, when he told my co-writer a story about going to Memphis when he was at a low ebb in his life. It was foggy that day, and he took a wrong turn downtown and ended up on the Mississippi River Bridge. After he crossed the river, he pulled off the road to turn around and it was then that he heard a train coming. He slapped my version of "Mystery Train" into his CD player and listened as the train cut through the fog.

"It was one of the highlights of my life," Marty explained. "Scotty is one of the most eloquent guitar players that ever picked up a guitar. He is the personification of soul in guitar playing. When John [Cash] died, the only other death in my life, musically speaking, was when Elvis Presley died. When John died, there was a lot of media around the event and a lot of folks calling me and I said no to most of it. I took my cue from Scotty. Of all the people that worked around Elvis, the one who handled it with the most dignity was Scotty. When Scotty talked about Elvis, it was for the right reasons, and when he showed up on behalf of Elvis, I felt like Scotty was still representing the man and not the cartoon figure. And when he didn't show up, it was for all the right reasons. I want Scotty to know that he has always been a beacon to me. He is a man of purpose."

I am moved by stories like that because it goes to the heart of why I play the guitar. Lord knows, it was never to get rich. No, for me, it's all about doing something with a guitar that affects people in a positive way. It's a way to leave a mark that fellow travelers can follow: *Scotty was here!*

* * *

In March 2004, I went to Europe on my first tour after the brain surgery. While I was on the plane coming back, my oldest friend James Lewis died. You met him in the first chapter of this book. We didn't see much of each other in later years, but he was still a big part of my life and I miss him.

That summer I went to Memphis to help celebrate the 50th anniversary of the recording of "That's Alright" at Sun Studio. On July 5, 2004, I pressed a button that started a simultaneous playing of the record on 1,500 radio stations around the world. When we went in for Elvis' audition in 1954, I never would have expected the 50th anniversary to be remembered, much less played on radio stations around the world. It gives me a great feeling to think that what we did will last for later generations.

Scotty in 2002. (Photo by Karen McBride)

NOTES

CHAPTER 1

The postcards exchanged by Scott and Mattie Moore are now in Scotty Moore's possession.

While researching this book, James Dickerson visited the old Moore homestead. It is now owned by James Lewis, who generously took time from his schedule to give Dickerson a tour of the house. Lewis's daughter currently lives in the house.

CHAPTER 2

All of the letters and telegrams referred to in this chapter can be found in *Foreign Relations*, 1948–1950, volumes 8, 9, and 10. These volumes, which are made available to select university libraries by the government, contain State Department communications no longer considered classified.

Facts on File contains excellent week-to-week summaries of developments in China during the months referred to in this book in its annual publications.

CHAPTER 3

All of the quotes from Marion Keisker in this book not otherwise identified were taken from interviews in the Jerry Hopkins Collection at the University of Memphis. Also in the collection is the letter to Hopkins from Keisker that challenges Sam Phillips's version of early events at the studio.

The quote from Jimmy Denson is taken from an interview given to Michael Donahue for *Mid-South* magazine.

As James Dickerson was working on this book, Tammy Wynette called to talk about her memories of Scotty. At the time she called, she was out on the road in her tour bus. An earlier conversation between Dickerson and Tammy's husband had been disconnected when the mobile phone on the tour bus entered a different cell area. This time, Tammy pulled the bus off the road to make the call. She said she was in the middle of nowhere. To Dickerson, it sounded like she was calling from a pay-phone booth.

CHAPTER 4

Unless otherwise stated, all quotes in this book attributed to Bob Neal were taken from interviews in the Jerry Hopkins Collection at the University of Memphis. A financial statement made out by Bob Neal for Scotty Moore and Bill Black is still in Scotty's possession.

Comments from Jack Clement were taken from interviews done by Dickerson in 1995 and 1986.

CHAPTER 5

Comments from Frank Page were taken from an interview done by Dickerson in 1995 and from interviews in the Jerry Hopkins Collection at the University of Memphis.

Comments from D. J. Fontana were taken from an interview done by Dickerson in 1995. He was most cooperative and offered to assist with the project in any way possible.

Comments from June Carter Cash were taken from James Dickerson's *Coming Home: 21 Conversations About Memphis Music.*

Information about Colonel Tom Parker's background was taken from Dirk Vellenga's *Elvis and the Colonel*, Peter Guralnick's *Last Train to Memphis*, and just about everyone interviewed for the book, all of whom had information and opinions about "The Colonel."

Marshall Grant was interviewed in 1995.

Bobbie Moore was interviewed in 1995.

Evelyn Black Tuverville was interviewed in 1995.

CHAPTER 6

Carl Perkins's account of the hospital visit was taken from the *706 ReUnion* album recorded by Scotty Moore and Perkins in 1992 at Sun Studio in Memphis. In addition to music, the album contains conversations between Scotty and Carl.

All comments from the Jordanaires, unless otherwise identified, were taken from a 1995 interview with Dickerson at Scotty Moore's house, where the singers had gathered to do overdubs on a tape in Scotty's home studio.

The account of Elvis Presley's fight at the service station was taken from published press reports.

CHAPTER 7

Fred Burch was interviewed in 1995 and Gerald Nelson was interviewed in 1996.

Comments from Reggie Young were taken from interviews done by Dickerson in 1995, 1985, and 1986.

Sharri Paullus was interviewed in 1995.

The account of Elvis's meeting with Marion Keisker was taken from interviews on file in the Jerry Hopkins Collection at the University of Memphis.

Vicki Hein was interviewed in 1995.

CHAPTER 8

Dickerson came across Scotty's blond Gibson in 1985 when Chips Moman moved back to Memphis after living in Nashville for a number of years. Dickerson wrote a story for *The Commercial Appeal* about Moman's ownership of the guitar and arranged for Moman to be photographed with it.

Herb O'Mell, Moman's assistant, told Dickerson the Smithsonian Institution had asked if it could display the guitar and had appraised it at $400,000. When the story was published, and Moman saw the price tag O'Mell had attached to the guitar, he was annoyed. He didn't mind showing off Scotty's guitar; he just didn't want the whole world to know how valuable it was. In November 1992, Moman asked for—and received—from Scotty written authentication of the guitar's history. Moman still owns the guitar. In 1996 Moman told Dickerson he would never sell the guitar, "not even for a million dollars."

John Carroll was interviewed in 1995.

Billy Sherrill was interviewed in 1996.

All comments from Sam Phillips were taken from interviews with Dickerson in 1985 and 1986, published press accounts, and interviews on file at the University of Memphis. All letters from Sam Phillips referred to in this book are in the possession of Scotty Moore.

CHAPTER 9

Emily Moore Sanders was interviewed in 1995.

Chips Moman was interviewed in 1996, 1985, and 1986.

CHAPTER 10

Tracy Nelson, Rose Drake, and Hugh Hickerson were interviewed in 1996.

Gail Pollock and Mary Ann Cosarelli were interviewed in 1995.

CHAPTER 11

Conrad Jones and Ronnie McDowell were interviewed in 1996.

Andrea Weil, Jerry Schilling, Gary Tallent, and Lee Rocker were interviewed in 1995.

Keith Richards was interviewed in 1996.

The week after Christmas 1995, Dickerson, Scotty, and Gail Pollock went to a Nashville nightclub to listen to Tracy Nelson perform. Scotty doesn't often go to nightclubs, but he remains a staunch Tracy Nelson fan—and he wanted to show Dickerson why he enjoys her music. Scotty and Gail met Dickerson in the parking lot of the tape plant, located just off Music Row. Dickerson left his car—a convertible—in the parking lot of the tape plant and rode in the car with Scotty and Gail to the nightclub. "Do you think my car will be safe here?" Dickerson asked.

"As safe as it would be anywhere," Scotty said.

Later that night—it was after midnight—Scotty and Gail drove Dickerson back to his car. The downtown streets were deserted at that time of the night, and no one was seen in the vicinity of the parking lot. After talking a few minutes, Dickerson got out of the car and Scotty and Gail drove away. When Dickerson got in his car, he discovered that someone had cut a hole in the roof and stolen items from the car.

As Dickerson pulled out of the parking lot and drove onto Music Row, a late model car with mismatched headlights pulled up behind him, pursuing him through the deserted city streets—past the old RCA building and the current address for Mercury Records. The chase lasted for several blocks, and Dickerson was able to lose his pursuers only because his smaller, faster car was more maneuverable than the land barge that stayed on his tail.

When the crime was reported to Nashville police, they said it sounded like a carjacking attempt.

NOTES

SCOTTY MOORE'S RECORDINGS WITH ELVIS PRESLEY

On the following Elvis Presley records, Scotty Moore acted as section leader or played lead guitar, rhythm guitar, or six-string bass.

1954-1955

Baby, Let's Play House

Blue Moon

Blue Moon of Kentucky

Good Rockin' Tonight

Harbor Lights

I Don't Care If the Sun Don't Shine

I Forgot to Remember to Forget

I Got a Woman

I Love You Because

I'll Never Let You Go (Little Darlin')

I'm Left, You're Right, She's Gone

Just Because

Milkcow Blues Boogie

Mystery Train

That's All Right

Tomorrow Night

Trying to Get to You

When It Rains, It Really Pours

You're a Heartbreaker

1956-1957

All Shook Up

Anyplace Is Paradise

Anyway You Want Me

Blue Christmas

Blue Suede Shoes

Blueberry Hill

Don't

Don't Be Cruel

Don't Leave Me Now

First in Line

Got a Lot o' Living to Do

Have I Told You Lately That I Love You

Heartbreak Hotel

Here Comes Santa Claus

Hot Dog

Hound Dog

How Do You Think I Feel

How's the World Treating You

I Beg of You

I Believe

I Need You So

I Want to Be Free

I Want You, I Need You, I Love You

I Was the One

I'll Be Home for Christmas

I'm Counting on You

I'm Gonna Sit Right Down and Cry (Over You)

Is It So Strange

It Is No Secret

Jailhouse Rock

Lawdy, Miss Claudy

(Let Me Be Your) Teddy Bear

Lonesome Cowboy

Long Tall Sally

Love Me

Loving You

Mean Woman Blues

Money Honey

My Baby Left Me

My Wish Came True

O' Little Town of Bethlehem

Old Shep

One Night (of Sin)

One Sided Love Affair

Paralyzed

Party

Peace in the Valley

Playing for Keeps

Ready Teddy

Rip It Up

Santa Bring My Baby Back (to Me)

Santa Claus Is Back in Town

Shake, Rattle and Roll

Silent Night

So Glad You're Mine

Take My Hand, Precious Lord

Tell Me Why

That's When Your Heartaches Begin

Too Much

Treat Me Nice

True Love

Tutti Frutti

When It Rains It Really Pours

When My Blue Moon Turns to Gold
  Again

White Christmas

Young and Beautiful

(You're So Square) Baby I Don't Care

1958-1959

As Long as I Have You

Crawfish

Dixieland Rock

Doncha' Think It's Time

Don't Ask Me Why

Hard Headed Woman

King Creole

Lover Doll

New Orleans

Steadfast, Loyal and True

Trouble

Wear My Ring Around Your Neck

Young Dreams

Your Cheatin' Heart

1960-1961

Almost Always True

Aloha Oe

Anything That's Part of You

Are You Lonesome Tonight?

Beach Boy Blues

Big Boots

Blue Hawaii

Can't Help Falling in Love

Crying in the Chapel

Didja' Ever

Dirty, Dirty Feeling

Doin' the Best I Can

Fame and Fortune

Fever

Follow That Dream

For the Millionth and the Last Time

Forget Me Never

Frankfort Special

Gently

G.I. Blues

The Girl of My Best Friend

Girl Next Door Went A-Walkin'

Give Me the Right

Good Luck Charm

Hawaiian Sunset

Hawaiian Wedding Song

He Knows Just What I Need

His Hand in Mine

His Latest Flame

Home Is Where the Heart Is

I Believe in the Man in the Sky

I Feel So Bad

I Got Lucky

I Gotta Know

I Met Her Today

I Slipped, I Stumbled, I Fell

I Want You with Me

I Will Be Home Again

I'm Comin' Home

I'm Gonna Walk Dem Golden Stairs

I'm Not the Marrying Kind

I'm Yours

If We Never Meet Again

In My Father's House

In My Way

In Your Arms

Island of Love

It Feels So Right

It's Now or Never

It's a Sin

Ito Eats

Joshua Fit the Battle

Judy

King of the Whole Wide World

Kiss Me Quick

Known Only to Him

Ku-U-I-Po

Like a Baby

Little Sister

Lonely Man

Mansion Over the Hilltop

Make Me Know It

A Mess of Blues

Milky White Way

Moonlight Swim

Night Rider

No More

Pocketful of Rainbows

Put the Blame on Me

Reconsider Baby

Riding the Rainbow

Rock-a-Hula Baby

Sentimental Me

Shoppin' Around

Slicin' Sand

Soldier Boy

Sound Advice

Starting Today

Steppin' Out of Line

Stuck on You

Such a Night

Surrender

That's Someone You Never Forget

There's Always Me

This Is Living

The Thrill of Your Love

Tonight Is So Right for Love

Tonight's All Right for Love

What a Wonderful Life

What's She Really Like

A Whistling Tune

Wild in the Country

Wooden Heart

Working on the Building

1962-1963

Anyone (Could Fall in Love With You)

Ask Me

Barefoot Ballad

Because of Love

Beyond the Bend

Blue River

Bossa Nova Baby

A Boy Like Me, A Girl Like You

The Bullfighter Was a Lady

273

Catchin' On Fast

C'mon Everybody

Cotton Candy Land

Dainty Little Moon Beams

Do the Vega

Earth Boy

Echoes of Love

El Toro

The Eyes of Texas

Finders Keepers, Losers Weepers

Fountain of Love

Fun in Acapulco

Girls, Girls, Girls

Gonna Get Back Home Somehow

Guadalajara (track only)

Happy Ending

How Would You Like to Be

I Don't Want To

I Don't Want to Be Tied

I Feel That I've Known You Forever

I Need Somebody to Lean On

I Think I'm Gonna Like It Here

If You Think I Don't Need You

I'm Falling in Love Tonight

(It's a) Long Lonesome Highway

Just for Old Time's Sake

Just Tell Her Jim Said Hello

Kissin' Cousins

The Lady Loves Me

Love Me Tonight

Malaguena (track only)

Mama

Marguerita

Mexico

Never Ending

Night Life

Night Rider (unreleased)

Once Is Enough

One Boy, Two Little Girls

One Broken Heart for Sale

Plantation Rock

Please Don't Drag That String Around

Relax

Return to Sender

Santa Lucia

She's Not You

Slowly But Surely

Smokey Mountain Boy

Something Blue

Song of the Shrimp

(Such an) Easy Question

Suspicion

Take Me to the Fair

Tender Feeling

Thanks to the Rolling Sea

There's Gold in the Mountains

(There's) No Room to Rhumba in a Sports Car

They Remind Me Too Much of You

Today, Tomorrow, and Forever (unreleased duet with Ann-Margret)

Vino, Dinero y Amor

Viva Las Vegas

The Walls Have Ears

We'll Be Together

We're Comin' in Loaded

Western Union

What Now, What Next, Where To

What'd I Say?

Where Do You Come From?

Witchcraft

A World of Our Own

1964-1965

Animal Instinct

Ask Me

Beginner's Luck

Big Love Big Heartache

Carny Town

Chesay

Come Along

Cross My Heart and Hope to Die

Do the Clam

Do Not Disturb

Down by the River Side

Fort Lauderdale Chamber of Commerce

Frankie and Johnny

Girl Happy

Go East, Young Man

Golden Coins

Hard Knocks

Hard Luck

Harum Holiday

Hey Little Girl

It Hurts Me

It's Carnival Time

It's a Wonderful World

I've Got to Find My Baby

Kismet

Little Egypt

Look Out, Broadway

The Meanest Girl in Town

Memphis, Tennessee

Mirage

My Desert Serenade

One Track Heart

Puppet on a String

Petunia, the Gardener's Daughter

Roustabout

Shake That Tambourine

Shout It Out

So Close, Yet So Far

Spring Fever

Startin' Tonight

What Every Woman Lives For

Wheels on My Heels

When the Saints Go Marching In

Wisdom of the Ages

Wolf Call

1966-1967

Adam and Evil

All I Needed Was the Rain

All That I Am

Am I Ready

Baby If You'll Give Me Your Love

Beach Street

Big Boss Man

City by Night

Clambake

Come What May

Confidence

Could I Fall in Love

Dominic (unreleased)

Double Trouble

Down in the Alley

Easy Come, Easy Go

Farther Along

The Girl I Never Loved

Guitar Man

Hey, Hey, Hey

High Heel Sneakers

A House That Has Everything

How Can You Lose What You Never
    Had?

How Great Thou Art

I Only Love One Girl

I'll Take Love

If the Lord Wasn't Walking by My
    Side

In the Garden

It Won't Be Long

275

Just Call Me Lonesome

Leave My Woman Alone
   (sound track only)

Long Legged Girl
   (With the Short Dress On)

Love Letters

The Love Machine

Never Say Yes

Old McDonald

Run On

She's a Machine

Sing You Children

Singing Tree (unreleased)

Smorgasbord

So High

Somebody Bigger Than You and I

Spinout

Stand by Me

Stay Away Joe

Stop Look and Listen

Suppose (unreleased)

Tomorrow Is a Long Time

We Call on Him

Where Could I Go But to the Lord

Where No One Stands Alone

Without Him

Who Needs Money

You Don't Know Me
   (unreleased movie version)

You Gotta Stop

You'll Never Walk Alone

Yoga Is as Yoga Does

1968

Goin' Home

Stay Away

Too Much Monkey Business

U.S. Male

GUITARS OWNED BY SCOTTY MOORE

Description	Date Purchased	Date Sold/Traded
1. Fender Esquire	1952	1953
2. Gibson ES 295	1953	July 7, 1955
3. Gibson L5 CES (blond) (serial number A-18195)	July 7, 1955	January 1957
4. Gibson Super 400 CESN (serial number A-24672)	January 1957	1963[1]
5. Gibson Super 400 (Sunburst) (serial number 62713)	October 1963	February 1986[2]
6. Gibson Super 100 CESN (serial number 080253002)	March 1987	currently in use

[1]This guitar is owned by record producer Chips Moman.
[2]This guitar is now on display at the Hard Rock Cafe in Dallas, Texas.

SELECT BIBLIOGRAPHY

BOOKS

Barber, Noel. *The Fall of Shanghai*. New York: Coward, McCann.

Bodde, Derk. *Peking Diary: A Year of Revolution*. New York: Henry Schuman, 1950.

Bronson, Fred. *The Billboard Book of Number One Hits*. New York: Billboard Publications, 1985.

Clubb, O. Edmund. *20th Century China*. New York: Columbia University Press, 1964.

Cotton, Lee. *Did Elvis Sing in Your Hometown?* Sacramento, CA: High Sierra, 1995.

Dewitt, Howard A. *Elvis: The Sun Years*. Popular Culture, 1993.

Dickerson, James. *Goin' Back to Memphis: A Century of Blues, Rock 'n' Roll, and Glorious Soul*. New York: Schirmer Books, 1996.

———. *Coming Home: 21 Conversations About Memphis Music*. Memphis: Scripps Howard, 1986.

Esposito, Joe. *Good Rockin' Tonight*. New York: Simon & Schuster.

Facts on File Yearbook. New York: Facts on File, 1948, 1949, 1950.

Fairbank, John King. *The Great Chinese Revolution: 1800–1985*. New York: Harper & Row.

Gardner, Steve. *Rambling Minds*. Toyko: Aoki Shoten, 1994.

Gill, Chris. *Guitar Legends*. New York: Harper Perennial, 1995.

Gruber, J. Richard. *Memphis: 1948–1958*. Memphis: Memphis Brooks Museum of Art, 1986.

Guralnick, Peter. *Last Train to Memphis: The Rise of Elvis Presley*. New York: Little, Brown, 1994.

Hannaford, Jim, and G. J. Rijff. *Inside Jailhouse Rock*. Holland, MI: Jim Hannaford Productions, 1994.

Harkins, John E. *Metropolis of the American Nile*. Oxford, MS: Guild Bindery Press, 1991.

Hopkins, Jerry. *Elvis: A Biography*. New York: Simon & Schuster, 1971.

Isenberg, Michael T. *Shield of the Republic*. New York: St. Martin's.

Key, V. O., Jr. *Southern Politics*. New York: Random House, 1949.

Lieberthal, Kenneth G. *Revolution and Tradition in Tientsin (1949–1952)*. Stanford, CA: Stanford University Press, 1980.

McAleer, Dave. *The All Music Book of Hit Singles*. London: Carlton Books, 1994.

Miller, William D. *Memphis During the Progressive Era*. Memphis: Memphis State University Press, 1957

Mooney, James L., ed. *Dictionary of American Naval Fighting Ships*. Washington, DC: Naval Historical Center, 1981.

Morgenthau, Hans J. *Politics Among Nations*. New York: Knopf, 1967.

Murphy, Bruce Allen. *Fortas: The Rise and Ruin of a Supreme Court Justice*. New York: Morrow, 1988.

Nash, Alanna, with Billy Smith, Marty Lacker, and Lamar Fike. *Elvis Aron Presley: Revelations from the Memphis Mafia*. New York: HarperCollins.

Presley, Priscilla Beaulieu, and Sandra Harmon. *Elvis and Me*. New York: Putnam's.

Rijff, Ger J., and Jan van Gestel. *Fire in the Sun*. Amsterdam: Tutti Frutti, 1991.

Salisbury, Harrison E. *The New Emperors*. Boston: Little, Brown.

Shaw, Arnold. *Dictionary of American Pop/Rock*. New York: Schirmer Books, 1982.

Smith, Gene. *Elvis's Man Friday*. Nashville: Light of Day, 1994.

Stambler, Irwin, and Grelun Landon. *The Encyclopedia of Folk, Country & Western Music*. New York: St. Martin's, 1969.

Stokesbury, James L. *A Short History of the Korean War*. New York: Morrow.

Swados, Harvey. *Standing Up for the People: The Life and Work of Estes Kefauver*. New York: Dutton, 1972.

Vellenga, Dirk, with Mick Farren. *Elvis and the Colonel*. New York: Delacorte Press.

Whitburn, Joel. *Billboard Top 1000 Singles (1955–1992)*. Milwaukee: Hall Leonard, 1993.

Wilson, Charles Reagan, and William Ferris. *Encyclopedia of Southern Culture*. Chapel Hill: University of North Carolina Press, 1989.

Worth, Fred, and Steve D. Tamerius. *All About Elvis*. New York: Bantam, 1981.

NEWSPAPERS

The *Commercial Appeal*, Memphis, Tennessee

The *Memphis Press-Scimitar*, Memphis, Tennessee

The *Nashville Banner*, Nashville, Tennessee

The *Nashville Tennessean*, Nashville, Tennessee

The *New York Times*, New York, New York

ARTICLES

Cronin, Peter, Scott Isler, and Mark Rowland. "Elvis Presley: An Oral Biography." *Musician* (October 1992).

Dickerson, James. "Presley Pal Still Pickin'." *CoverStory* 2, no. 44 (1993).

———. "Perkins & Friends." *Nine-O-One Network* (September/October 1986).

———. "Aspiring Musicians Beat a Hopeful Path to Publishing Office." *The Commercial Appeal*. August 26, 1985.

Donahue, Michael. "That's All Right, Mama." *Mid-South* (August 11, 1981).

James, Steve. "The Acoustic Roots of Rock." *Acoustic Guitar* (July/August 1994).

Johnson, Robert. "The Elvis Diary." *Sixteen* (May 1957).

Joyce, Mike. "All on the Mall: A Day of Diverse Music and So Forth." *Washington Post*. July 5, 1995.

Kienzle, Rich. "Riffs, Amps, or Butts." *Guitar Player* (March 1990).

Kyle, Dave. "An Interview With Ray Butts." *Vintage Guitar* (1994).

Martin, Neville. "The King and I." *Guitarist* (November 1992).

Randall, Nancy. "Elvis—The Memory Lives. *Nine-O-One Network* (December 1987).

———. "Elvis." *Nine-O-One Network* (July/August 1987).

———. "The Men Who Shot Elvis." *Nine-O-One Network* (July/August 1987).

Woods, Kevin. "Scotty Moore." *Vintage Guitar* (December 1993).

RECOMMENDED RECORDINGS

Bill Black's Combo. *Movin'—The Untouchable Guitar*. Hi Records

Moore, Scotty. *The Guitar That Changed the World*. Epic Records. Produced by Billy Sherrill *

Moore, Scotty, and Carl Perkins. *706 ReUnion: A Sentimental Journey*. Belle Meade Records. Produced by Scotty Moore**

Moore, Scotty, with Carl Perkins, Willie Rainsford, D. J. Fontana, the Jordanaires, and Tracy Nelson. *Moore Feel Good Music.* Belle Meade Records. Produced by Scotty Moore**

Presley, Elvis. *The Top Ten Hits.* RCA Records

————. *The Complete Sun Sessions.* RCA Records

————. *The Number One Hiits.* RCA Records

Rocker, Lee. *Big Blue.* Black Top

Starr, Ringo. *Beaucoup of Blues.* Apple Records. Reissued by Capitol Records in 1995. Produced by Pete Drake. Engineer: Scotty Moore

Various Artists. *It's Now or Never—The Tribute to Elvis.* Mercury Records. Produced by Don Was

RECOMMENDED VIDEOS

"Elvis '68 Comeback Special." Lightyear Entertainment. Produced and directed by Steve Binder

*No longer available

**Available only by mail order from Belle Meade Records, 1609 McGavock Street, Nashville, TN 37203

INDEX

285

Printed in the United States
80393LV00001B/109-114